PRO TOOLS 110

Pro Tools Fundamentals II

For Pro Tools 12.8 Software

Frank D. Cook

Avid Learning Partner Program
PRO TOOLS **12**

Copyright and Disclaimer

Copyright © 2017 NextPoint Training, Inc. and its licensors. All rights reserved. Printed in USA.

No part of this document may be reproduced or transmitted in any form or by any means, electronic or mechanical, including photographing, photocopying, or recording, for any purpose without the express written permission of NextPoint Training, Inc.

The media provided with this book, and any accompanying course material, is to be used only to complete the exercises contained herein. No rights are granted to use the footage/sound materials in any commercial or non-commercial production or video.

All product features and specifications are subject to change without notice.

Trademarks

Avid, Digidesign, Pro Tools, VENUE, Media Composer, Sibelius, and all related product names and logos are registered trademarks of Avid Technology, Inc. in the United States and/or other countries. All other trademarks are the property of their respective owners.

Acknowledgements

Avid Worldwide Training would like to thank all Avid Certified Instructors for their ongoing suggestions and comments, based on their experience in the classroom and their professional expertise, which have resulted in the continued improvement of Avid courseware.

PT110, Version 12.8

PN: 9320-65299-01

ISBN-13: 978-1-943446-49-0

pd 9/15/2017
110v12.8-Book.doc

The sale of this book without its cover is unauthorized. If you purchase this book without a cover, you should be aware that it was reported to the publisher as "unsold and destroyed." Neither the author nor the publisher has received payment for the sale of this "stripped" book.

About the Author

This book and the associated coursework was developed by **Frank D. Cook**, as the second in a series of courses designed to prepare students fro Pro Tools Certification under the Avid Learning Partner program.

Frank is a musician, educator, and longtime Pro Tools user. The owner of Insource Writing Solutions and NextPoint Training, Inc., Frank has worked in the technical publications and education industries for more than 20 years. As a writer, editor, technical publications manager, and business owner, Frank has authored and contributed to hundreds of guides, manuals, reports, textbooks, and other publications for clients in a wide variety of industries.

Frank has been a consultant for Digidesign/Avid for over twelve years. During this time, he has helped define Avid's training strategy and has developed extensive curriculum for Avid's official training and certification programs. Frank also teaches Pro Tools courses as an adjunct professor at Sacramento City College and American River College in Sacramento, California, and is an Avid Master Instructor.

Other course books by Frank D. Cook include:

- *Audio Production Basics with Pro Tools | First*, with co-author Eric Kuehnl

- *Pro Tools 101: Pro Tools Fundamentals I*

- *Pro Tools 201: Pro Tools Production I*

- *Pro Tools 210M: Pro Tools Production II (Music Production)*

- Pro Tools 310M: Advanced Music Production Techniques

About NextPoint Training

NextPoint Training, Inc. provides advanced training, software tools, and learning resources for educators and students studying Pro Tools and other media applications. Our products include audio textbooks (such as *Audio Production Basics with Pro Tools| First*) and the Elements|ED learning platform (ElementsED.com). On the Elements|ED site, students and educators can find material to supplement this and other textbooks.

Contents

Introduction xi

    About this Book xi

    Online Resources for this Course xi

        Course Videos xii

        Practice Quizzes xii

    Course Prerequisites xii

    Avid Audio Training Paths xiii

    Conventions and Symbols Used in this Book xiii

    Cross-Platform Issues xv

Lesson 1. Getting Started 1

    About This Course 2

        Requirements for Exercises 2

        Software and Hardware 2

    Starting Work in Pro Tools 2

        Accessing Existing Sessions and Projects 2

        Configuring the Playback Engine 4

        Configuring Pro Tools Hardware Settings 6

        Configuring I/O Settings 8

    Opening a Session or Project and Adding Tracks 14

        Opening a Recently Used Pro Tools Document 14

        Adding Tracks as You Work 14

        Configuring Track Routing 15

    Edit and Mix Window Display Options 16

        Changing the Display of the Mix and Edit Windows 16

        Using the I/O View 18

        Using the Comments View 18

        Using Collaboration Tools (Project Documents Only) 19

    Track List Display Options 20

        Showing and Hiding Tracks 20

        Using the Track List Pop-Up Menu 21

    Review/Discussion Questions 22

Exercise 1. Setting Up a Session 24

Lesson 2. Managing Session Data and Media Files 31

    Pro Tools Software Capabilities 32

        Basic Specifications 32

        Pro Tools HD Software 32

    Working with Digital Video 32

        Setting Up Video Tracks 33

        Video Playback on a Secondary Monitor 33

vi   PT110: Pro Tools Fundamentals II

Using Workspace Browsers 34
    Browser Features 34
    Workspace Browser Overview 34
    Workspace Browser Functionality 35
    Waveform Display 35
    Auditioning Audio Files 36

Using Soundbase 38
    Searching for Files with Soundbase 38
    Searching Using Tags 39

Importing Files and Session Data 40
    Considerations for Importing Files 40
    Importing Files Using a Workspace Browser 41
    Importing Files Using the Import Commands 45
    Importing Tracks and Other Session Data 47
    Batch Importing Files 49

Working with Clip Groups 49
    Creating Clip Groups 50
    Clip Group Icons 52
    Ungrouping Clips 52
    Regrouping Clips 53
    Clip Groups in the Clip List 53

Review/Discussion 54

Exercise 2. Working with Media Files 56

Lesson 3. Recording MIDI and Audio 63

Setting Up the Session 64
    Displaying Conductor Rulers 64
    Adding Meter and Tempo Events 64
    Creating a Linear Tempo Change 67
    Recording with a Click 68

Recording Selections 70
    Creating a Selection 70
    Using Pre- and Post-Roll 75

Loop Recording Audio and MIDI 77
    Loop Recording Differences: Audio Versus MIDI 78
    Capturing Loop Record Takes 78

Auditioning Loop Record Takes 79
    Setting the Match Criteria 79
    Selecting Alternate Takes 80

Recording MIDI Using Loop Playback with MIDI Merge 81

Review/Discussion 82

Exercise 3. MIDI Recording 83

Lesson 4. Working with MIDI & Virtual Instruments **89**

   Understanding Track Timebases 90

      Sample-Based Operation Versus Tick-Based Operation 90

      Track Timebases 91

      Tick-Based Timing and Note Values 92

   Virtual Instruments 92

      Using Plug-In Virtual Instruments 93

      Rendering Virtual Instruments 93

   MIDI-Compatible Tracks and Track Views 95

      Viewing MIDI Data in the Edit Window 95

      MIDI-Compatible Tracks in the Pro Tools Mix Window 97

   Auditioning and Playing Back MIDI 98

      MIDI Thru Option 98

      Default Thru Instrument Option 99

      MIDI Thru Setting versus Default Thru Instrument Setting 100

   Editing MIDI Data 100

      Editing MIDI Clips 100

      Editing MIDI Notes with the Pencil Tool 101

      Editing Existing MIDI Notes 104

      Deleting MIDI Notes 107

   Review/Discussion 108

Exercise 4. Using Virtual Instruments **110**

Lesson 5. Working with Elastic Audio **115**

   Elastic Audio Basics 116

      Enabling Elastic Audio on a Track 116

      Auto-Enabling Elastic Audio for New Tracks 118

      Understanding Elastic Audio Analysis 113

      Conforming Clips to the Session Tempo Map 119

      Warp Indicators 120

      Removing Clip Warping 120

   Elastic Audio Track Views 121

      Elastic Audio Markers 121

   Warping Sound with Elastic Audio 123

      Using Warp View 123

      Types of Manual Warping 124

   Using Elastic Audio to Tighten a Rhythmic Performance 127

      How Quantizing Affects Elastic Audio Events 127

      Improving the Quantization Results 128

   Using Elastic Audio to Experiment with Tempo 128

      Applying Tick-Based Timing to Elastic Audio-Enabled Tracks 128

      Applying Tempo Changes 129

viii   PT110: Pro Tools Fundamentals II

Improving the Quality of Warped Audio 129
    Editing Event Markers in Analysis View 130
    Adjusting Event Sensitivity 131
    Using X-Form 133
Using Elastic Audio for Pitch Changes 133
    Pitch Shifting with the Elastic Properties Window 133
    Pitch Shifting with the Transpose Window 134
    Changing and Undoing Pitch Transposition 135
Review/Discussion 136

Exercise 5. Using Elastic Audio for Dialog **138**

Lesson 6. Editing and Fine-Tuning a Performance **143**
Using the Smart Tool 144
    Activating the Primary Smart Tool Functions 144
    Creating Fades Using the Smart Tool 145
    Smart Tool Fade Settings 145
Working with Fades 146
    Using the Fades Dialog Boxes 146
    Editing Existing Fades 151
Creating Rhythmic Changes for Audio and MIDI Data 154
    Using Input Quantize 154
    Quantizing Existing Material 155
    Adjusting the Groove and Feel 157
MIDI Real-Time Properties 159
    Using the Real-Time Properties View 159
    Using the Real-Time Properties Floating Window 159
    Enabling Real-Time Properties 160
    Quantizing with Real-Time Properties 161
Review/Discussion 163

Exercise 6. MIDI Real-Time Properties **164**

Lesson 7. Additional Editing and Media Management **169**
Clip Looping 170
    Working with Clip Loops 170
    Creating Clip Loops 171
    Modifying Clip Loop Settings 172
    Editing Clip Loops 172
    Considerations for Working with Clip Loops 174
    Unlooping Clips 175
Editing Techniques 175
    Working with the Grid 175
    Using Layered Editing 177
AudioSuite Overview 178
    AudioSuite versus Insert Processing 178
    AudioSuite Features 178
    Using AudioSuite Plug-Ins 179

Contents   ix

Working with the Clip List 185
   Finding a Clip in the Clip List 186
   Cleaning Up the Clip List 188
   Exporting Selections 192
Review/Discussion 195

Exercise 7. Working with Clip Loops and Editing on the Grid **197**

Lesson 8. Basic Mixing and Signal Flow **203**
Track Colors, Icons, and Status Indicators 204
   Track Color Coding 204
   Track Type Icons 205
   Track Status Indicators 206
Using Inserts for Effects Processing 207
   Inserts on Audio Tracks and Aux Inputs 207
   Inserts on Master Faders 207
   Plug-In Inserts 207
   Hardware Inserts 208
Using Sends and Returns for Effects Processing 209
   Creating a Send 209
   Setting the Send Level 210
   Changing the Default Send Level Preference 210
   Send Display Options 211
   Creating a Return 212
Working with Sends 215
   Using the Send Window 215
   Moving and Copying Sends 218
   Changing and Removing Sends 219
Using Native Plug-Ins 219
   Using Gain-Based Processors 219
   Using Time-Based Processors 219
   Using the Plug-In Window 220
Master Fader Tracks 221
   Uses of Master Faders 222
   Creating Master Faders 222
Review/Discussion 223

Exercise 8. Adding Music and Effects Processing **225**

Lesson 9. Writing and Editing Automation **231**
Understanding Automation 232
   Groups and Automation 232
   Automation Playlists 232
Working with Automation 233
   Automation Modes 233
   Enabling and Suspending Automation 234
   Writing Automation Selectively 235

x   **PT110: Pro Tools Fundamentals II**

Playing Automation..236
Viewing Automation...236
Graphical Editing of Automation Data...237
Automation Displays...238
Creating and Adjusting Breakpoint Automation Data...238
Drawing Automation...239
Cutting, Copying, and Pasting Automation Data..241
Cutting Automation Versus Deleting Automation...241
Using Cut, Copy, and Paste Commands...242
Using Paste Special Mode...243
Removing Automation from a Track..244
Deleting Breakpoints on the Displayed Automation Graph (Recap).................................244
Clearing Automation for the Displayed Automation Graph...244
Clearing Automation for All Automation Graphs...244
Review/Discussion..245

Exercise 9. Using Automation **247**

Lesson 10. Using Advanced Mixing Techniques and Creating Final Media **253**
Working with Track Subsets...254
Using the Do-To-Selected Function..254
Submixing Tracks...255
Routing Signals Using Paths and Selectors..256
Grouping Tracks..259
Understanding Mix and Edit Groups...259
Creating a Mix or Edit Group...261
Activating and Deactivating Groups...262
Working with Groups..263
Identifying Group Membership...263
Selecting Members of a Group..265
Modifying a Group..265
Deleting a Group..266
Using the All Group...267
Groups and Automation..268
Groups and Elastic Audio..268
Creating Final Media..268
Creating a CD-Compatible Bounce..268
Creating an Archive...270
Review/Discussion..272

Exercise 10. Mixing Techniques **274**

Index **281**

Introduction

This book forms the foundation for the second course designed to prepare students for the Avid User Certification exam for Pro Tools. The Pro Tools 110 course is offered worldwide by Avid Learning Partner schools. The course is designed to be taught either as an intensive three-day workshop or as a traditional course with classes spanning several weeks or months.

About this Book

Pro Tools 110: Pro Tools Fundamentals II expands upon the basic principles taught in Pro Tools 101 and introduces the core concepts and skills you will need to operate a Pro Tools 12.8 system running mid-sized sessions with dozens of tracks. The lessons in this course are followed by exercises that take you step-by-step through the main Pro Tools functions described in each lesson.

This course book was designed for classes that include hands-on experience with Pro Tools. All Pro Tools 110 examples and exercises were written to work with Pro Tools 12.8 systems available at press time.

Book Contents

The text and screenshots in this book generally represent the user experience on a Mac-based Pro Tools 12 system. The primary operations described in the text are available on all standard Pro Tools 12.8 systems. However, certain features discussed are available only when running Pro Tools HD software.

Some configurations described in this book require an audio interface, such as an Mbox Pro. Although no specific hardware is required for the course, certain concepts and illustrations are based on the functionality available with an Mbox Pro.

Exercise Requirements

Students can complete the exercises in this book as they progress through the course. The exercises are designed to work on any Pro Tools 12.8 system. Some exercises may require the use of a MIDI controller or other components not included with Pro Tools. The hardware and software requirements for the exercises are stated in the exercise overviews.

The Download Media

This book makes use of media files for the included exercises. The media files can be downloaded by pointing your browser to alpp.us/PT110-128 and downloading the PT110 Exercise Media (v12.8) folder. Note that the above URL address is *case sensitive*, so be sure to enter it exactly as written.

Software Requirements

Students should have access to a Pro Tools 12.8 or later system to complete the exercises. (Current systems running Pro Tools HD 12.8 software can also be used.)

Online Resources for this Course

Supplemental resources are available online to help you master the material covered in this course book and prepare for the Avid User Certification exam. Online resources include video training on Lynda.com and practice quizzes on ElementsED.com.

Course Videos

A video training course covering all of the lessons in this book is available through Lynda.com. The video course, *Pro Tools 12 Essential Training: 110*, includes over 50 videos developed specifically to complement this course book.

The Pro Tools 110 video training course is available for online viewing here: alpp.us/PT110_Online.

Practice Quizzes

The PT110 Study Guide module on ElementsED.com provides access to study resources for students, including unlimited practice quizzes covering the contents of this course book.

Students can select the chapters, difficulty level, and number of questions for each practice quiz. Upon submitting a quiz, students will receive detailed feedback with the quiz results, along with a list of study suggestions detailing the sections in this book that require further review.

To access the PT110 Study Guide, sign up for a free account at www.elementsed.com.

Course Prerequisites

Prerequisites include successful completion of the Pro Tools 101 course. This course requires a basic understanding of computer operations, digital audio, MIDI recording concepts, and Pro Tools fundamentals.

Computer Skills:

- Identifying the components of a computer and their functions in relation to audio
- Using the mouse, standard menus, and keyboard commands
- Locating, moving, and renaming files and folders
- Opening, saving, and closing session files
- Restarting the computer and its components

Audio and MIDI Concepts:

- Disk-based, random access audio recording and playback
- Multi-track recording
- Basic mixing and signal routing
- Digital audio concepts: sample rate and bit depth
- MIDI controller connections, data types, and signal flow

Pro Tools Fundamentals:

- The Pro Tools session file structure
- Opening, navigating, and saving Pro Tools sessions
- Creating new tracks in Pro Tools
- Assigning Inputs and Outputs in the Pro Tools Mix and Edit windows
- Using Mix window controls such as Volume, Mute, Solo, and Pan

- Using Edit tools such as the Zoomer, Trim, Selector, and Grabber tools
- Using Slip, Shuffle, Spot, and Grid Edit modes
- Using Transport window controls to play back and record audio and MIDI

Avid Audio Training Paths

Avid's audio coursework includes programs supporting certification in dedicated focus areas, including Pro Tools, Sibelius, Control Surface Operation, and Live Sound. Course components are designed to be completed individually and in sequence. However, individual training partners may offer the same course content through somewhat different class configurations.

Descriptions of each of the courses offered through the Avid Learning Partner program are available on the Avid website. (Go to www.avid.com/education.)

User Certification

Pro Tools 110 is the second course in the Avid Certified User training curriculum. The 100-level coursework prepares students to operate a Pro Tools system in an independent production environment.

Certification path for Avid Certified User: Pro Tools

Next Steps

Following completion of the Avid Certified User coursework and exams, students can proceed to the 200-level courses to pursue Avid Certified Operator status. The 200-series Pro Tools courses include the following:

- Pro Tools 201: Pro Tools Production I
- Pro Tools 210M: Pro Tools Production II (Music Production Techniques)
- Pro Tools 210P: Pro Tools Production II (Post Production Techniques)

Upon successful completion of the 200-series coursework, students are eligible to take Avid's Pro Tools Operator Certification exam in either music or video post-production.

Conventions and Symbols Used in this Book

This section describes the conventions and symbols used in this course book.

Procedures and Lists

Procedures and lists appear in one of the following forms.

Numbered procedures and lists:

1. These are used when the order of steps or items is critical.
2. When used, steps are listed in sequence.

Bulleted procedures and lists:

- These are used when the order of steps or items is not critical

  – Or –

- When more than one option is available

  – Or –

- When only one step or item is required

Menu and Key Commands

The following are examples of the conventions used to indicate menu choices and keyboard commands:

Convention	Action
FILE > SAVE SESSION	Choose SAVE SESSION from the FILE menu
CONTROL+N	Hold down the CONTROL key and press the N key
COMMAND-CLICK	Hold down the COMMAND key and click the mouse button
Right-click	Click with the right mouse button
Press [1]	Press 1 on the numeric keypad

Icons

The following icons are used to call attention to tips, important notices, shortcuts, and cross-references.

Tips provide helpful hints, introduce related operations or concepts, or describe alternative methods of working.

Important notices warn of conditions that may affect audio, system performance, Pro Tools session data, or connected hardware.

Shortcuts provide useful keyboard, mouse, or control surface shortcuts that can help users work more efficiently.

Cross-references alert the reader to another section, book, or Avid Guide that provides additional information on the current topic.

Sidebars

The format shown below is used for sidebar text to present supplemental information related to the current topic. Sidebars often provide information on Pro Tools processing that takes place "under the hood" to help you understand what to expect when applying a particular operation. Sidebars are also used to provide suggested techniques for working with a particular function and often contain mnemonic tips, visualization techniques, and associations designed to help you remember keyboard commands and shortcuts.

> ### Sidebars for Pro Tools Course Books
>
> Sidebars are used to provide additional, supplemental information about a topic. Sidebars often contain FYI-type information that will help you work faster or achieve better results. Sidebars can be a few sentences to a few paragraphs in length.

Cross-Platform Issues

This course book applies to both Mac and Windows Pro Tools systems. Most Pro Tools controls, tools, procedures, and menus are similar on all systems. There are, however, some differences in keyboard commands and file naming conventions that readers should be aware of when moving between different platforms.

Keyboard Commands

Many keyboard commands in Pro Tools use *modifier keys*, which are keys pressed in combination with other keys or with a mouse action. The following table summarizes equivalent keys on Mac and Windows:

Mac OS	Windows
Command key (⌘)	Ctrl (Control) key
Option key (⌥)	Alt key
Control key (^)	Start (Win) key (⊞)
Return key	Enter key on main (not numeric) keypad
Delete key	Backspace key

Laptop Computers and Numeric Keypad Commands

Many commands in Pro Tools software are accessible from the numeric keypad of a full-size computer keyboard. If you are using a laptop computer, numeric keypad operations may not be available. In those cases, you can add a USB or Bluetooth numeric keypad to the computer.

File Naming Conventions and File Extensions

Some general differences exist in the way files are named and recognized by Mac and Windows operating systems. Pro Tools can help you avoid conflicts by enforcing conventions that are compatible with both systems whenever possible.

For cross-platform compatibility, all files in a session must have a 3-letter file extension added to the file name. Session files for Pro Tools 10 and later have the extension *.ptx*. Pro Tools 7 through 9.x session files have the extension *.ptf*. Pro Tools 5.1 through 6.9 session files have the extension *.pts*, and Pro Tools 5 sessions have the extension *.pt5*. WAV files have the *.wav* file extension, and AIFF files have the *.aif* file extension.

LESSON 1

Getting Started

This lesson introduces you to the software you will be using for the Pro Tools 110 course and provides an overview of typical hardware systems that the course is designed for. The lesson covers information on the I/O settings for your Pro Tools session and the hardware settings for your system. It also includes details on setting up a session and adjusting the display of the Edit and Mix windows.

GOALS

- Use the Dashboard to open projects and sessions
- Configure hardware options using the Hardware Setup dialog box
- Work with I/O settings using the I/O Setup dialog box
- Use shortcuts to add new tracks to a session
- Configure display options for the Mix and Edit windows

Key topics from this lesson are included in the *Pro Tools 12 Essential Training: 110* course on Lynda.com, available here: alpp.us/PT110_Online.

This lesson provides tips for setting up a system for optimal results as you continue to work on your sessions and projects. You will be introduced to basic settings in the Playback Engine, Hardware Setup, and I/O Setup dialog boxes. You will also review options for quickly adding tracks and options for adjusting the display of your Edit and Mix windows.

About This Course

This course is designed to introduce the core concepts and skills required to operate a Pro Tools 12.8 system running midsized sessions. The material is geared towards students who have a solid understanding of Pro Tools' primary functions, but whose experience may be limited in some areas.

This book addresses typical conditions that you might encounter when working on real-world projects, such as working on sessions with large track counts, configuring specialized track routing with customized I/O settings, and performing mixing and editing operations that require advanced features of Pro Tools software.

The text and screenshots in this book generally represent the user experience on a Mac-based Pro Tools system. Most of the operations discussed are available on all standard Pro Tools software systems. Features that require Pro Tools HD software or specific hardware are noted as such.

Many of the features discussed in this book are available in Pro Tools I First software, which is available for free on Avid.com. Readers who do not own Pro Tools 12 software can use Pro Tools I First to try out the available features; however, a paid version of Pro Tools 12 or Pro Tools I HD 12 is required to complete the course exercises.

Requirements for Exercises

You will be able to complete all of the exercises in this book using standard Pro Tools 12.8 software. Some exercises steps may require a microphone or MIDI controller; however, alternative steps are provided for uses who do not have access to the required hardware.

Software and Hardware

Although parts of the Pro Tools 110 course cover Pro Tools HD software functions, the course is designed to be completed using a standard Pro Tools system (non-HD). No specific audio interface is required; however, your system must be capable of stereo audio playback at a minimum.

Starting Work in Pro Tools

Once you've launched Pro Tools 12.8 (or later), you will be presented with the Dashboard. As discussed in the *Pro Tools 101* course, the Dashboard is your starting point for creating a new local session or cloud-based project. In Pro Tools 12.8 and later, you can also create offline projects from the Dashboard. These are project documents that are stored in your local cache and not backed up to your Avid Cloud account. The offline projects feature allows you to create unlimited project documents without impacting your available cloud storage. Then you can cloud-enable projects selectively whenever you need to work remotely from a different system or if you decide to share a project with a collaborator.

Accessing Existing Sessions and Projects

You also use the Dashboard to open an existing session or project document. Clicking **RECENT** in the left sidebar will show you a list of your recently used sessions and projects (when signed in). Clicking on **PROJECTS** in the left sidebar will show you a list of all project documents that are available to you, based on your user account. In order to access or create project documents (cloud-enabled or not), you must be signed in to your Avid Master Account.

To sign in to your Avid Master Account:

1. Click the **SIGN IN** button in the top right corner of the Dashboard.

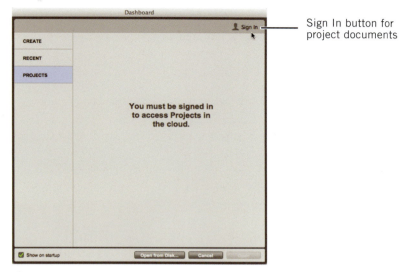

Figure 1.1 Clicking on the Sign In button in the Dashboard

An Account Sign In dialog box will display.

 You must have an active internet connection to sign in. Once signed in, you'll be able to access project documents from your local cache without an internet connection.

2. In the Sign In dialog box, enter the username and password for your Avid Master Account. Then click the **SIGN IN** button at the bottom.

Figure 1.2 User info in the Account Sign In dialog box

When sign-in completes, your available project documents will display on the Projects page of the Dashboard.

If another Pro Tools user has shared a project with you as a collaborator, that project will display in your projects list, along with your own projects.

Before opening or creating a project or document, you can take certain steps to optimize your system. These include configuring the Playback Engine settings, configuring the hardware settings for your audio interface, and configuring the I/O settings.

Configuring the Playback Engine

As discussed in the *Pro Tools 101* book, Pro Tools software provides various settings for optimizing host-based performance. You can configure these settings using the Playback Engine dialog box. You can also use the Playback Engine dialog box to switch between your available audio interface options. It is helpful to select the desired audio interface before creating a Pro Tools document or opening an existing document.

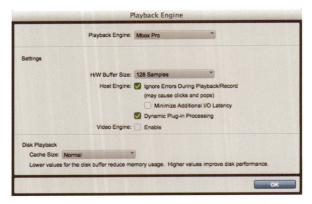

Figure 1.3 Playback Engine dialog box in Pro Tools 12.8

Playback Engine Selector

The Playback Engine selector at the top of the dialog box allows you to choose the audio device that Pro Tools will use for recording and playback. The available options are determined by the audio interfaces you have connected and the type of system you are using.

Changing the Playback Engine setting can be useful to switch between multiple connected audio interfaces, or to switch to or from your computer's built-in audio (Aggregate I/O). Choosing the desired audio interface in advance will help ensure that the I/O settings match when you create or open a Pro Tools document.

 If you change devices with a Pro Tools session open, the session will automatically save and close. Once you dismiss the Playback Engine dialog box, the session will reopen using the new device.

Hardware Buffer Size Selector

The Hardware Buffer Size (H/W Buffer Size) determines the number of samples passed from the audio interface to the computer's CPU at once for host-based processing tasks, such as Native plug-in processing. In Pro Tools 11 and later, this setting only affects tracks using the low-latency processing domain. These include tracks that are record-enabled and tracks receiving live input (such as tracks using input monitoring).

Setting the Hardware Buffer Size

Lowering the H/W Buffer Size will reduce monitoring latency when recording. However, this can also limit the processing power available for plug-in processing and virtual instruments on record-enabled tracks.

Increasing the H/W Buffer Size will allocate more processing power to record-enabled tracks. However, this can also cause unwanted latency during recording and related activities.

As a general rule, you should set your H/W Buffer Size as low as your session will allow when tracking, given the number of tracks you are recording and types of processing that you need for the tracks. If needed, the H/W Buffer Size can be adjusted as you work.

Considerations for the Hardware Buffer Size

Factors that affect the minimum H/W Buffer Size setting you can use include the following:

- The number of Audio tracks being recorded simultaneously. Recording a large number of tracks at once places greater demands on the system and may require a larger buffer size.

- The number and type of plug-ins in use on record-enabled or input-monitored tracks. Native plug-ins can place a high demand on the system. If you are recording on tracks with processing-intensive effects, you may need to increase the H/W Buffer Size to prevent errors.

- The number of virtual instruments in use in the session. Because virtual instruments may be operating in the low-latency domain, they can require higher H/W Buffer Size settings.

 See the discussion on "Auditioning and Playing Back MIDI" in Lesson 4 for tips on reducing the impact of virtual instruments on CPU processing.

- The number and type of Native plug-ins being used on Aux Input tracks. Certain Aux Input tracks may be operating in the low-latency domain, if they are receiving "live" audio from an external source.

Host Engine Error Suppression

Pro Tools systems provide the option to have the software continue playing and recording despite any host processing errors that may occur. This is enabled using the **IGNORE ERRORS DURING PLAYBACK/RECORD** checkbox in the Playback Engine dialog box.

Error suppression should generally be enabled in current versions of Pro Tools software to avoid interruptions during playback and recording.

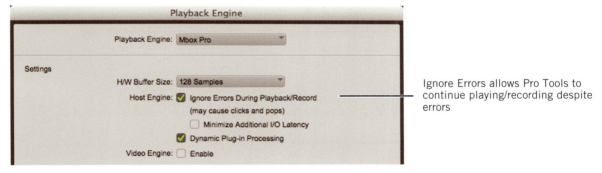

Figure 1.4 Settings section in the Playback Engine dialog box

 Be sure to disable error suppression if you use Pro Tools to print a final mix from real-time playback. Failure to do so can result in pops and clicks in the audio.

Cache Size Selector

The Cache Size setting in the Playback Engine dialog box allocates memory for Pro Tools to pre-buffer audio for playback and recording. The default setting (Normal) is designed to optimize disk performance for general use, dynamically growing the disk cache based on the number of tracks in the session.

You can also set a fixed Cache Sizes to load more session audio into RAM for cached playback. Lower values conserve RAM usage, while higher values improve disk performance.

6 PT110: Pro Tools Fundamentals II

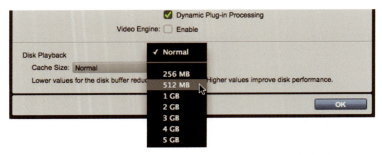

Figure 1.5 Setting the Cache Size in the Playback Engine dialog box

Working with a large RAM cache is especially useful when using shared media storage. With a sufficient amount of RAM allocated, you can cache the entire Pro Tools timeline. This allows for audio playback and recording without any disk access restrictions or bottlenecks.

Configuring Pro Tools Hardware Settings

Once you've selected your audio interface in the Playback Engine dialog box, you can set various options for that device in the Hardware Setup dialog box (**SETUP > HARDWARE**). These include the default sample rate, the current clock source, and other hardware-specific features.

Depending on your active audio interface, you will be able to configure the settings either directly in the Hardware Setup dialog box or in a dedicated control panel that you access from Hardware Setup.

Setting the Default Sample Rate

If you specify a sample rate for your audio interface, this setting will be used as the default whenever you create a new session or project. You can select this setting in Hardware Setup when no session or project is open.

 You can also choose a specific sample rate for a new Pro Tools session by selecting the desired setting in the New Session dialog box.

To change the default sample rate:

1. With no document open, choose **SETUP > HARDWARE**. The Hardware Setup dialog box will display.

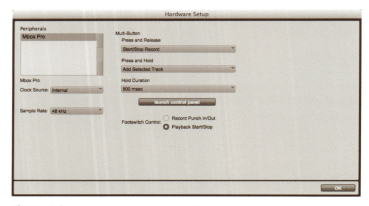

Figure 1.6 Hardware Setup for an Mbox Pro

2. Select a sample rate from the **SAMPLE RATE** pop-up menu on the left side of the dialog box.

3. Click **OK** to close the Hardware Setup dialog box and commit the change.

Changing the Clock Source

The clock source will be set to **Internal** in the Hardware Setup dialog box by default, meaning that the sample clock is derived from the current audio interface. The internal clock setting is appropriate for general-purpose use of your audio interface.

If you use your audio interface to receive digital input from a device connected to the available S/PDIF, ADAT, or AES/EBU connections on your interface or if you synchronize your system with other devices, such as non-linear video systems, you will need to select an external clock source.

The options for external clock will vary based on the type of audio interface you are using and the types of digital connections available. The following discussion uses an Mbox Pro as an example, which can receive external clock from the S/PDIF input or Word Clock connector on the included breakout cable.

To change the clock source:

1. Select a source from the **Clock Source** selector in the Hardware Setup dialog box.

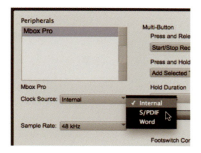

Figure 1.16 Clock Source options for an Mbox Pro audio interface

The Clock Source options available on an Mbox Pro include the following:

- **Internal.** Use this setting when recording analog signals directly into your analog inputs.
- **S/PDIF.** Use this setting when recording through the S/PDIF inputs from an external digital device. This will synchronize the Pro Tools sample clock to that device.
- **Word.** Use this setting when synchronizing Pro Tools to external equipment using Word Clock.

2. Click **OK** to close the Hardware Setup dialog box and commit the change.

 Your digital input device must be connected and powered on for Pro Tools to synchronize to it. If the input device is not powered on, leave the Clock Source set to Internal.

Using a Dedicated Control Panel

When using an audio interface that includes a dedicated control panel, the Hardware Setup dialog box will display a **Launch Control Panel** button. If you are using the built-in audio on your computer (such as Pro Tools Aggregate I/O), Hardware Setup will display a **Launch Setup App** button. Each of these buttons can be used to configure your hardware settings outside of Pro Tools.

Clicking **Launch Control Panel** will launch the associated control panel software for the selected audio interface. Clicking **Launch Setup App** will open the Mac's Audio MIDI Setup utility; from there, you can use the Audio Devices window (**Window > Audio Devices**) to configure the Aggregate I/O settings as desired.

Configuring I/O Settings

When you create a new session or project document in Pro Tools, you are able to specify the document parameters in the Dashboard. As you learned in the Pro Tools 101 course, you can select **Stereo Mix** in the I/O Settings pop-up menu to ensure that your document will be created with default input and output paths that match your active audio interface.

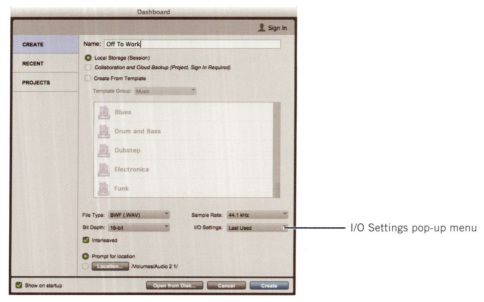

Figure 1.17 Dashboard in Pro Tools 12.8

However, sometimes it is useful to modify your I/O settings with customized names and bus paths. Although you can customize I/O settings at any time, it is helpful to configure your desired settings before creating or opening a Pro Tools document.

Customizing I/O Settings

You can modify your I/O settings in various ways, such as by renaming the signal paths and adding or removing busses. This allows you to customize the inputs, outputs, and busses that are available in the Pro Tools mixer.

> **Example 1.1: Customizing I/O Settings for Effects Sends**
>
> If you use Pro Tools for music production, you may find that you use similar effects processing from one session to the next. Rather than using whatever bus happens to be available when you need to create a delay or reverb send, you might want to create dedicated busses in your I/O settings to use for these purposes.
>
> To do so, you can create two new stereo bus paths, giving them meaningful names (such as *Reverb* and *Delay*). The next time you create a session with the **Last Used** I/O settings, the Reverb and Delay busses will be included.

Accessing I/O Settings

The current I/O settings can be displayed at any time, whether a session is open or not, by selecting **Setup > I/O**. The I/O Setup dialog box will display.

Lesson 1 ■ Getting Started   9

Figure 1.18 I/O Setup dialog box showing the default input paths for an Mbox Pro audio interface

Saving I/O Settings

Any changes you make in I/O Setup are saved on your system as your Last Used I/O settings. This enables you to use a custom I/O configuration for the next session you create or open.

I/O settings are also saved within each session and project document. This ensures that when you open a document, its previously configured settings (custom busses and path names, etc.) remain available.

Pro Tools uses the Last Used I/O settings by default whenever you create a new session or project document. When you open an existing session or project, Pro Tools uses the *system* settings for the **INPUT**, **OUTPUT**, and **INSERT** pages, and it uses the *session* settings for the **BUS** page.

System Settings versus Session Settings

When you create a **new** session or project with the Last Used I/O, Pro Tools uses your system settings on all pages of the I/O Setup dialog box in order to reflect any customizations you've made. System settings are interface-specific. This means that if you select a different audio interface at any point, Pro Tools will begin using the system settings for that audio interface going forward.

When you open an **existing** session, Pro Tools retains the *session's* settings on the Bus page, along the system settings for the Input, Output, and Insert pages. This means that any customizations made to bus paths in a document will override your customized system settings when the document is opened.

Adding and Removing Busses

The I/O Setup dialog box lets you add or remove busses to use for effects sends, submixing, or other signal routing purposes. At times, you may want to add new busses to use for dedicated purposes; at other times you may want to delete some existing busses to keep the bus menus more manageable.

To add busses to a session:

1. In the I/O Setup dialog box, select the **BUS** tab.

2. Click on the **NEW PATH** button just below the bus list. The New Paths dialog box will open.

Figure 1.19 Clicking on the New Path button to add busses in I/O Setup

3. In the New Paths dialog box, specify the number of busses to add, the desired bus format (mono or stereo), and a path name to use for the bus or busses.

Figure 1.20 Specifying details for four new stereo effects send busses

4. Click **CREATE**. The new busses will be added to the bottom of the bus list in I/O Setup. When you add multiple busses with the same path name, the new busses are numbered sequentially.

Figure 1.21 Effects send busses added to I/O Setup

5. When finished adding busses, click **OK** to close the I/O Setup dialog box and commit the changes you've made.

To delete busses from a session:

1. In the I/O Setup dialog box, select the **BUS** tab.
2. In the bus list, select the busses you wish to delete.

> **To select multiple busses, Shift-click on successive bus names (for a contiguous selection) or Command-click (Mac) / Control-click (Windows) (for a non-contiguous selection).**

3. Click on the **DELETE PATH** button below the bus list. The selected busses will immediately be removed from the bus list.

Figure 1.22 Clicking the Delete Path button to remove selected busses

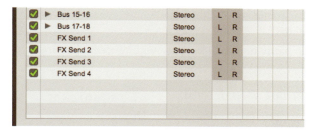

Figure 1.23 Bus list after deleting busses

4. When finished deleting busses, click **OK** to close the I/O Setup dialog box and commit the changes you've made.

Renaming Signal Paths

A signal path is a named group of inputs, outputs, or busses based on a specific channel format. For example, the main stereo outputs for your system may use a signal path called *Out 1-2*, *Analog 1-2*, or *Built-In Output 1-2*, depending on your active audio interface or your computer's built-in sound options. This signal path represents a pair of mono outputs (the left and right channels) that are grouped together as a stereo pair.

The default signal paths in Pro Tools use generic names, such as *Analog 1-2* and *Bus 1-2*. These names are shown in I/O Setup and correspond to the labels that you see when you use Input, Output, and Send selectors.

Figure 1.24 Default input paths for the Mbox Pro as displayed in the I/O Setup dialog box

You can rename signal paths at any time to make them more descriptive and to better reflect their use in a given session.

To rename stereo paths in I/O Setup:

1. In the I/O Setup dialog box, select the tab containing the signal paths you wish to rename (**INPUT**, **OUTPUT**, or **BUS**).

2. If needed, click a disclosure triangle next to a stereo path name to display its subpaths (individual mono paths within the stereo path).

Figure 1.25 Click a disclosure triangle to display mono subpaths.

3. Double-click on a path name to change it. The name field will become highlighted, allowing you to enter a new name.

4. Type the desired name and press **ENTER** or **RETURN** when finished.

5. Repeat the above steps to rename other signal paths.

> **To automatically move to the next path while renaming multiple paths, press the Tab key.**

6. When finished renaming signal paths, click **OK** to close the I/O Setup dialog box and commit the changes you've made.

The signal path names from I/O Setup appear as input, output, and send options in Pro Tools channel strips in the Mix window.

The example in Figure 1.26 below shows input paths as they might appear after customizing the I/O settings.

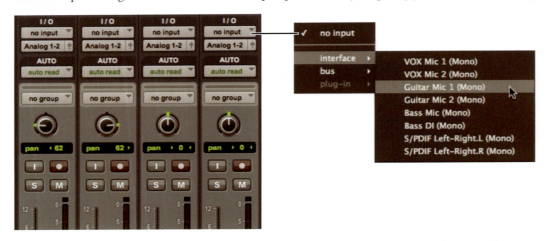

Figure 1.26 Input paths displayed in a track Audio Input Path selector in the Pro Tools Mix window

Setting the Audition Path

The Audition Path setting is used for all of Pro Tools' audition and preview functions. These functions include auditioning clips in the Clip List; auditioning files in Soundbase, Workspace browsers, and the Import Audio dialog box; auditioning fades in the Fades dialog box; and previewing effects in AudioSuite plug-in windows.

The Audition Path selector in the I/O Setup dialog box lets you specify the Output path to use for playing back auditions. The Audition Path defaults to your main monitor path. You can change this setting, if your audio interface has sufficient I/O, to perform auditions without disturbing playback through the main outputs.

To change the Audition Path for Pro Tools:

1. Choose **Setup > I/O**.

2. Click on the **Output** tab.

3. Click the **Audition Path** selector near the bottom of the dialog box and select an alternate Output path.

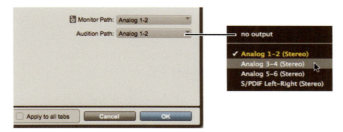

Figure 1.27 Setting a new stereo Audition path for an Mbox Pro

4. When finished, click **OK** to accept the change and close the I/O Setup dialog box.

Setting the Default Output Bus

The Default Output Bus selector in the I/O Setup dialog box can be used to set the output bus assignment that Pro Tools uses by default for new tracks that you create. You can select a different default output bus for each supported track format (mono, stereo, etc.).

 The Default Output Bus can be set to an internal mix bus or an output bus.

To specify a default output for new tracks in the I/O Setup dialog box:

1. Choose **Setup > I/O**.

2. Click on the **Bus** tab.

3. Click the **Default Output Bus** selector and select a format and destination.

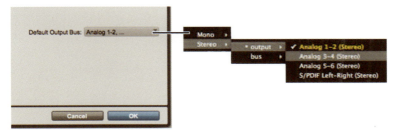

Figure 1.28 Setting a new default output path for stereo tracks

4. When finished, click **OK** to accept the change and close the I/O Setup dialog box.

Opening a Session or Project and Adding Tracks

Once you've configured your system as desired, you can create a new session or project document or open an existing document. The Pro Tools 101 book provides details on creating a new Pro Tools document, so here we'll focus on opening a work-in-progress to do some additional recording, editing, and mixing.

Opening a Recently Used Pro Tools Document

To open a session or project that you have worked on recently from the current system, choose **FILE > OPEN RECENT** and select the document from the displayed submenu. If the document is not shown in this menu, choose **FILE > CREATE NEW** or **FILE > OPEN PROJECT** to display the Dashboard. Then click on **RECENT** in the left sidebar to display a list of recently used sessions and projects.

The File > Open Recent submenu shows only the last 10 Pro Tools documents used on the system. The Recent list in the Dashboard is a longer, scrollable list.

The recent files list includes all sessions that have been opened recently on the system (regardless of who used the system), but it shows only projects that have been opened recently by the currently logged in user.

To prevent other users from gaining access to the projects in your Avid Master Account, be sure to log out when finished working on borrowed systems or systems in a shared lab or workgroup environment.

Adding Tracks as You Work

In the Pro Tools 101 course, you learned how to use the New Tracks dialog box to add tracks to a session or project document. This dialog box provides a great way to add a whole set of tracks at once, especially if you know in advance how many different tracks of each type you are likely to need.

However, it is also common to add tracks one at a time as you work. Pro Tools lets you do this quickly using various double-click shortcut operations.

Adding a New Track Like the Previous

If you have already added one or more tracks since opening your session, you can quickly add another track that matches the last track you created. The newly added track will have the same type (Audio, Instrument, Aux Input, etc.) and channel width (mono or stereo) as the previously added track.

To add a new track matching the last track created, double-click in one of the following locations:

- In an empty area of the Mix window, below or to the right of any current tracks
- In the empty area of the Edit window, below any current tracks
- In the empty area below any current tracks in the Track List

If you haven't added any new tracks since opening the session, double-clicking in one of the above locations will create a new stereo Audio track by default.

Adding a New Track of a Specific Type

By using modifiers in combination with the double-click shortcut, you can quickly add a track of a specific type (Audio, Instrument, Aux Input, or Master Fader). The channel width of the newly added track will generally match that of any previously added track (with the exception of Instrument tracks, which are always added as stereo tracks when using the double-click shortcut).

To add a new track of a specific type, use one of the following double-click shortcuts:

- Audio Track: COMMAND+DOUBLE-CLICK (Mac) or CTRL+DOUBLE-CLICK (Windows)
- Instrument Track: OPTION+DOUBLE-CLICK (Mac) or ALT+DOUBLE-CLICK (Windows)
- Auxiliary Input Track: CONTROL+DOUBLE-CLICK (Mac) or START+DOUBLE-CLICK (Windows)
- Master Fader: SHIFT+DOUBLE-CLICK (Mac or Windows)

If you haven't added any new tracks since opening the session, the above operations will create a new stereo track of the specified type by default.

 Using multiple modifiers in combination with the double-click shortcut will add one track of each type, based on the modifier relationship. For example, using COMMAND+OPTION+DOUBLE-CLICK on a Mac will simultaneously add a new Audio track and a new Instrument track.

Configuring Track Routing

After adding a new track, you will commonly need to configure the input or output routing of the track. For example, suppose you've added a new Aux Input track to use as an effects return using a bus send from various source tracks. After renaming the track, you will need to route the proper bus to the track's input.

Figure 1.29 Routing an effects send to an Aux Input track using a custom bus path

After completing the routing, you may want to customize the signal path with a more descriptive name. You can quickly rename a signal path from any input, output, or send selector where the bus has been assigned.

To rename a signal paths from an input, output, or send selector:

1. Right-click on the path selector and choose RENAME from the pop-up menu.

Figure 1.30 Renaming the path "FX Return 1" from the right-click menu for the Input Path selector

2. In the resulting Rename I/O dialog box, type a new name for the signal path. (See Figure 1.31.)

Figure 1.31 Specifying a new name in the Rename I/O dialog box

3. Click **OK** to apply the new path name. The new name will appear in the path selector and will replace the previous name in the I/O Setup dialog box.

Edit and Mix Window Display Options

As you continue your work, you may find it useful to show or hide various views in the Mix or Edit windows. This section discusses some useful view options and introduces shortcuts for modifying your window views. These options give you greater control over how Pro Tools displays its windows, tracks, and track data.

Changing the Display of the Mix and Edit Windows

The Mix and Edit windows can be customized to show or hide optional components to suit your needs and working preferences. Various selections in the View menu (Mix Window Views, Edit Window Views, and Rulers) allow you to toggle component parts on and off in the associated window.

Items that are checked in the submenus are currently displayed. Selecting a view will toggle its display state.

Figure 1.32 Using the View menu to select the I/O view in the Edit window

Using View Selectors

As an alternative to using the View menu, it is often quicker to use the View selector controls provided in the Mix and Edit windows to toggle the desired views on/off. The available controls include the Edit Window View selector, the Ruler View selector, and the Mix Window View selector.

Each View selector provides access to options that mirror those available under the View menu.

To display or hide a view in the Edit window, do the following:

1. Click on the **Edit Window View selector** above the track display area in the Edit window.

2. Select the view to toggle on/off from the pop-up menu.

Figure 1.33 Using the Edit Window View selector to display the I/O view

To display or hide a Ruler in the Edit window, do the following:

1. Click on the **Ruler View selector** in the Main Timebase Ruler display in the Edit window.

2. Select the ruler to toggle on/off from the pop-up menu.

Figure 1.34 Using the Ruler View selector to display or hide rulers

To display or hide a view in the Mix window, do the following:

1. Click on the **Mix Window View selector** in the lower-left corner of the Mix window.

2. Select the view to toggle on/off from the pop-up menu.

Figure 1.35 Using the Mix Window View selector to display the Comments view

   You can also access the list of available views by right-clicking on the label for any displayed view in the Mix or Edit windows. This is often faster than using a View selector, especially when working in the Mix window.

   Option-click (Mac) or Alt-click (Windows) on the label at the top of a view column in the Edit window or above a view row in the Mix window to hide the view. The clicked view will disappear from the display in the window.

Mix Window Track Width

The Mix window allows you to globally change all channel strips to a narrower width. This allows you to view more tracks on screen at once in the Mix window and reduces the amount of scrolling you will need to do when working on a large session.

To change the Mix window display:

- Choose **VIEW > NARROW MIX**. The Mix window channel strips will change to a narrow display.

- To return to the normal width, choose **VIEW > NARROW MIX** a second time.

Figure 1.36 Mix window in normal width view (left) and Narrow Mix view (right)

 Press OPTION+COMMAND+M (Mac) or CTRL+ALT+M (Windows) to toggle between the two Mix window display options.

Using the I/O View

I/O controls are typically visible in the Mix window. These controls can also be displayed in the Edit window, using the optional I/O view. This view displays each track's input and output assignment, track volume, and pan settings.

Figure 1.37 I/O view displayed in the Edit window

Using the Comments View

The Comments view is available in both the Mix and Edit windows, allowing you to display comments that have been entered for a track. After showing the Comments view, you will see any previously entered comments displayed with each track in your session.

Lesson 1 ■ Getting Started   19

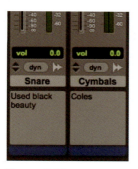 

Figure 1.38 Comments view displayed in the Mix window (left) and Edit window (right)

Using Collaboration Tools (Project Documents Only)

When working on a project document, the Edit window will display Global Track Collaboration tools in the Edit window toolbar, along with Track Collaboration controls at the head of each track. The Track Collaboration controls can also be displayed in the Mix window, above the I/O section.

The collaboration tools are only necessary when you want to share a project with other Pro Tools users for remote collaboration. Since this is often not the case, you can generally hide the collaboration tools to reduce clutter and distraction in the Mix and Edit windows.

Global Track Collaboration Tools

The Global Track Collaboration tools are displayed in the Edit window toolbar. These tools are used for posting and receiving all shared track data when collaborating. When working on an offline project (without cloud backup), these controls will be inactive and grayed out on screen.

Figure 1.39 Global Track Collaboration tools in the Edit window

To hide the Global Track Collaboration tools:

1. Click on the Edit window toolbar pop-up menu at the top-right edge of the window.

Figure 1.40 Displaying the Edit window toolbar pop-up menu

2. Click on **Track Collaboration** to deselect it. The Global Track Collaboration tools will be hidden in the Edit window toolbar.

Individual Track Collaboration Controls

The Track Collaboration controls for individual tracks are displayed at the head of each track in the Edit window. You can use these controls to share a track with a collaborator, to take or release ownership of a track, to upload changes on a shared track, or to download changes made by a collaborator into your local copy.

Figure 1.41 Track Collaboration controls at the head of a track

To hide the Track Collaboration controls in the Edit window:

1. Click on the **EDIT WINDOW VIEW SELECTOR** above the track display area in the Edit window.
2. Click on **TRACK COLLABORATION** to deselect it. The Track Collaboration view will be hidden at the head of the tracks.

To hide the Track Collaboration controls in the Mix window:

1. Click on the **MIX WINDOW VIEW SELECTOR** in the bottom left corner of the Mix window.
2. Click on **TRACK COLLABORATION** to deselect it. The Track Collaboration view will be hidden in the Mix window.

 You can also right-click above the Track Collaboration controls in the Mix window to deselect it from the list of available views.

Track List Display Options

The Track List, located in the left side column of both the Edit and Mix windows, displays the names of all the tracks in a session. This list provides a quick reference to view and select tracks and also lets you modify your display by showing and hiding individual tracks and changing the track order.

Showing and Hiding Tracks

Hiding a track allows you to remove the track from view without deleting it. When you hide a track, the track remains in the session, but it does not display in the Edit and Mix windows.

 Hidden tracks continue to play back even while not displayed.

Track Show/Hide status is linked between the Mix and Edit windows. (The Score Editor and MIDI Editor windows have independent track Show/Hide functionality.) Hiding a track in the Edit window also hides it in the Mix window but does not hide it in the Score Editor or MIDI Editor.

To hide a track, do the following:

- In the Track List, click the **TRACK SHOW/HIDE** icon (solid black dot next to the track name). The icon will dim, and the track will disappear from the Edit and Mix windows.

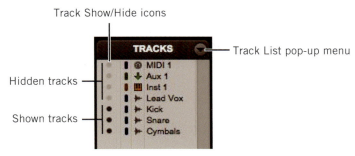

Figure 1.42 The Pro Tools Track List

In the example above, the tracks MIDI 1, Aux 1, Inst 1, and Lead Vox are hidden in the Mix and Edit windows, but they will continue to play back in the session.

To show a hidden track, do the following:

- In the Track List, click the dimmed **TRACK SHOW/HIDE** icon for the track you want to show. The icon will turn solid black, and the track will reappear in the Edit and Mix windows.

Using the Track List Pop-Up Menu

In addition to the Track Show/Hide icons, the Track List includes a pop-up menu that provides access to track-specific commands. These commands are not available under Pro Tools' main menus.

 Context-focused pop-up menus are available throughout the Pro Tools user interface, providing access to commands not available through the main menus. Pop-up menu locations are signified by a circle icon containing a down-pointing triangle.

To show or hide all tracks, all selected tracks, or tracks of a certain type:

1. Click the Track List pop-up menu.

2. Choose a display option from the pop-up menu or the available submenus. Available options include showing only tracks of a certain type, hiding only tracks of a certain type, showing or hiding all selected tracks, and showing or hiding all tracks.

Figure 1.43 Displaying only Audio tracks

After changing the displayed tracks from the pop-up menu, you can restore the previous track display by clicking on the Track List pop-up menu a second time and selecting **RESTORE PREVIOUSLY SHOWN TRACKS**.

Review/Discussion Questions

1. How can you sign in to your Avid Master Account when starting work in Pro Tools? What is required to sign in to your account? (See "Starting Work in Pro Tools" beginning on page 2.)

2. Why is it important to select the audio interface you want to use prior to creating or opening a session? What dialog box can you use for this purpose? (See "Playback Engine Selector" beginning on page 4.)

3. What is the H/W Buffer Size setting in the Playback Engine dialog box used for? What kinds of tracks are affected by this setting? (See "Setting the Hardware Buffer Size" beginning on page 4.)

4. What dialog box can you use to configure the available options for your connected audio interface? What are some of the options you can configure in this dialog box? (See "Configuring Pro Tools Hardware Settings" beginning on page 6.)

5. How can you specify the I/O settings that Pro Tools will use when you create a new session? (See "Configuring I/O Settings" beginning on page 8.)

6. Where are changes to Pro Tools I/O settings saved? Are they stored in the session or on the system? (See "Saving I/O Settings" beginning on page 9.)

7. What dialog box can you use to rename signal paths? (See "Renaming Signal Paths" beginning on page 11.)

8. How can you configure an audition path in Pro Tools? (See "Setting the Audition Path" beginning on page 12.)

9. What are some ways to open a recently used project or session on a system? (See "Opening a Recently Used Pro Tools Document" beginning on page 14.)

10. What shortcut operations are available for adding individual tracks to your session? (See "Adding Tracks as You Work" beginning on page 14.)

11. What options are available for changing the display of the Mix and Edit windows? What are some of the optional views available in each window? (See "Changing the Display of the Mix and Edit Windows" beginning on page 16.)

12. How can you easily show or hide tracks in Pro Tools? What is the difference between hiding a track and deleting a track? (See "Showing and Hiding Tracks" beginning on page 20.)

13. What are some options available in the Track List pop-up menu? (See "Using the Track List Pop-Up Menu" beginning on page 21.)

To review additional material from this chapter, see the PT110 Study Guide module available through the Elements|ED online learning platform at ElementsED.com.

EXERCISE 1

Setting Up a Session

In Lesson 1, you learned how to work with I/O settings and how to use various shortcut operations to add tracks. In this exercise, you will use some of these techniques to familiarize yourself with the controls in I/O Setup and to prepare a session with proper I/O paths.

Duration: 20 Minutes

Downloading the Media Files

To complete the exercises in this book, you will need to download the associated media files or obtain them from your instructor. Be sure to save the files to a location that you will have ongoing access to as you complete the exercises and projects in this book.

To download the media files, point your browser to http://alpp.us/PT110-128.

*Note: The above URL is **case sensitive**.*

Modifying the System I/O

To get started with this exercise, you will modify your system I/O settings for inputs, outputs, and bus paths.

Modify your system input paths:

1. Launch Pro Tools and dismiss the Dashboard, if it appears, by clicking CANCEL.

2. With no session open, choose SETUP > I/O to open the I/O Setup dialog box.

3. Select the INPUT page from the tabs at the top of the dialog box.

    The Input page will display the system settings, based on the hardware you are currently using and any customizations that may have been made on the system. (See Figure 1.44.)

Exercise 1 ■ Setting Up a Session   25

Figure 1.44 The Input page of I/O Setup showing the default input paths for an Mbox Pro

4. Double-click on the top input path to rename it. The path name will become highlighted within a text field for editing.

Figure 1.45 Input path selected for renaming

5. Rename the signal path as **Custom 1-2**. Press **Return** or **Enter** when finished, keeping the I/O Setup dialog box open.

Figure 1.46 Renamed input path

Modify the outputs and bus paths:

1. Switch to the Output page by clicking on the **Output** tab at the top of the dialog box.

2. Press **Command+A** (Mac) or **Ctrl+A** (Windows) to select all of the output paths.

26 PT110: Pro Tools Fundamentals II

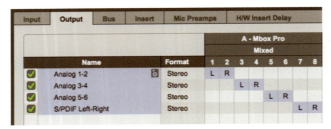

Figure 1.47 Output paths selected (Mbox Pro shown)

3. Click the **Delete Path** button below the path list on the left. All selected output paths will be removed.

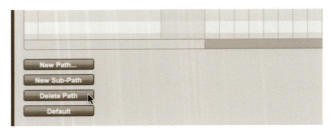

Figure 1.48 Clicking on the Delete Path button to remove selected output paths

4. Next, switch to the Bus page by clicking on the **Bus** tab.

5. Reset the bus paths to defaults by clicking the **Default** button below the path list on the left.

Figure 1.49 Clicking the Default button to reset the bus paths

The path list will update to show the default internal mix busses: **Bus 1-2** through **Bus 23-24**.

6. When finished, commit the changes you've made by clicking **OK** to close the I/O Setup dialog box.

Creating a Session

Next, you will create a new session from the Off To Work template file included with the course exercise media and save it on your system in the class files location specified by your instructor.

Open the template and save the session:

1. Choose **File > Open Session**.

2. Navigate to the Exercise Media folder and open the *Off To Work.ptxt* template file
   [PT110 Exercise Media (v12.8) > 01 Off To Work > Off To Work.ptxt].

   A dialog box will open displaying default parameters based on the template. (See Figure 1.50.)

Exercise 1 ■ Setting Up a Session   27

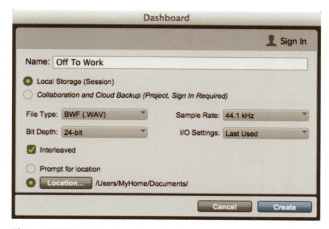

Figure 1.50 Dialog box for selecting parameter settings for the new session

3. Name the session 110 Exercise 1 [Your Initials] and select the **Prompt for location** option near the bottom of the dialog box.

4. Click **Create** to proceed. A second dialog box will open, prompting you to choose a save location.

5. Navigate to an appropriate location and click **Save**. A new session will open with a single GTR track.

Configuring Your I/O

In this part of the exercise, you will reset the I/O settings to their defaults and observe the effects that this has on the session.

Resetting I/O

To get started, you will reset the I/O to defaults on the Input, Output, and Bus pages of the I/O Setup dialog box.

Reset the Input page to defaults:

1. Choose **Setup > I/O** to open the I/O Setup dialog box; then select the **Input** page.

2. Click the **Default** button below the path list on the left. The input paths will reset to their defaults.

> **Discussion Point #1**
>
> What did the input paths look like before you reset them? Did this reflect the system settings or the session settings?

Reset the Output and Bus pages:

1. Select the **Output** page in the I/O Setup dialog box.

2. Notice that the Audition Path is set to **None**. This page reflects the Last Used system settings, so the session has no output paths available.

3. Click the **Default** button below the path list on the left. The default output paths will appear.

> ### Discussion Point #2
> What does the Audition Path setting display after resetting the output paths to default? What is the purpose of this setting and why might you want to change it?

4. Next, select the **Bus** page in the I/O Setup dialog box.
5. Scroll through the path list to examine the currently included busses.
6. Click the **Default** button below the path list on the left. The path list will update to display the default output busses and internal mix busses.
7. When finished, commit the changes you've made by clicking **OK** to close the I/O Setup dialog box.

> ### Discussion Point #3
> Before resetting the output paths, did they reflect the system settings or the session settings? How did they change when you clicked the Default button?

Adding a New Track

In this part of the exercise you will add a new Audio track to your session for use with the **Drums_01** clip in the session's Clip List. You will also reset the Outputs for the session for proper playback.

Add an Audio track to the session:

1. Press **Command** (Mac) or **Ctrl** (Windows) while double-clicking in the Edit window, below the GTR track. A new stereo Audio track will be added to your session.
2. Double-click the track nameplate and rename the track **Drums**.
3. **Option-click** (Mac) or **Alt-click** (Windows) on each of the clips in the Clip List (Drums_01 and GTR_01) to audition them.

    Note that the GTR_01 clip has silence at the beginning, so you will need to hold down the mouse until playback begins.

4. Drag the **Drums_01** clip from the Clip List onto the **Drums** track and position it at the beginning of the session.
5. Press the **Spacebar** to play back the tracks in your session. You will likely hear only the drums.

> ### Discussion Point #4
> What output path was used on the new track that you added for the drums? Why do you think you cannot hear the GTR track during playback?

Correct the GTR output path:

1. In the I/O view of the Edit window, compare the output for the GTR track to that of the Drums track. Note that the output of the GTR track is set to 1-2, which is an inactive output.

2. Reassign the GTR track output by clicking on the **AUDIO OUTPUT PATH SELECTOR** and choosing **OUTPUT > ANALOG 1-2 (STEREO) –> ANALOG 1-2** (or the main stereo output path for your hardware).

Figure 1.51 Assigning the GTR track to the main stereo outputs

Finishing Up

Before exiting Pro Tools, listen to the session to ensure proper playback. Also be sure to save the work you have done for future use or to submit for a grade.

Listen to your work and save the session:

1. Press **RETURN** (Mac) or **ENTER** (Windows) to return to the start of the session.

2. Press the **SPACEBAR** to begin playback. Listen to the session to ensure that the tracks all play back through your main outputs.

3. If any track is not included in the playback, diagnose and correct the issue before moving on. Ask your instructor for assistance if you cannot determine the source of the problem.

4. Once you've verified playback, save and close the session (**FILE > CLOSE SESSION**). That completes this exercise.

 Remember that you cannot close a Pro Tools session by closing its windows. You must choose CLOSE SESSION from the FILE menu.

LESSON 2

Managing Session Data and Media Files

This lesson covers the capabilities of standard Pro Tools software and draws some comparisons to Pro Tools|HD software. It also discusses various ways to use the Workspace browser and Soundbase features and presents techniques for locating, auditioning, importing, and working with files in a Pro Tools session. The lesson ends with a discussion of clip groups and related topics.

GOALS

- Understand the capabilities of a Pro Tools 12 system
- Locate files using Workspace browsers
- Explore sound libraries using Soundbase
- Audition audio in a browser
- Import files in multiple ways
- Work with clip groups

Key topics from this lesson are included in the *Pro Tools 12 Essential Training: 110* course on Lynda.com, available here: alpp.us/PT110_Online.

Pro Tools projects often contain a large number of media files and can grow in both size and complexity as you work. As such, managing the associated data and media files can present a challenge. This lesson will help you understand the capabilities of Pro Tools in music and post-production work environments. It discusses techniques you can use to locate specific files. It also presents information on importing and working with various types of media files in your current session or project document. Lastly, it shows you how to combine clips from your media files into clip groups to simplify the processes of selecting and manipulating the clips.

Pro Tools Software Capabilities

Standard Pro Tools software provides a rich feature set for working with audio, along with the ability to import a Video track for reference during post-production tasks. Pro Tools|HD software expands on the features provided with standard Pro Tools, adding support for surround mixing and basic video editing.

This section describes some of the capabilities of standard Pro Tools software and provides a summary of some key differences in Pro Tools|HD.

Basic Specifications

Pro Tools 12 provides sampling rates of up to 192 kHz with bit depths of up to 32-bit floating point. Standard Pro Tools software powers up to 128 simultaneous mono or stereo Audio tracks and provides up to 32 channels of simultaneous I/O.

Pro Tools HD Software

Standard Pro Tools systems can be upgraded to Pro Tools|HD software at any time. Pro Tools|HD offers higher track counts and hardware options that expand your available I/O. Pro Tools|HD Native systems provide up to 64 channels of I/O, while Pro Tools|HDX systems provide up to 192 channels of I/O.

Pro Tools|HD also provides numerous software features and enhancements. Some key Pro Tools|HD software features include the following:

- Full surround mixing capabilities, up to 7.1.2 Dolby Atmos formats

- Advanced automation features, including Snapshot automation and Glide automation commands

- Video editing features

Working with Digital Video

Standard Pro Tools software allows you to import a single video clip into your session, which automatically creates a Video track. Although you can make selections on the Video track with the Selector tool and move (reposition) the video clip with the Grabber tool, all other editing functions are disabled.

With Pro Tools|HD software, various additional editing features and functions are enabled for working with digital video, including the following:

- Ability to import multiple video clips into a session (on a Video track or in the Clip List)

- Ability to include multiple Video tracks in the Timeline (only one can be played back at a time)

- Ability to edit video clips (e.g., cut, copy, paste, and delete selections) on a Video track

Other video editing capabilities include non-destructive editing, multiple undos, editing across multiple tracks, separating and healing clips, and more.

Lesson 2 ■ Managing Session Data and Media Files   33

> ### A Word about Editing Video
>
> While it is possible to perform simple video edits using Pro Tools HD software, it is important to recognize that Pro Tools is not a substitute for a dedicated video editing application, such as Avid Media Composer, Apple Final Cut Pro, or Adobe Premiere Pro. The video editing capabilities provided in Pro Tools are primarily geared toward the needs of audio professionals who work in post-production. As such, common video editing techniques such as adding dissolves and transitions are not possible in Pro Tools.
>
> When doing professional post-production work with video, it is important to set the Pro Tools Timecode ruler to match the frame rate of your video clips. This can be done using the Timecode Rate selector in the Session Setup window (**Setup > Session**). It is also useful to set your main timebase to use the Timecode ruler (**View > Main Counter > Timecode**) and to set your Grid to **Timecode: 1 frame**.

Setting Up Video Tracks

In standard Pro Tools software, a Video track will be created whenever you import a compatible video file; it is not possible to create a Video track any other way. The imported file will automatically be placed on the track.

With Pro Tools|HD software, however, you can create Video tracks with or without video clips on them and add or remove video clips as needed.

 Additional details on managing and editing digital video in Pro Tools|HD are provided in the Pro Tools 210P course book.

Video Playback on a Secondary Monitor

With current versions of Pro Tools, it is possible to display full-screen video playback from the Video window on a separate connected DVI computer monitor, HDMI screen, or projector. To do so, the video monitoring device must first be connected to your computer as a secondary display.

To use the Video window for full-screen playback:

1. Select **Window > Video**, or press **Command+[9]** (Mac) or **Ctrl+[9]** (Windows) on the numeric keypad to open the Video window.

2. Click on the title bar area of the Video window and drag the window to the desired connected DVI computer monitor or other secondary display.

3. Right-click inside the Video window display area and select **Fullscreen** from the pop-up menu.

Figure 2.1 Selecting the fullscreen display option in the Video window

The window will expand to fill the screen on the secondary display, with the title bar hidden.

Using Workspace Browsers

Workspace browsers are database management tools for Pro Tools, offering search and import capabilities as well as tools for managing data inside and outside of your session. Workspace browsers combine a browser-style interface with an integrated databasing engine, optimized for Pro Tools media management.

Browser Features

Some of the features of Workspace browsers include the following:

- Search across one or more mounted drives (volumes), using a combination of file properties.
- Audition audio files.
- Use Elastic Audio features to audition and conform audio files to the session tempo.
- Drag and drop files into an open session.

 Additional Workspace browser features and functionality are covered in the 200-level Pro Tools courses.

Workspace Browser Overview

Workspace browsers provide access to features optimized for media management. Browsers let you search and sort audio files, video files, and sessions.

Workspace browser windows provide a unified interface that can be focused on a variety of specific locations. Available focus areas for a Workspace browser include:

- Sound Libraries (installed sample packs and loop libraries)
- Volumes (storage drives)
- Session (currently open Pro Tools document)
- Catalogs (user-created file collections)
- User (current user's home directory)

The main elements of a Workspace browser include the Toolbar area, Locations pane, and Workspace pane.

Figure 2.2 Main elements of a Pro Tools Workspace browser

The browser window provides useful information and controls for searching and auditioning files:

- The Title bar at the top of the window shows the browser focus and/or the name of the targeted volume, session, or catalog.

- The Toolbar provides access to View Presets 1 through 5, browser navigation and preview tools, Search tools, tagging functions, and the Browser pop-up menu.

- The Locations pane displays the available focus areas: Sound Libraries, Volumes, Session, Catalogs, and User locations.

- The Workspace pane shows search results, including columns of metadata (file properties) for volumes, folders, and files.

In this course, we focus primarily on the functionality provided when a Workspace browser is focused on volumes.

Information on functionality specific to other browser focus areas is provided in the Pro Tools 200-level courses.

Workspace Browser Functionality

A Workspace browser provides access to all your mounted volumes as well as the folders and files they contain. The Workspace browser window allows you to do the following:

- Access, view, and search the contents of all mounted volumes.

- Designate volumes for record and playback, playback only, or transfer only.

- View, manage, audition, and import individual files from any mounted volume.

- Locate and open a session from any mounted volume.

It is also possible to create and update indexes for your drives from a Workspace browser. Indexing your drives allows them to be searched very quickly from within a Workspace browser.

For any of the above function, you will start by opening a Workspace browser window.

To open a new Workspace browser, do one of the following:

- Choose **WINDOW > NEW WORKSPACE > DEFAULT**.

- Press **OPTION+I** (Mac) or **ALT+I** (Windows).

Refer to Lesson 4 of the Pro Tools 101 course for information on using the Workspace browser to locate and open a session.

Waveform Display

The Waveform column of a Workspace browser shows the waveforms that have been calculated for audio files. (See Figure 2.3.) Waveforms will display under any of the following conditions:

- The waveform has previously been calculated and stored

- The file has been imported into a session (waveforms are automatically calculated on import)

- The file has been auditioned in a Workspace browser (waveforms are calculated on playback)

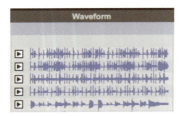

Figure 2.3 Waveform displays in a browser

Waveforms are not shown if they have not yet been calculated.

If an audio file item does not have a waveform, the waveform can be calculated by selecting the file and choosing **Calculate Waveform** from the Workspace browser pop-up menu or pressing the **spacebar** to audition the file.

Auditioning Audio Files

Audio files can be auditioned from within Workspace browsers in various ways. Auditioning allows you to preview audio files before importing to help you identify files correctly. Audio files can be previewed at the session tempo using the Elastic Audio capabilities of the software. Files can also be previewed in context, allowing you to audition files while Pro Tools is playing back a session.

Auditioning follows the Audition Path selected in the Output pane of the Pro Tools I/O Setup dialog box (see Lesson 1). The audition level can be adjusted using the Volume control in the browser Toolbar.

Basic Previews

To audition audio in a browser, do any one of the following:

- Select an audio file in the Workspace pane and press the **spacebar**. Playback will begin from the start of the file. Press the **spacebar** a second time to stop the preview.

  > The option for **Spacebar Toggles File Preview** must be selected in the Browser pop-up menu to start and stop previews with the spacebar.

- Select an audio file in the Workspace pane and click on the **Preview** button in the browser Toolbar. Playback will begin from the start of the file. Click a second time to stop the preview.

Figure 2.4 Clicking the Preview button in a Browser toolbar

- Click on the **Play** icon to the left of a waveform display. Playback will begin from the start of the file. Click the **Play** button again or press the **spacebar** to stop the preview.

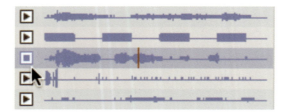

Figure 2.5 Auditioning an audio file using the Play icon

- Click anywhere in a waveform display to begin playback mid-file. (See Figure 2.6.) Playback will begin at the selected point. Press the **SPACEBAR** to stop the preview.

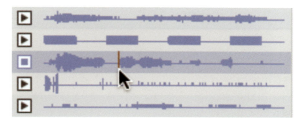

Figure 2.6 Auditioning from a specific location within an audio file

Previewing at the Session Tempo

To preview audio files at the session tempo, do the following:

1. Enable the **AUDIO FILES CONFORM TO SESSION TEMPO** button (metronome) in the browser Toolbar.

Figure 2.7 Enabling the Audio Files Conform to Session Tempo function on the Toolbar

> The option for **AUDIO FILES CONFORM TO SESSION TEMPO** can also be toggled on/off by selecting it from the Browser pop-up menu.

2. Right-click on the **METRONOME** icon to select the appropriate Elastic Audio processor.

> For information on Elastic Audio processor options, see Lesson 5.

3. Place the insertion point in the session at the location where you want to preview the file.

4. Activate preview using any of the audition methods described above. The selected audio file will play back using the tempo in effect for the session at the insertion point.

When **AUDIO FILES CONFORM TO SESSION TEMPO** is enabled, Pro Tools will perform Elastic Audio analysis on any unanalyzed audio files that you preview. Once analyzed, the **KIND** column in the Workspace pane will display a metronome icon next to the *Audio File* description and will show the file's duration in Bars|Beats and its native tempo in BPM.

Previewing in Context

To preview audio files in context with your session, do the following:

1. Enable **AUDIO FILES CONFORM TO SESSION TEMPO** as described above.

2. Activate playback of your session by pressing the **[0]** (zero) key on your numeric keypad.

3. Activate preview using any of the audition methods previously described. The selected audio file will begin playback on the next downbeat in your session.

To enable continuous playback of previewed files, select LOOP PREVIEW from the Browser menu or right-click the PREVIEW button and select LOOP PREVIEW from the pop-up menu.

> **Example 2.1: Importing a Drum Loop**
>
> A common technique in music production is to supplement the rhythm for a portion of a song with an imported drum or percussion loop. When searching for an appropriate loop to import, it can be helpful to hear how the loop candidates will sound when played with your session.
>
> To do so, you can focus a Workspace browser on your loop library, and enable both the AUDIO FILES CONFORM TO SESSION TEMPO option and the LOOP PREVIEW option. With a file selected in your loop library, you can press [0] to begin Pro Tools playback followed by SPACEBAR to begin loop preview. The selected file will loop repeatedly as the session plays back.
>
> During playback, you can use the UP ARROW and DOWN ARROW keys on your alphanumeric keypad to select the previous or next file in your library. Subsequently selected files will begin previewing immediately after the currently playing loop ends.

Using Soundbase

Soundbase is a Workspace browser window that allows you to find audio files using tags. Tags are descriptive labels that are saved as metadata (file properties) within a WAV or AIFF audio file. You can add tags to WAV or AIFF files from any Workspace browser window, or you use audio files from a pre-tagged sound library.

> **Loopmasters Sample Pack**
>
> Pro Tools 12.7 and later come with the Avid Loopmasters Sample Pack 1.0, a fully tagged 2 GB collection of loops and samples. The Loopmasters installer is included separately and can be installed from your Avid Master Account or through the Avid Application Manager. When you run the installer, the sample pack content is installed in the default Sound Libraries location (*user directory* > Documents > Pro Tools > Sound Libraries).

Searching for Files with Soundbase

Pro Tools provides two options for searching your Sound Libraries using tags: you can open a new Soundbase window or you can change the focus of an open Workspace browser.

To open a new Soundbase window:

- Choose WINDOW > NEW WORKSPACE > SOUNDBASE or press CONTROL+OPTION+I (Mac) or START+ALT+I (Windows).

    A new Soundbase window will open with Advanced Search mode active. (See Figure 2.8.)

By default, Soundbase windows open with the Tags pane displayed at the top and various Advanced Search rows preconfigured for common music-production criteria.

Lesson 2 ■ Managing Session Data and Media Files 39

Figure 2.8 Default configuration of a Soundbase window

To search Sound Libraries using an open Workspace browser:

- To access Soundbase functionality from an open Workspace browser, click on **Sound Libraries** in the Locations pane on the left.

    The Tags pane will display at the top of the browser window, and the Sound Library location will be focused for searching. The search mode (Quick Search or Advanced Search) and criteria will remain as previously configured in the Workspace browser.

Searching Using Tags

Tags can be used for searching within your Sound Libraries (using Soundbase) or for searching in other locations (using standard Workspace functionality). Tags are available only for audio files, so tag-based search results will always be limited to audio results.

To search using Tags:

1. Activate a Soundbase search as described above or click on the Tags pane icon at the top of any Workspace browser window.

    Figure 2.9 Clicking on the Tags pane icon (shown inactive)

    The icon will highlight in blue, and the Tags pane will display.

2. Click any tag in the Tags pane to show only audio files with that tag in the browser. The displayed results will be filtered by the active tag (or tags). (See Figure 2.10.)

You can also begin typing a Tag name in the Tag Search field to select from a list of matching Tags.

Figure 2.10 Files with the Drums tag shown in a Workspace browser

3. (Optional) Click on additional tags to add additional filters to the Tag Search field.

You can modify your active search at any time to remove a tag or to exclude results based on matching tags.

To remove Tags, do one of the following:

- Click the **X** on the right side of any tag in the Tag Search field. The tag will be removed from the search criteria.

- Press the **Esc** key to clear all tags from the Tag Search field and clear the search criteria.

To exclude results based on matching tags:

- **Option-click** (Mac) or **Alt-click** (Windows) on any tag in the Tag Search field or in the Tags pane to exclude files from the search results based on that tag.

 For additional information on using tags and Soundbase, see the latest Pro Tools Reference Guide.

Importing Files and Session Data

As discussed in the *Pro Tools 101* book, you can drag and drop audio files from a Workspace browser (or an Explorer or Finder window) to the Timeline, to a track, to the Track List, or to the Clip List. This section provides additional details on importing media and other session data.

Considerations for Importing Files

Many formats of audio files can be imported into Pro Tools sessions, including the following:

- AIFF and WAV (native formats)

- SD I and SD II
- MP3
- AAC audio (AAC, Mp4, and M4a file extensions)

 Pro Tools cannot import protected AAC or MP4 files with the M4p file extension. These files are protected under the rules of digital rights management.

- QuickTime
- MXF audio
- REX 1 and REX 2 files
- ACID files

Referenced Files versus Copied Files

By default, files added to a session by drag and drop will *reference* the original media, if possible. However, files will be copied or converted and placed in the session's Audio Files folder under either of the following conditions:

- The file is not in a Pro Tools native file format (.wav or .aiff).
- The sample rate does not match your session.

Force-Copying Media

If no conversion is necessary, Pro Tools will reference the original version of the media. However, you can choose to force-copy media while importing by using key commands or by enabling the **AUTOMATICALLY COPY FILES ON IMPORT** preference setting.

To manually force-copy files on import:

- Hold **OPTION** (Mac) or **ALT** (Windows) while dragging files into your session. Copies will be created in the session's Audio Files folder.

To automatically force-copy files on import:

1. Choose **SETUP > PREFERENCES** and select the **PROCESSING** tab.
2. Enable the **AUTOMATICALLY COPY FILES ON IMPORT** checkbox.
3. Click **OK** to close the Preferences dialog box.

Importing Files Using a Workspace Browser

Workspace browsers can be used for importing audio, MIDI, or video files into Pro Tools. Files can be imported to the Clip List and onto tracks, providing similar functionality to the Import commands. In each case, you will need to first locate the files you want, using the search capabilities of the Workspace browser.

> **Example 2.2: Assembling a Drum Track**
>
> After importing a drum loop to use for a song intro, you may find that you would like to import other, similar loops to the same track to provide variation for different song sections, such as at the first verse and at the chorus. You can search in the Workspace browser to locate appropriate files; then you can either drag and drop the files into the Clip List for later use or drag them directly onto the track where you want to use them. If you place your Edit cursor at the desired song location prior to importing, when you drag and drop files to the target track they can be placed at the correct location automatically.

To locate files using a Workspace browser:

1. Choose **WINDOW > NEW WORKSPACE > DEFAULT** or press **OPTION+I** (Mac) or **ALT+I** (Windows).

2. In the Workspace browser, click the **ADVANCED SEARCH** button (magnifying glass with a plus sign).

3. Select the location you want to search by doing one of the following:

   - **To search across all connected drives:** click on the **VOLUMES** folder in the Locations pane.

   - **To search only a specific location:** click the disclosure triangle next to the **VOLUMES** folder to show all connected drives and optionally expand the drives to see their contents; then click on the target location (drive or folder) to select it.

   - **To search within multiple separate locations:** Click the disclosure triangle next to the **VOLUMES** folder and optionally expand the target drives. Then click on the **SEARCH CHECKED** icon (checkbox) at the top of the Locations pane to activate selection boxes and place a check next to each target location.

Figure 2.8 Selecting multiple search locations in a Workspace browser

4. Use the Advanced Search settings to specify **[KIND]** from the first drop-down list, **[IS]** from the second drop-down list, and either **[AUDIO FILE]**, **[MIDI FILE]**, or **[VIDEO FILE]** from the third drop-down list.

5. The search results will appear below in the Workspace pane.

Importing to the Clip List or to Tracks

To import items into the Clip List:

1. Select the files to import from the search results in the Workspace browser.

2. Drag and drop the files onto the Clip List in the Edit window.

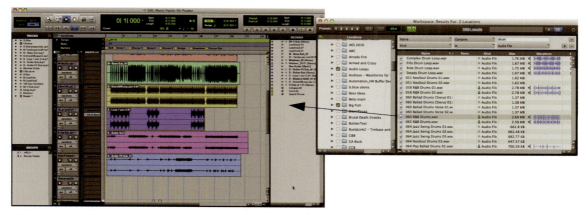

Figure 2.9 Dragging files from a Workspace browser to the Clip List

When importing MIDI or video files, you will be prompted by an Import Options dialog box, allowing you to specify additional options, if needed.

3. If prompted, verify that the destination is set to Clip List and click **OK**.

To import items into an existing track:

1. Select a file to import from the search results in a Workspace browser.

2. Drag and drop the selected file onto an existing, compatible track at the desired location. The file will be imported and placed where it is dropped.

Figure 2.10 Dragging files from a Workspace browser into a Drums track

When importing video files, you will be prompted by a Video Import Options dialog box, allowing you to specify additional options that you may need.

Figure 2.11 The Video Import Options dialog box

It is also possible to import files from a Workspace browser and create new tracks in the process. This would be useful, for example, to import multiple audio files onto separate tracks to construct a layered sound effect.

To import items as new tracks:

1. Select the files to import from the search results in a Workspace browser.

2. Do one of the following:

    - Shift-drag the items and drop them anywhere in the Edit window.
    - Drop the items onto empty space in the Edit window, if available, below the existing tracks.
    - Drop the items on the Track List.

    When importing MIDI or Video files, you will be prompted by an Import Options dialog box, allowing you to specify additional options, as needed.

3. If prompted, verify that **NEW TRACK** is selected as the destination, select other options as applicable, and click **OK**.

 When importing MIDI to a track, you can choose to include the tempo map and key signature map from the MIDI file. This can be beneficial in music production if you wish to update your session with performance information from a file, such as when replacing pre-production sketches with a final MIDI composition.

 Importing the tempo map and key signatures with a MIDI file will overwrite the current session tempo map and the contents of the Key Signature ruler, respectively, wiping out the existing data. Use this option with caution.

Spotting Files During Import

In post-production work, it is often useful to import audio or video files to a specific timecode location in your session. When importing sound effects files, for example, you may want to spot the sound effect to a specific frame in a video reference file. This can easily be achieved by importing while working in Spot mode.

To import and spot items into a track:

1. Enable Spot mode by clicking on the **SPOT** button in the Edit window toolbar.

     You do not need to enable Spot mode when importing a video file, since you can choose the import location in the Video Import Options dialog box.

2. Select the file to import from the search results in a browser window.

3. Drag and drop the file onto a Track playlist in the Pro Tools Timeline. One of the following will happen, depending on the file type you're importing:

    - When importing an audio or MIDI file, the Spot dialog box will appear. (See Figure 2.13.)

- When importing a video file, the Video Import Options dialog box will appear.

4. For video files, select **Spot** from the Location drop-down menu in the Video Import Options dialog box and click **OK**.

   The Spot dialog box will appear.

   Figure 2.12 The Spot dialog box

5. In the Spot dialog box, enter the appropriate Time Scale (such as Timecode) and Start location (where you want to spot the imported item) and click **OK**.

Importing Files Using the Import Commands

In the Pro Tools 101 class, you used the **File > Import** commands to import audio or video files into a session. The Import command can also be used to import MIDI files, clip groups, and session data into your current session.

The Import commands available in Pro Tools are as follows:

Command	Keyboard Shortcut	Function
File > Import > Audio	Command+Shift+I (Mac) Ctrl+Shift+I (Windows)	Allows you to import an audio file or clip to the Clip List or to a new track in your session
File > Import > MIDI	Command+Option+I (Mac) Ctrl+Alt+I (Windows)	Allows you to import a MIDI file to the Clip List or to a new track in your session
File > Import > Video	Command+Option+Shift+I (Mac) Ctrl+Alt+Shift+I (Windows)	Allows you to import a video file*
File > Import > Clip Groups	None	Allows you to import a clip group to a new track or to the Clip List in your session
File > Import > Session Data	Option+Shift+I (Mac) Alt+Shift+I (Windows)	Allows you to import entire tracks and associated media files from one Pro Tools session into another

*Importing video to the Clip List requires Pro Tools HD software.

To use an Import command:

1. Select **File > Import** and choose the appropriate command from the Import submenu.

PT110: Pro Tools Fundamentals II

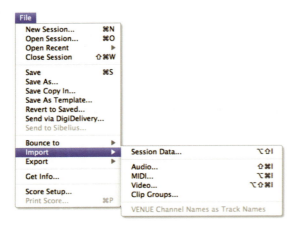

Figure 2.13 The Import submenu

When importing audio, the Import Audio dialog box will open (as discussed in *Pro Tools 101*). In all other cases, an Open dialog box will appear, allowing you to choose a file of the appropriate type.

Figure 2.14 Open dialog box as displayed when importing a MIDI file

2. Navigate to and select the desired file, then click **OPEN**. The Import Options dialog box will appear. This dialog box allows you to select a destination for the file and provides other relevant options.

> **When importing session data, the Import Session Data dialog box appears instead of the Import Options dialog box. See "Importing Session Data" later in this lesson.**

3. Select an option in the Destination section of the Import Options dialog box:

   - Select **CLIP LIST** to import the file to the Clip List without placing it on a track.
   - Select **NEW TRACK** to import the file and place it onto a new track in the session.

4. If importing to a new track, choose the import location using the Location pop-up menu.

Figure 2.15 Location pop-up menu in the MIDI Import Options dialog box

5. Select other options in the Import Options dialog box, as desired, and click **OK**. The file will be imported to the selected destination. New tracks will be created as needed for the imported file based on the Import Options you chose.

Selecting Import Options

The Video Import Options dialog box allows you to simultaneously import audio from a QuickTime video file. To import audio with the video file, select the **IMPORT AUDIO FROM FILE** checkbox.

Figure 2.16 Import audio checkbox in the Video Import Options dialog box

 To import audio from a QuickTime file without importing the video, use the **FILE > IMPORT > AUDIO** command. In the Import Audio dialog box, select the QuickTime file containing the desired audio.

Selecting an Import Location

The Location pop-up menu in each of the Import Options dialog boxes allows you to specify a location for any file you are importing to a new track. The import location options are as follows:

- **Session Start.** Select this option to place the imported file at the start of the session.

- **Song Start.** Select this option to place the imported file at the song start location, if different from the session start.

- **Selection.** Select this option to place the imported file at the start of an existing Edit selection or at the Edit cursor location if no Edit selection exists.

- **Spot.** Choose this option to place the file at a specific location using the **SPOT** dialog box.

Importing Tracks and Other Session Data

The **IMPORT > SESSION DATA** command allows you to import entire tracks from another Pro Tools session or template file into your current document. This command provides powerful options for reusing and combining session attributes.

> ### Example 2.3: Importing Tracks from a Collaborator
> In larger productions, it is sometimes useful to work on separate copies of a session with one or more collaborators. After recording basic tracks, for example, you might give a copy of the session to another Pro Tools operator to edit the drums while you continue recording supplemental tracks or begin vocal edits. When the drum editing is finished, you can use the Import Session Data command to import the edited drum tracks back into your master session, replacing the unedited drum tracks.

To import tracks from another session:

1. From within your current session, choose **FILE > IMPORT > SESSION DATA** or press **OPTION+SHIFT+I** (Mac) or **ALT+SHIFT+I** (Windows).

2. In the resulting dialog box, select the session or template file to import data from, and click **OPEN**. The Import Session Data dialog box will open. (See Figure 2.17.)

> You can also drag a session file from a Workspace browser into your current session's track playlist area or Track List to access the Import Session Data dialog box.

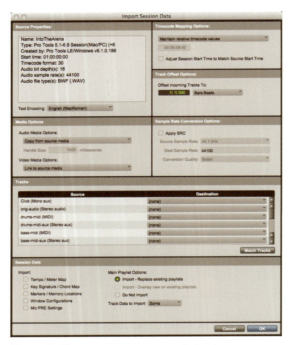

Figure 2.17 Import Session Data dialog box

3. In the Tracks section of the dialog box, do one of the following:

   - Select tracks to add to your session by clicking on the track names or by clicking the pop-up menu to the right of each track name and selecting **NEW TRACK** as the destination.

   > To import all tracks, Option-click (Mac) or Alt-click (Windows) on any track pop-up menu and select New Track.

   - Select tracks to replace in your session by clicking the pop-up menu to the right of each track name and selecting the equivalent matching track in your session as the destination. Only tracks that match by track type and channel format will be shown in the pop-up menu as potential matches.

   - Automatically select tracks to replace in your session by clicking the **MATCH TRACKS** button. Tracks with a matching track type, channel format, and name will auto-select.

    Be sure to verify auto-selected tracks prior to committing them. The Match Tracks button may match tracks with similar names that are not equivalent, targeting tracks that you do not wish to replace.

4. Select the appropriate Import options in the **Session Data** section on the bottom of the dialog box.

5. Click **OK** when you are finished. The selected tracks will be imported to the current session.

 Imported tracks are made inactive if their source media is unavailable or if the current session does not contain an equivalent output path.

Batch Importing Files

As described in the Pro Tools 101 course, you can drag audio files from a Finder window (Mac) or a File Explorer window (Windows) onto the Pro Tools application icon or directly to the Clip List in your session to batch import the files.

To batch import files:

1. Open a session or create a new session.

2. From an Explorer or Finder window, locate the files you want to import.

3. Select the files and drag them directly into the Clip List. Audio files will immediately appear in the Clip List in the session; MIDI or video files will produce the MIDI Import Options or Video Import Options dialog box, respectively.

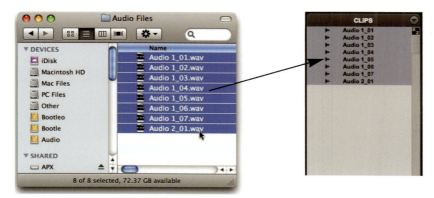

Figure 2.18 Batch importing audio files from the Mac Finder

 Pro Tools does not support dragging multiple file types into the application simultaneously. You can batch import in groups of the same file type only.

4. If applicable, select **CLIP LIST** as the destination in the Import Options dialog box and click **OK**. The imported files will appear in the Clip List.

After importing, you can **OPTION-CLICK** (Mac) or **ALT-CLICK** (Windows) on any audio or MIDI clip in the Clip List to audition it.

 Refer to the Pro Tools 101 course for more information on batch importing audio.

Working with Clip Groups

Oftentimes, the work you do on imported or recorded clips will involve many edits and adjustments, resulting in a large number of separate, small subset clips. One popular way to combine the subset clips together is to use the Consolidate command in Pro Tools (**EDIT > CONSOLIDATE CLIP**).

However, this is not always the best approach, as it creates a new parent file on disk from the selected subset clips, consuming additional disk space and making it difficult or impossible to go back and make adjustments to your original edits. A more flexible alternative is to use a clip group.

A clip group is a collection of any combination of audio, MIDI, or video clips that is grouped together to facilitate selecting, moving, and working with the grouped clips simultaneously. A clip group looks and acts like a single clip, similar to a consolidated clip, but it maintains the separate subset clips within the grouped object.

Clip groups are particularly useful for assembling parts and sections to facilitate composition and arranging. For example, you might group the clips of a brass section during the chorus to copy it to the next chorus.

 Clip groups have no relation to and are completely independent of Mix and Edit groups, which are covered in Lesson 10.

The clip group file type is identified with a *.cgrp* extension and has its own icon.

Figure 2.19 The clip group icon in Pro Tools

Creating Clip Groups

Clip groups can be created on a single track, on multiple adjacent tracks, or on multiple non-adjacent tracks. Clips on any Audio, MIDI, Instrument, or Video track can be included in a clip group. Clip groups let you combine multiple clips into "macro" clips for groove and tempo manipulation, editing, and arranging.

You can create a clip group from any selection on one or more tracks. The following rules apply when creating a clip group:

- The size of the selection determines the size of the clip group.
- The selection can start and end on any clip boundary, empty space, or in the middle of a clip. There is no minimum number of clips required for a clip group.
- Selections starting or ending within a clip will separate the clip at the selection boundary when you create a clip group.
- Clip groups will include all clips between the first and last selected clip on a track.

Multitrack clip groups (clip groups created across multiple tracks) are useful for grouping parts, such as multi-miked drum tracks, and for composing and arranging. Multitrack clip groups can be created across any combination of Audio, MIDI, Instrument, and Video tracks, and can include both tick-based and sample-based tracks. These clip groups appear as a single object across adjacent tracks.

> **Example 2.4: Using Clip Groups for Drums**
>
> Clip groups can be handy for working with and arranging drums. Consider a drum track that has been sliced into many individual sections by Beat Detective. With clip groups, you can create track segments of various sizes, such as 8-bar sections, or verses and choruses. You can then rearrange the song using these groups without having to repeatedly select all the individual clips.

Lesson 2 ■ Managing Session Data and Media Files 51

> Clip groups can start anywhere, including in empty space or in the middle of a clip, so you can use them to turn tracks into blocks that start and end on the bar regardless of where the actual clips start and end. This practice simplifies song arrangement.

To create a clip group:

1. Make a selection on one or more tracks.

   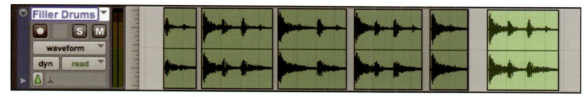

   Figure 2.20 Selecting clips to be grouped on a single Audio track

   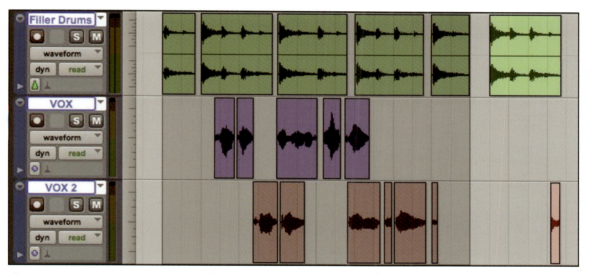

   Figure 2.21 Selecting clips to be grouped across multiple tracks

2. Choose **CLIP > GROUP** or press **OPTION+COMMAND+G** (Mac) or **CTRL+ALT+G** (Windows).
   The clip group will appear as one clip, with a clip group icon in the lower left corner. Clip groups also appear in the Clip List.

   Figure 2.22 A clip group on an Audio track and in the Clip List

Clip Group Icons

A variety of different types of clip groups can be created, including audio, MIDI, video, mixed multitrack, and non-contiguous multitrack clip groups. (See Figures 2.23 through 2.26.) Pro Tools represents each type with a different icon in lower left corner of the clip in the Edit window and in the Clip List. Each icon includes a media-type symbol inside of a shaded box or container. (See Figure 2.26.)

Figure 2.23 A clip group on a MIDI track

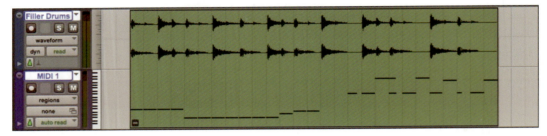

Figure 2.24 A mixed multitrack clip group

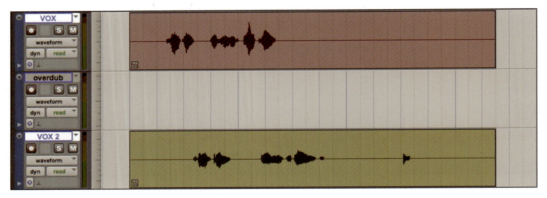

Figure 2.25 A non-contiguous clip group

Figure 2.26 Clip group icons (left to right: Audio, MIDI, Video, Non-contiguous, and Mixed Multitrack)

 Clip groups can be created from empty selections. This can be useful when working in Shuffle mode to preserve the gaps between clips or to create placeholders for later use.

 Multitrack clip groups create nested clip groups of multiple clips by track before grouping across tracks.

Ungrouping Clips

Clip groups can be ungrouped at any time using the Ungroup command to return the nested clips to their original state. When you have multiple nested clip groups, the Ungroup command ungroups the topmost clip group only, preserving any underlying clip groups.

To ungroup a clip group:

1. Select the clip group.

2. Choose **CLIP > UNGROUP** or press **OPTION+COMMAND+U** (Mac) or **CTRL+ALT+U** (Windows). The clip group will disappear, revealing all underlying clips and any nested clip groups.

Pro Tools also allows you to ungroup all nested clip groups simultaneously with the **UNGROUP ALL** command.

To ungroup a clip group and all of its nested clip groups:

1. Select the clip group.

2. Choose **CLIP > UNGROUP ALL**. The clip group will disappear, revealing all underlying clips.

Regrouping Clips

The **REGROUP** command undoes the last Ungroup command and regroups the individual clips back to their former clip group state. This lets you ungroup a grouped clip, edit its underlying clips in any way desired, and regroup it to continue working on higher-level composition and arranging.

To regroup a clip group:

1. Select any clip from the ungrouped clip group.

2. Choose **CLIP > REGROUP** or press **OPTION+COMMAND+R** (Mac) or **CTRL+ALT+R** (Windows).

    - If you used the Ungroup All command, the **REGROUP** command re-creates all previous nested clip groups.

    - If you regroup an ungrouped clip group that is used more than once in the session, the Change All dialog box opens. (See Figure 2.33.)

Figure 2.27 The Change All dialog box

3. In the Change All dialog box, do one of the following:

    - Choose **MODIFY** to apply your changes to all other instances of the same clip group.

    - Choose **COPY** to create a copy and apply your changes only to the copied clip group.

Clip Groups in the Clip List

Clip groups are included in the Clip List. Clicking on the disclosure triangle will reveal the clip group's component files. A multitrack clip group will display indicators after the clip group name showing the types of tracks that have been used to create it. For example, a display showing Group 01 (4A 2M Channels) indicates that Group 01 consists of four audio channels and two MIDI channels.

Clip groups can be auditioned in the usual way by holding **OPTION** (Mac) or **ALT** (Windows) and clicking on the clip group name in the Clip List.

Review/Discussion

1. What are some of the features enabled by Pro Tools HD software? (See "Pro Tools HD Software" beginning on page 32.)

2. What is required to import and arrange multiple video clips on a Video track? (See "Working with Digital Video" beginning on page 32.)

3. Name the areas of focus available for Workspace browsers in Pro Tools. (See "Workspace Browser Overview" beginning on page 34.)

4. What are some of the functions that you can perform using a Workspace browser? (See "Workspace Browser Functionality" beginning on page 35.)

5. How can you audition files from a browser? How can you audition them in context with your session? (See "Auditioning Audio Files" beginning on page 36.)

6. What is Soundbase? What are tags in Soundbase? (See "Using Soundbase" beginning on page 38.)

7. What are some available destinations when importing audio from a Workspace browser or Soundbase? (See "Importing Files Using a Workspace Browser" beginning on page 41.)

8. What are some of the different types of media you can import into Pro Tools (in addition to audio files)? (See "Importing Files Using the Import Commands" beginning on page 45.)

9. What command allows you to import entire tracks from another Pro Tools session into your current session? (See "Importing Tracks and Other Session Data" beginning on page 47.)

10. What types of clips can be grouped together as a clip group? Can clips of different types be combined into a single clip group? (See "Working with Clip Groups" beginning on page 49.)

11. How many clips are required for a clip group? Can clip groups contain silence? (See "Creating Clip Groups" beginning on page 50.)

12. What kind of icon is used to indicate a clip group? Where is the icon located? (See "Clip Group Icons" beginning on page 52.)

13. What do the UNGROUP and UNGROUP ALL commands do? How would you go about reassembling a clip group after using one of these commands? (See "Ungrouping Clips" beginning on page 52.)

 To review additional material from this chapter, see the PT110 Study Guide module available through the Elements|ED online learning platform at ElementsED.com.

EXERCISE 2

Working with Media Files

In Lesson 2, you learned about various options for importing media into a Pro Tools document. In this exercise, you will create a new session and import media into it in various ways. You will use the imported media to create audio background elements for the intro segment of a short film.

Duration: 15 Minutes

Getting Started

For this exercise, you will work with a video segment from the short film Agent MX Zero.

To get started, you will create a new, blank session and save it to the class files location specified by your instructor.

Create the Exercise 2 session:

1. Launch Pro Tools and choose **FILE > CREATE NEW** (or click **CREATE** on the left side of the Dashboard).

2. Name the new session 110 Exercise 2 [Your Initials] and select the session parameters as follows:

    - File Type: WAV
    - Bit Depth: 24
    - Sample Rate: 48 kHz
    - I/O Settings: Stereo Mix
    - Interleaved: Enabled (checked)

3. Click **CREATE** to proceed. A second dialog box will open, prompting you to choose a save location.

4. Navigate to an appropriate location and click **SAVE**. A new session will open with the Edit window displayed.

Creating the Video Track

In this part of the exercise, you import a video clip using the **IMPORT VIDEO** command. This will automatically create a video track in the session. You will then configure the session to work with Timecode that matches the frame rate of the imported video file.

Import a video clip:

1. Choose **FILE > IMPORT > VIDEO**. An Open dialog box will appear, allowing you to navigate to the video clip you wish to use.

2. Navigate to the Exercise Media folder and select the MXZero.mov file within the 02 MX Zero folder [PT110 Exercise Media (v12.8) > 02 MX Zero > MXZero.mov].

Exercise 2 ■ Working with Media Files   57

The Video Import Options dialog box will display.

3. Select **Session Start** for the **Location** and verify that the option to **Import Audio from File** is disabled (unchecked). Then click **OK** to import the video file into the session.

Figure 2.28 Video Import Options dialog box configured for importing the MXZero movie

A second dialog box will open, prompting you to launch the Video Engine, if not already running.

Figure 2.29 Video Engine dialog box

4. Click **Yes** in the dialog box to enable the Video Engine. A progress bar will display as the Video Engine launches, and the Video track will appear in the Edit window.

5. Choose **Window > Video** to display the Video window, if not already shown.

6. Size and position the Video window so that it doesn't obscure the tracks or the Edit window toolbar. (Try the lower right corner of the screen.)

Configure Timecode settings for the session:

1. Set the Main Time Scale for the session to Timecode, if not already active, by choosing **View > Main Counter > Timecode**.

2. Open the Session Setup window by choosing **Setup > Session**.

3. Use the **Timecode Rate** pop-up menu to select 23.976 FPS for the session, to match the imported video file.

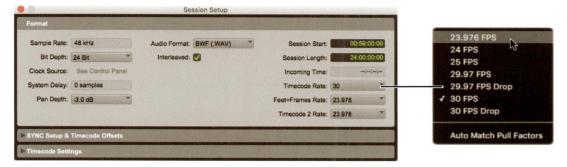

Figure 2.30 Setting the Timecode Rate in Session Setup

4. Close the Session Setup window when finished.

Importing Audio Tracks

In this part of the exercise, you will import audio tracks to use with your session using the IMPORT SESSION DATA command. The basic audio tracks you will use have already been assembled in the MXZ_Audio.ptx session.

Import the audio tracks:

1. Choose FILE > IMPORT > SESSION DATA. An Open dialog box will appear, allowing you to navigate to the session file you wish to use for importing tracks.

2. Again navigate to the 02 MX Zero folder within the Exercise Media folder [PT110 Exercise Media (v12.8) > 02 MX Zero].

3. Select the MXZ_Audio.ptx session file and click OPEN. The Import Session Data dialog box will display, showing the tracks available to import.

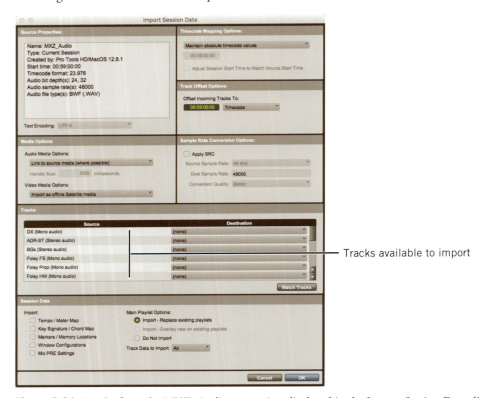

Figure 2.31 Tracks from the MXZ_Audio.ptx session displayed in the Import Session Data dialog box

4. Option-click (Mac) or Alt-click (Windows) on the name of any track listed in the Import Session Data dialog box to select all tracks to import.

5. At the bottom of the dialog box, verify that the following settings are selected:

   - MAIN PLAYLIST OPTIONS: Set to Import - Replace existing playlists
   - TRACK DATA TO IMPORT: Set to All

6. Click OK to import all selected tracks and media. The Audio tracks will display below the Video track that you created earlier.

Importing from a Workspace Browser

In this part of the exercise, you will import a gunshot sound effect and place it in the session. Then you will use the Spot dialog box to position the file at the proper location.

View the scene where gunshot sounds are needed:

1. Place the session in **GRID** mode, if not already active, and set the **GRID VALUE** to **1 second**.

2. Make a selection on the Video track from 01:00:07:00 to 01:00:16:00.

    > Refer to the Timecode ruler as well as the Start, End, and Length fields in the Counters area of the Edit window toolbar as timing references to make the proper selection.

3. Press the **SPACEBAR** to audition the selection and view the onscreen action.

Open and configure a Workspace browser window:

1. To open a Workspace browser focused on Volumes, do one of the following:

    - Choose **WINDOW > NEW WORKSPACE > DEFAULT**.
    - Press **OPTION+I** (Mac) or **ALT+I** (Windows).

    A Workspace browser window will display.

2. Activate **ADVANCED SEARCH** mode by clicking the "magnifier plus" button in the Workspace browser toolbar. The button will be highlighted in blue when Advanced Search is active.

Figure 2.32 Advanced Search button in the Workspace toolbar: inactive (left) and active (right)

A filter row will appear below the browser toolbar.

3. Use the selectors in the displayed filter row to specify **<KIND> <IS> <AUDIO FILE>**.

4. Click the **PLUS** symbol at the end of the row to add a second filter row.

5. Use the selectors in the second row to specify **<NAME> <CONTAINS>**; enter the word **gunshot** as the search term.

Figure 2.33 Filter and search criteria specified in the Workspace browser

Search results will begin to appear in the bottom pane of the Workspace browser.

Import the appropriate file to your session:

1. Audition each of the gunshot files displayed in the browser using one of the following techniques:

   - Select each file in turn and press the **SPACEBAR**.
   - Select each file in turn and click on the **PREVIEW** button in the browser Toolbar.

   Figure 2.34 Clicking the Preview button in the toolbar

   - Click on the **PLAY** icon to the left of the waveform display for each file.

2. Select the gunshot file containing a series of three shots with a long, reverberated decay on the final shot.

3. Verify that the **AUDIO FILES CONFORM TO SESSION TEMPO** button (metronome icon) is NOT active in the browser toolbar. (Button should display in dark grey.)

4. Drag the selected file into your session, placing it anywhere on the **FX Guns** track.

5. Close the Workspace browser window when finished.

Spot the gunshot file to the proper Timecode location:

1. **RIGHT-CLICK** on the imported file and select **SPOT** from the pop-up menu. The Spot dialog box will display.

2. In the dialog box, enter Timecode location 01:00:08:13 in the **Start** field.

   Figure 2.35 Start location specified in the Spot dialog box

3. Click **OK** to spot the file to the proper location on the track.

4. Play the selection to verify the results.

Finishing Up

To finish up, you can play back the session to hear the results in context with the video. Also be sure to save the work you have done before closing the session.

Listen to your work and save the session:

1. Press **RETURN** (Mac) or **ENTER** (Windows) to return to the start of the session.

2. Press the **SPACEBAR** to begin playback. During playback, note the different audio elements playing from each track.

3. When finished, stop playback.

4. Save and close the session. That completes this exercise.

Remember that you cannot close a Pro Tools session by closing its windows. You must choose CLOSE SESSION from the FILE menu.

LESSON 3

Recording MIDI and Audio

Recording performances is central to working with Pro Tools. Whether you are recording MIDI or audio, live performances on-location or musicians in studio, rock music, ADR, or Foley, knowing how to get the best results quickly is key to your success. This lesson covers different options available for recording MIDI and audio in Pro Tools.

GOALS

- Set up your session for recording
- Make selections for recording
- Work with different MIDI input recording options
- Perform loop recording operations
- Select different loop record takes

Key topics from this lesson are included in the *Pro Tools 12 Essential Training: 110* course on Lynda.com, available here: alpp.us/PT110_Online.

Many Pro Tools projects require extensive recording of both audio and MIDI data into your session. Whether your projects use the default tempo and meter or include tempo changes and compound meter, knowing how to set up your session and understanding the different options available will help you achieve a successful recording.

Setting Up the Session

In the Pro Tools 101 course, you learned about Time Scales and how to set the default tempo and meter for your session. In the following section, you will learn how to create additional Tempo and Meter changes, how to gradually change the tempo, and how to generate a click from a MIDI device. These techniques can be useful to map out your session prior to recording or to adjust the session after recording the basic tracks, to match your session timeline to the recorded material.

The Pro Tools 210M course provides detailed information on working with key changes in a session.

Displaying Conductor Rulers

The Meter and Tempo Rulers indicate the location and degree of any changes in meter or tempo throughout the session.

To display Meter and Tempo Rulers in a session:

- Choose **VIEW > RULERS** and choose the rulers you want to view.

    – Or –

- Click the **RULER VIEW SELECTOR** in the Edit window, and choose the rulers you want to view.

Figure 3.1 Enabling ruler displays with the Ruler View selector

Adding Meter and Tempo Events

When you create a session in Pro Tools, the meter defaults to 4/4 and the tempo defaults to 120 beats per minute (BPM). You can change meter and tempo using the corresponding rulers. Meter and tempo events can be inserted anywhere along the timeline. They are stored and appear in the Meter Ruler and Tempo Ruler, respectively.

You can make precise meter and tempo changes using the Time Operations window, the Graphic Tempo Editor, and the Tempo Operations window. These operations are covered in the Pro Tools 201 and 210M books.

To add meter and tempo events to a session, do one of the following:

- Click the **ADD METER CHANGE** button or **ADD TEMPO CHANGE** button (plus sign) at the left of the Meter ruler or Tempo ruler, respectively.

Figure 3.2 Adding a meter change (left) and a tempo change (right)

– Or –

- While holding the **CONTROL** key (Mac) or **START** key (Windows), move the cursor into the Meter ruler or Tempo ruler (the cursor changes to the Grabber with a "+") and click at the location where you want to insert the event. (This technique can also be used to add events to the Markers ruler.)

Figure 3.3 Manually inserting a tempo change

– Or –

- (Meter events only) Double-click the **CURRENT METER** display in the MIDI Controls section of either the Edit window toolbar or the Transport window.

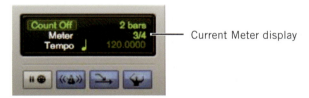 — Current Meter display

Figure 3.4 Meter display in the MIDI Controls section

After initiating a meter change or tempo change using one of the above steps, the Meter Change dialog box or Tempo Change dialog box will open, respectively.

For a meter change, do the following:

1. In the Meter Change dialog box, enter the **LOCATION** and **METER** for the change. (See Figure 3.5.)

   Optionally select the **SNAP TO BAR** option to cause the inserted meter event to fall cleanly on the first beat of the nearest measure.

Figure 3.5 Meter Change dialog box

2. Select a note value for the number of clicks to sound in each measure. For a dotted-note click value, select the dot (.) option.

3. Click **OK** to insert the new meter event. The meter event will appear as a small triangle in the Meter ruler. The triangle can be selected, copy/pasted, and double-clicked to edit the event.

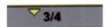

Figure 3.6 Inserted meter event

For a tempo change, do the following:

1. In the Tempo Change window, enter the **LOCATION** and **BPM** value for the tempo change.

    Select the **SNAP TO BAR** option to place the inserted tempo event cleanly on the first beat of the nearest measure.

Figure 3.7 Tempo Change dialog box

2. To base the BPM value on something other than the default quarter note, select the desired note value from the Resolution pop-up menu.

3. Click **OK** to insert the new tempo event. The tempo event will appear as a small triangle in the Tempo ruler. The triangle can be dragged to move the event and can be double-clicked to edit the event.

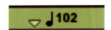

Figure 3.8 Inserted tempo event

 Refer to the *Pro Tools 101* book for information on setting the base meter and tempo.

Creating a Linear Tempo Change

The Tempo Operations window lets you define tempo events over a range of time (or measures). The time range is specified in Bars|Beats (default) or in the time format chosen for your Main Time Scale. To open the Tempo Operations window, choose EVENT > TEMPO OPERATIONS > TEMPO OPERATIONS WINDOW.

> **Example 3.1: Creating a Gradual Tempo Change**
>
> In music composition and production, it is common to have sections where the tempo gradually increases (an *accelerando*) or gradually decreases (a *ritardando*) across several measures. Using the Tempo Operations window in Pro Tools, you can achieve these effects in your session's tempo map. Simply specify the starting and ending measures in the Selection fields and the starting and ending BPM values in the Tempo fields before applying the change.

Linear Tempo Operations

Use the Linear page of the Tempo Operations window to create tempos that change evenly (linearly) over a selected range of time.

To open the Linear Tempo Operations page:

- Choose EVENT > TEMPO OPERATIONS > LINEAR. The Linear page of the Tempo Operations window will open.

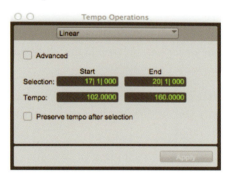

Figure 3.9 Linear Tempo Operations page

Linear Page Default Options

The options displayed on the Linear page of the Tempo Operations window include the following:

- **ADVANCED**—When this checkbox is selected, the selection range changes to the Main Time Scale format, and additional options become available.

- **SELECTION START AND END**—These fields specify the Start and End point for the tempo change. When an Edit selection is made, the Start and End fields will display the selection boundaries.

- **TEMPO START AND END**—These fields specify the starting and ending tempos for the identified range. The tempo will gradually ramp up or down between these two values across the selection.

- **PRESERVE TEMPO AFTER SELECTION**—If selected, the **original** tempo setting is preserved at the selection end point after the tempo operation. If unselected, the last tempo event created by the tempo operation continues to the end of the session or until the next tempo event.

The option to Preserve Tempo After Selection is commonly misunderstood. Note that this option preserves the original, underlying tempo (start tempo) and not the ending tempo resulting from the tempo change operation.

Linear Page Advanced Options

When the Advanced checkbox is selected, the parameters displayed on the Linear page of the Tempo Operations window change to provide additional options.

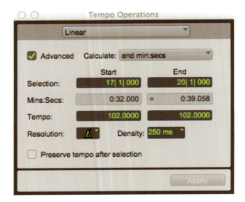

Figure 3.10 Advanced view of the Linear page

The following Advanced options are available:

- **CALCULATE**—This option lets you calculate one of the parameters—the selection end time or the starting or ending tempo—based on settings you choose for the other parameters. Depending on the Calculate option selected, different fields will be enabled in the window.

- **SELECTION START AND END**—These fields display the start and end points for the tempo change using the Main Time Scale. When an Edit selection is made, the Start and End fields display the selection boundaries. Changing start or end values changes the selection range.

- **ALTERNATE START AND END**—The fields below the Selection Start and End fields display the selection start and end locations in an alternate Time Scale.

- **TEMPO START AND END**—These fields display the tempo, in beats per minute (BPM), for the start and end points of the selected range.

- **RESOLUTION**—This pop-up menu lets you choose the note value for your tempo curve.

- **DENSITY**—This pop-up menu lets you specify the density of the tempo change events written to the Tempo Ruler.

Recording with a Click

As discussed in the Pro Tools 101 course, recording your audio at the session tempo allows you to take advantage of some useful editing functions in Pro Tools, such copying, pasting, and arranging measures and song sections in Grid mode.

 You can also generate a tempo map for a session after you have recorded audio. However, recording to a click while in Bars|Beats can save you significant editing time.

Using the Click Plug-In

Pro Tools provides a built-in click generator in the Click II plug-in. The Click II plug-in is assigned automatically when you create a click track. The click can be enabled and disabled from the MIDI Controls area in either the Edit window or the Transport window or toggled on/off from the Options menu. The click can also provide a countoff for recording and playback.

To enable/disable the click, do one of the following:

- In the MIDI Controls, click the **METRONOME** button to toggle the click on/off.

Figure 3.11 Metronome button in the MIDI Controls

– Or –

- Select **OPTIONS > CLICK**. This has the same effect as clicking on the Metronome button.

 Press the [7] key on the numeric keypad to toggle the metronome click on/off.

To use a countoff for recording or playback:

- Click the **COUNT OFF** button in the MIDI Controls so that it becomes highlighted.

Figure 3.12 Count Off button in the MIDI Controls

 Press the [8] key on the numeric keypad to toggle the Count Off control on/off.

Using a Different Sound Source for the Click

Although the Click II plug-in provides various click sounds to choose from, at times you (or the performers you are working with) may want to have a different sound for the metronome. The Click/Countoff Options dialog box in Pro Tools lets you configure click playback from any virtual instrument in your session.

To configure a click from a virtual instrument:

1. Open the Click/Countoff Options dialog box by choosing **SETUP > CLICK/COUNTOFF** or by double-clicking either the **METRONOME** button or the Count Off value displayed in the MIDI Controls.

2. In the Click/Countoff Options dialog box, set the following values:

   - **Accented fields:** Set the note, velocity, and duration for the accented notes.
   - **Unaccented fields:** Set the note, velocity, and duration for the unaccented notes.

- **Output pop-up menu:** Select a virtual instrument in the session to use for the click.

 To set the Accented and Unaccented note values, you can select each field and play the corresponding note on a connected MIDI keyboard.

When the click plays in your session, the accented note will sound on the first beat of each measure, and the unaccented note will sound on the remaining beats.

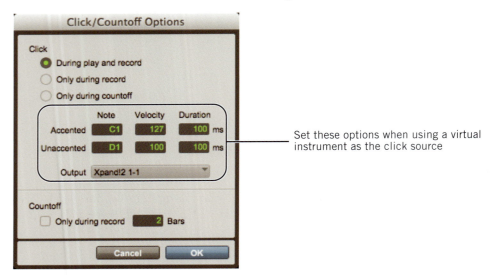

Figure 3.13 Click/Countoff Options dialog box with Xpand!2 selected as the click output source

3. Using the radio buttons at the top of the dialog box, select whether the click will be played DURING PLAY AND RECORD, ONLY DURING RECORD, or ONLY DURING COUNTOFF.

4. Specify the count off duration to use (when Countoff is enabled) at the bottom of the dialog box. To hear the countoff only when recording, select the checkbox to the left; to hear the countoff during both playback and recording, clear the checkbox.

5. Click **OK** to accept the changes.

Recording Selections

After completing your initial tracking, you will commonly need to perform additional recording in selected areas to allow the talent to correct a mistake or to try out different takes. Pro Tools offers a selection-based punch-in capability that provides a very powerful and precise way to re-record a portion of a track without affecting material on the track that you wish to keep.

By making a selection prior to beginning to record on a track, you can control the portion of the track that gets recorded. Combining this process with appropriate pre- and post-roll settings allows you to create automatic punch-in and punch-out points for recording takes and overdubs in the studio.

Creating a Selection

Pro Tools provides numerous ways to create and modify selections. Any selection that you create can subsequently be used for recording takes and overdubs within the selected timeline range.

Using Clips to Create Timeline Selections

One of the easiest ways to create a selection is simply to select one or more existing clips. If a clip or series of clips matches the time location and duration that you wish to use for recording (on the same track or on a different track), you can use these clips to create the appropriate timeline selection.

With the Timeline and Edit selections linked, select a clip or clips that represent the desired transport range for recording.

To use a clip selection to record on another track:

1. Select the GRABBER tool (F8) in the toolbar area of the Edit window.
2. Click on a clip on any track to select it.
3. If desired, SHIFT-CLICK on another clip on the same track or a different track to extend the selection.
4. Start a record pass on any record-enabled track or tracks. The length and timeline location of the record take will correspond with the area of the selection.

Making a Selection On-The-Fly During Playback

Another useful selection technique involves selecting a range of material on the fly during playback. This allows you to make a selection by ear while listening to your session, such as while playing back a record take.

To make a selection by ear during playback:

1. Begin playback of the session near the area you are interested in.
2. Press the DOWN arrow key on the keyboard at the point where you want your selection to start. The edit cursor will move to the marked start location.
3. Press the UP arrow key at the point where you want your selection to end. The Timeline Out Point will move to the marked end location and the selected area will be highlighted.

> Pressing an arrow key a second time during playback will update the In/Out point and cancel the previously marked point.

> If you press the UP arrow key to mark the Out point without having pressed the DOWN arrow, the playback start point will be used as the start of the selection.

Using Timeline Selection In and Out Points to Adjust a Selection

After making an initial selection, you can fine-tune it using the Timeline Selection In and Out Points in the Main Timebase ruler. When tracks are record-enabled, Timeline Selection In and Out Points appear as red markers in the ruler. If no tracks are record-enabled, the In and Out Points are blue.

Figure 3.14 Red Timeline Selection In and Out Points (with Pro Tools record-enabled)

The Timeline Selection In and Out Points can be moved, either separately or together, to select a range.

To set the record range by dragging the Timeline Selection Points:

1. If you want the dragged In and Out Points to snap to Grid lines, set the Edit mode to GRID.
2. Drag the TIMELINE SELECTION IN POINT to the desired start point of the range. (See Figure 3.15.)

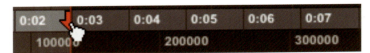

Figure 3.15 Dragging the Timeline Selection In Point (start time) in the Main Timebase ruler

3. Drag the **Timeline Selection Out Point** to the desired end point of the range.

 To move a selection while maintaining the selection length, hold **Option** (Mac) or **Alt** (Windows) while dragging either the In or Out Point. The In and Out points will move in tandem to the new location.

Using Memory Locations for Selections

As discussed in the *Pro Tools 101* book, memory locations can be used to bookmark locations for quick recall. Memory locations store time properties either in markers (playback locations) or in selections (edit locations).

Memory locations can also store and recall general properties, including the following:

- Zoom settings
- Pre-/post-roll times (discussed later in this chapter)
- Track show/hide status
- Track heights

You can view markers and create memory locations using the Markers ruler (**View > Rulers > Markers**). You can also view, create, modify, and delete all types of memory locations (markers, selections, zoom settings, etc.) in the Memory Locations window (**Window > Memory Locations**).

Figure 3.16 The Memory Locations window

Adding Memory Locations

You have already learned several ways to add marker memory locations to your session. Here is a quick recap of some of your options.

To add a memory location to your session, do one of the following:

- Click the **Add Marker/Memory Location** button (plus sign) at the head of the Markers ruler.
- **Control-click** (Mac) or **Start-click** (Windows) on the Markers ruler at the location where you want to add a memory location.
- Press the **[Enter]** key on the numeric keypad.

Any of the above actions will display the New Memory Location dialog box, allowing you to specify the name and parameters for the memory location.

Automatically Naming Memory Locations Added During Playback

You can also add memory locations on the fly during playback. This can be a quick way to mark areas that need to be edited or re-recorded.

To save time during this process, you can have Pro Tools automatically name the memory locations as you create them. This prevents the New Memory Location dialog box from displaying each time you add a marker.

> **Example 3.2: Creating an Edit List**
>
> After completing initial tracking (or any long record take), it can be useful to listen through the tracks individually and compile a list of required edit locations. Rather than scrambling to write down timeline locations during playback, or starting and stopping playback repeatedly, you can add temporary markers at each location where an edit or punch-in is required.
>
> If you configure the Memory Locations window to auto-name memory locations, you will be able to simply press the [**Enter**] key (numeric keypad) during playback any time you hear something that needs further attention. Pro Tools will instantly mark the spot for you, and you will be able to easily return to the marked spots later by recalling the associated memory locations.

To enable auto-naming of memory locations added during playback:

1. Display the Memory Locations window (**Window > Memory Locations**).

2. Click on the Memory Locations pop-up menu in the upper-right corner of the window.

Figure 3.17 The Memory Locations pop-up menu

3. Select **Auto-Name Memory Location** from the pop-up menu. (See Figure 3.18.)

Figure 3.18 Enabling Auto-Name Memory Locations

With this option enabled, pressing [ENTER] during playback will instantly add successively numbered markers to the Markers ruler. After completing a playback pass, you can edit and rename the newly added markers by double-clicking on them in the Markers ruler or in the Memory Locations window.

To disable the Auto-Name Memory Location option, deselect it from the Memory Locations pop-up menu.

Creating a Selection from Marker Memory Locations

If markers already exist in your session, you can use them to make a selection and set your record range. For example, to re-record the second chorus of a song, you can recall the **CHORUS 2** marker and then hold **SHIFT** while recalling the **VERSE 3** marker. This provides a quick way to select the target range.

The process of holding the **SHIFT** key to make a selection can be used with all methods of recalling memory locations:

- Clicking the marker symbol on the Markers ruler
- Clicking the entry in the Memory Locations window
- Typing a period, the memory location number, and a second period on the numeric keypad

Using Selection-Based Memory Locations

You can also store any selection you create for future use. To do this, simply create a *selection* memory location in your session (as opposed to a marker memory location).

To create a selection-based memory location:

1. Create an Edit selection using any of the techniques you've learned thus far.
2. Initiate a new memory location using any available method (for example, press the [ENTER] key on the numeric keypad).
3. In the New Memory Location dialog box, click the **SELECTION** radio button under Time Properties.

Figure 3.19 Time Properties set to Selection in the New Memory Location dialog box

4. Enable any of the General Properties that you wish to have recalled with the selection memory location.

 Additional details on using General Properties with memory locations are provided in the *Pro Tools 201* book.

5. Provide a descriptive name for the memory location and click **OK**. The new memory location will be added to your session.

After creating a selection-based memory locations, you can recall the selection by clicking on the associated entry in the Memory Locations window or by typing **[PERIOD], [MEMORY LOCATION NUMBER], [PERIOD]** on the numeric keypad.

 Selection-based memory locations are not represented on the Markers ruler.

Any selection-based memory locations stored in your session can be recalled at any time and used as the basis for a record range.

Using Pre- and Post-Roll

When recording over a section of existing material, musicians typically want to hear playback begin prior to the start of the record range. It can also be helpful to allow playback to continue for a period past the end of the record range. The pre-roll and post-roll values in Pro Tools allow you to specify how much audio to play prior to the selection (pre-roll) and after the selection (post-roll).

Setting pre- and post-roll values creates an automatic punch-in and punch-out on record-enabled tracks for the selected area. Pre- and post-roll times appear as flags in the Main Timebase ruler. When pre- and post-roll are enabled, the flags are yellow; otherwise they are white.

Figure 3.20 Yellow pre- and post-roll flags (enabled) at bars 1 and 5 in the Main Timebase ruler

Pre- and post-roll amounts can be entered in the Transport window, set from a track's playlist or Timebase ruler, or recalled with a memory location that includes pre- and post-roll values.

Setting Pre- and Post-Roll in the Transport Window

Pre- and post-roll can be enabled and set from the corresponding fields in the Transport window.

To set and enable the pre- and post-roll times in the Transport window:

1. With the Transport window displayed, select **VIEW > TRANSPORT > EXPANDED**, if not already selected.

2. In the Transport window, click in the pre-roll field to select it.

3. Type in the pre-roll amount and press **FORWARD SLASH [/]** on the numeric keypad to move to the post-roll field. The Pre-roll button becomes highlighted, indicating that pre-roll is enabled.

 You can use the period (.) or Left/Right arrow keys to move through the different time fields for pre and post-roll. Use the Up/Down arrow keys to increase or decrease the numerical values.

4. Type in the post-roll amount and press **RETURN** (Mac) or **ENTER** (Windows). The Post-roll button becomes highlighted, indicating that post-roll is enabled.

Figure 3.21 Pre-roll and Post-roll buttons enabled (highlighted) in the Transport window

With the pre- and post-roll values set, you can toggle the functions on or off at any time. To toggle pre- or post-roll on or off, click the appropriate button in the Transport window so it becomes highlighted or unhighlighted (enabled or disabled, respectively).

Setting Pre- and Post-Roll in a Playlist

When the Timeline and Edit selections are linked (**OPTIONS > LINK TIMELINE AND EDIT SELECTION**), you can use the Selector tool to set the amount of pre- and/or post-roll and enable or disable pre- and post-roll by clicking in a track's playlist.

To set and enable the pre- and post-roll by clicking in a playlist:

1. Create a selection on any track or tracks.

2. With the **SELECTOR** tool, **OPTION-CLICK** (Mac) or **ALT-CLICK** (Windows) in a track playlist before the selection start point to enable pre-roll and set the pre-roll value.

3. With the **SELECTOR** tool, **OPTION-CLICK** (Mac) or **ALT-CLICK** (Windows) in a track playlist after the selection end point to enable post-roll and set the post-roll value.

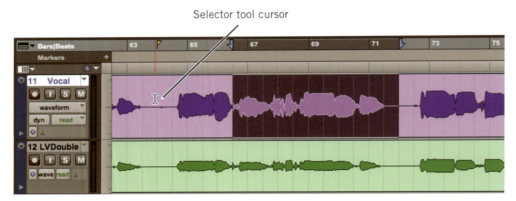

Figure 3.22 Enabling pre-roll by Option-clicking in the playlist of the Vocal track (note the pre-roll flag in the ruler)

To disable pre- and post-roll by clicking in a playlist:

1. Create a selection on any track or tracks.

2. With the **SELECTOR** tool, **OPTION-CLICK** (Mac) or **ALT-CLICK** (Windows) in the front half of the selection on a track playlist to collapse/disable the pre-roll.

3. With the **SELECTOR** tool, **OPTION-CLICK** (Mac) or **ALT-CLICK** (Windows) in the back half of the selection on a track playlist to collapse/disable the post-roll.

Setting Pre- and Post-Roll in the Timebase Ruler

You can set the pre- and post-roll amount in the Timebase ruler by dragging the pre-roll and post-roll flags. This lets you adjust the amount of pre- or post-roll or reset the pre- and post-roll values to zero.

Lesson 3 ■ Recording MIDI and Audio   77

The pre- and post-roll flags can be moved in the ruler, either separately or at the same time, to set their location.

To set the pre- and post-roll amounts by dragging in the ruler:

1. If you want pre-/post-roll to snap to Grid lines, set the Edit mode to **Grid**.

2. Drag the pre-roll and post-roll flags to new locations in the ruler.

Figure 3.23 Dragging a pre-roll flag in a Timebase ruler

 To set pre- and post-roll values to the same amount, **Option-drag** (Mac) or **Alt-drag** (Windows) on either flag in the ruler. Both flags will adjust accordingly as you drag.

Enabling Pre-/Post-Roll from the Options Menu

Oftentimes you will find yourself toggling pre- and post-roll on and off repeatedly. To speed up the process, pre- and post-roll can be enabled and disabled together using a command under the Options menu.

To toggle both pre- and post-roll on or off from the Options menu:

- Select **Options > Pre/Post-Roll**. When this option is selected, both pre- and post-roll will be enabled; when it is cleared, both will be disabled.

 Press **Command+K** (Mac) or **Ctrl+K** (Windows) to toggle pre- and post-roll on/off from the keyboard.

Example 3.3: Recording Multiple Takes of a Guitar Solo

When trying to capture the perfect take for a particularly challenging part of a performance, you may find yourself repeatedly toggling pre- and post-roll on/off. For each take of a guitar solo, for example, the guitarist will likely want to hear a bar or two of pre-roll. Immediately after each take, the guitarist may ask to hear the performance, in which case you will want to turn off pre-roll to save time during playback.

If the guitarist requires multiple takes before being satisfied with the performance, you can find yourself toggling Pre/Post Roll on and off over and over again. In these situations, it is well worth your time to use the associated keyboard shortcut (Command+K or Ctrl+K) and commit it to memory.

Loop Recording Audio and MIDI

Loop recording is a Pro Tools feature that allows you to record take after take while the same section of the session repeats continuously. This is a convenient option for quickly recording multiple takes of a section without losing spontaneity. Loop recording is always non-destructive.

To begin loop recording, you must first specify the start and end points for the loop by making a Timeline selection. If your selection does not cover an entire clip on the record-enabled track, Pro Tools automatically separates the selection as new a clip when recording begins.

You can listen to track material leading up to the loop record range by enabling pre-roll. The pre-roll setting, if enabled, is used only during the first record pass. Pre-roll times are ignored on each successive loop. To compensate for this, you may want to make the loop range slightly longer than the area that you need to record. Later, you can trim back the recorded takes to the appropriate length.

Loop Recording Differences: Audio Versus MIDI

Although the record process is the same for loop recording audio and loop recording MIDI, the resulting recorded clips differ slightly:

- When loop recording audio, Pro Tools creates a single audio file that comprises all takes. Takes appear as individual subset clips in the Clip List and are numbered sequentially.

- If an audio record pass is interrupted before reaching the midpoint of the loop, the entire take for that pass is discarded.

- When loop recording MIDI, new clips are created each time a new record pass begins. However, if no MIDI input is received during a pass, no additional clip is added during the next pass.

- If a MIDI record pass is interrupted mid-take, the entire clip is retained, regardless of where the record pass was stopped.

Capturing Loop Record Takes

To perform a loop record process, the Pro Tools record mode must first be set to Loop Record and a timeline selection must be made to delineate the record range. Recording can then be initiated on any Audio, MIDI, or Instrument track.

The preference setting for AUTOMATICALLY CREATE NEW PLAYLISTS WHEN LOOP RECORDING automatically copies each take to a new playlist in the track. This facilitates using Playlists view for auditioning and selecting alternate takes.

Adding playlists and using Playlists view are discussed in the Pro Tools 200-level courses.

To loop record on an Audio, MIDI, or Instrument track:

1. Select **OPTIONS > LOOP RECORD**, or right-click on the **RECORD** button and select **LOOP** from the pop-up menu. When Loop Record mode is enabled, a loop symbol appears in the Record button.

Figure 3.24 Loop Record mode enabled

Press OPTION+L (Mac) or ALT+L (Windows) to toggle Loop Record mode on/off from the keyboard, or press [5] on the numeric keypad.

2. Record-enable the target track by clicking its Record Enable button.

3. Make sure **OPTIONS > LINK TIMELINE AND EDIT SELECTION** is selected.

4. With the **SELECTOR** tool, drag in the target track's playlist to set the desired loop range.

5. To hear track material up to the start point of the loop, enable and set the pre-roll time.

6. Click the **RECORD** button in the Transport controls followed by the **PLAY** button, or press an appropriate keyboard shortcut (such as **[3]** on the numeric keypad).

7. Allow loop recording to continue until a sufficient number of takes has been captured.

 To cancel all recorded takes while loop recording, press COMMAND+PERIOD (Mac) or CTRL+PERIOD (Windows).

8. When you have finished recording, click the **STOP** button in the Transport controls or press the **SPACEBAR**.

If you stop recording audio before reaching the midpoint of the loop on an Audio track, Pro Tools discards the current take. If you record more than half of the take, Pro Tools keeps the take when you stop recording.

The recorded takes appear as clips in the Clip List and are numbered sequentially. The most recently recorded take remains in the record track.

Auditioning Loop Record Takes

After recording multiple passes of audio or MIDI using Loop Record mode, Pro Tools lets you access the record passes, or takes, using the Alternate Takes menu. This menu allows you to easily select, audition, and compare takes created from different record passes.

Setting the Match Criteria

The clips that appear in the Takes List are determined by the currently active match criteria. You can set these criteria to filter out unrelated clips when selecting or working with alternate takes.

To specify the match criteria:

1. Do one of the following:

   - **COMMAND-CLICK** (Mac) or **CTRL-CLICK** (Windows) with the **SELECTOR** tool anywhere within a take and select **ALTERNATES MATCH CRITERIA** from the pop-up menu.

   - Right-click the take with the **SELECTOR** or **GRABBER** tool, and select **MATCHING ALTERNATES > MATCH CRITERIA** from the pop-up menu.

   The Alternates Match Criteria window will open. You can use this window to filter the results that display in the Alternate Takes List.

Figure 3.25 The Alternates Match Criteria window showing default settings

2. In the Match Criteria window, select the filter criteria that you want to make active.

Main Filters. The following filters can be selected in any combination. Only clips that match ALL of the selected criteria will display.

- **TRACK ID**—Shows only audio clips recorded to the current track, based on the track ID. Do not apply this filter when working with MIDI takes.
- **TRACK NAME**—Shows only clips that share the same root name with the track.
- **CLIP RATING**—Shows only clips that have the same rating as the selected clip.

 Clip rating is covered in the Pro Tools 210M course.

Time Stamps. Only one of the time stamp filters can be active at any time.

- **ALL**—Shows any clips that include the time location of the Edit cursor or Edit selection.
- **CLIP START**—Shows any clips that have the same start time as the selected clip.
- **CLIP START AND END**—Shows any clips that have the same start and end times as the selected clip. This ensures that the Alternate Takes List includes only clips that match the loop record range.
- **WITHIN SELECTION**—Shows any clips that are entirely within the Edit selection.
- **NONE**—No other filter criteria are applied beyond the main filters.

Selecting Alternate Takes

After specifying the match criteria, you can access each of your clip passes from the Alternate Takes List or the Right-click Matching Alternates submenu.

To select an alternate take, do one of the following:

- **COMMAND-CLICK** (Mac) or **CTRL-CLICK** (Windows) with the **SELECTOR** tool on a selected clip and select a different take from the Alternate Takes pop-up menu.

Figure 3.26 The Alternate Takes pop-up menu

- Right-click the clip with the **SELECTOR** or the **GRABBER** tool, and select an alternate take from the Matching Alternates submenu in the pop-up menu.

Lesson 3 ■ Recording MIDI and Audio   81

Figure 3.27 The Matching Alternates submenu

Recording MIDI Using Loop Playback with MIDI Merge

When recording on a MIDI or Instrument track, you have the option of using MIDI Merge mode. This allows you to add MIDI data to an existing MIDI clip. However, MIDI Merge mode is not compatible with Loop Record mode.

For drum machine–style layered loop recording, you can use Loop Playback with MIDI Merge enabled. With this method, MIDI data is added to the clip with each pass as Pro Tools loops across the selected record range. This is a great option for recording MIDI drums. For example, you can record hi-hats on the first pass and add kick and snare on subsequent passes.

To record using MIDI Merge with Loop Playback:

1. In the Options menu, deselect **LOOP RECORD** mode.

2. Enable Loop Playback by selecting **OPTIONS > LOOP PLAYBACK** or pressing **COMMAND+SHIFT+L** (Mac) or **CTRL+SHIFT+L** (Windows).

     You can also press [4] on the numeric keypad to toggle Loop Playback on or off.

    When Loop Playback is enabled, a loop symbol will appear in the Play button.

3. Record-enable the target MIDI or Instrument track.

4. Click the **MIDI MERGE** button in the MIDI Controls so it becomes highlighted in blue.

    Figure 3.28 MIDI Merge button enabled (highlighted in blue)

5. Select the record range.

6. Click **RECORD** in the Transport controls and press **PLAY**. Pro Tools will loop across the selected range, allowing you to add to your MIDI recording with each successive record pass.

Review/Discussion

1. What menu would you use to display Conductor rulers, such as Meter and Tempo? How can you display rulers without using a main menu? (See "Displaying Conductor Rulers" beginning on page 64.)

2. What are the default tempo and meter for all Pro Tools sessions? (See "Adding Meter and Tempo Events" beginning on page 64.)

3. What modifier key would you hold while clicking on a ruler to add a meter or tempo change to your session? (See "Adding Meter and Tempo Events" beginning on page 64.)

4. What main menu provides access the Tempo Operations window? What is the purpose of the Linear page in the Tempo Operations window? (See "Creating a Linear Tempo Change" beginning on page 67.)

5. What is the purpose of the note, velocity, and duration fields for accented and unaccented notes in the Click/Countoff dialog box? When would you need to set these options? (See "Using a Different Sound Source for the Click" beginning on page 69.)

6. Describe at least three different ways to make a selection for recording. (See "Creating a Selection" beginning on page 70.)

7. Describe three ways to set the pre- and post-roll values. What modifier do you use to set pre- and post-roll by clicking in a track playlist? (See "Using Pre- and Post-Roll" beginning on page 75.)

8. What keyboard shortcut can you use to toggle Pre/Post Roll on and off? (See "Enabling Pre-/Post-Roll from the Options Menu" beginning on page 77.)

9. What are some differences in the way audio and MIDI clips are created when loop recording? How would you go about enabling loop recording for audio or MIDI? (See "Loop Recording Differences: Audio Versus MIDI" and "Capturing Loop Record Takes" beginning on page 78.)

10. How can you access the Alternate Takes List? How can you restrict, or filter, the results displayed in the Alternate Takes List? (See "Setting the Match Criteria" beginning on page 79.)

11. How can you perform a MIDI Merge recording while looping? (See "Recording MIDI Using Loop Playback with MIDI Merge" beginning on page 81.)

To review additional material from this chapter, see the PT110 Study Guide module available through the Elements|ED online learning platform at ElementsED.com.

EXERCISE 3

MIDI Recording

In this exercise, you will select a basic MIDI drum recording from various loop record takes that have been completed in advance. Then you will use MIDI Merge mode to perform additional record passes and enhance the drum performance. Parts of this exercise require the use of a MIDI keyboard or other MIDI controller.

Duration: 20 Minutes

Getting Started

To get started with this exercise, you will create a session from a template file provided with the course exercise media and save it to the class files location specified by your instructor.

Open the template and save the session:

1. Launch Pro Tools and choose **FILE > OPEN SESSION** (or choose **OPEN FROM DISK** from the Dashboard).

2. Navigate to the Exercise Media folder and open the *Waiting Here.ptxt* template file [PT110 Exercise Media (v12.8) > 03 Waiting Here > Waiting Here.ptxt].

    A dialog box will open displaying default parameters based on the template.

3. Name the session 110 Exercise 3 [Your Initials] and select the **PROMPT FOR LOCATION** option near the bottom of the dialog box.

4. Click **CREATE** to proceed. A second dialog box will open, prompting you to choose a save location.

5. Navigate to an appropriate location and click **SAVE**. The session will open with the Edit window displayed.

Preparing the Session

Before starting to work, you will need to display the Transport window and configure it for the session.

Display and configure the Transport window:

1. Display the Transport window, if needed, by choosing **WINDOW > TRANSPORT**.

    You can also display the Transport window by pressing COMMAND+[1] (Mac) or CTRL+[1] (Windows) on the numeric keypad.

2. Choose **VIEW > TRANSPORT** (or click the **TRANSPORT WINDOW POP-UP**) and verify that the following display settings are active. (See Figure 3.29.)

    - **COUNTERS**
    - **MIDI CONTROLS**
    - **EXPANDED TRANSPORT**

Figure 3.29 Transport window with Counters and MIDI Controls shown (Expanded view)

Selecting a Loop Record Take

For this part of the exercise, you will select a basic pattern on the MIDI Drums track from among several existing loop record takes.

Before you can select from the loop record takes, you will need to configure the Alternates Match Criteria to show only clips that match the current source clip.

Configure the Alternates Match Criteria:

1. If needed, display the Edit window by pressing **COMMAND+=** (Mac) or **CTRL+=** (Windows).

2. Zoom in on the playlists by clicking **ZOOM PRESET 2**.

3. Select the MIDI Drums-01 clip at the start of the MIDI Drums track.

   This clip represents the first take of a previously completed loop recording.

4. Using the **SELECTOR** tool, **COMMAND-click** (Mac) or **CTRL-click** (Windows) on the selected clip. The Alternate Takes list will appear.

5. Select **ALTERNATES MATCH CRITERIA** from the top of the Alternate Takes list. (See Figure 3.30.)

Figure 3.30 Selecting Alternates Match Criteria from the Alternate Takes list

The Alternates Match Criteria window will open. (See Figure 3.31.)

6. In the Alternates Match Criteria window, select **TRACK NAME** as the main filter and **CLIP START AND END** as the time-stamp criteria.

Figure 3.31 Alternates Match Criteria set for selecting loop record takes

7. Close the Alternates Match Criteria window when finished.

• • •

You are now ready to begin auditioning the loop record takes. For this part of the exercise, you will use Loop Playback to listen to the selection while alternating through the record takes to select your preferred option.

 The MIDI Drums track uses the Xpand!2 virtual instrument plug-in for playback.

Audition the loop record takes:

1. Choose **OPTIONS > LOOP PLAYBACK** to enable loop playback mode, if not already active.

2. Select the MIDI Drums-01 clip and press the **SPACEBAR** to begin playback. Pro Tools will begin playing the selected range in a continuous, repeating pattern.

3. While loop playback continues, **COMMAND-CLICK** (Mac) or **CTRL-CLICK** (Windows) on the selected clip with the **SELECTOR** tool and select the next take from the Alternate Takes list (MIDI Drums-02).

   The selected take will appear on the track playlist and will begin playing back.

4. Repeat this process to audition each of the loop record takes.

5. When you find the take that you wish to use, stop playback.

> **Discussion Point #1**
>
> Why was it necessary to use the Alternates Match Criteria window before auditioning takes? What affect did it have on the results displayed in the Alternate Takes list?

Recording with MIDI Merge

For the next part of this exercise, you will use a MIDI keyboard to record additional parts for your drum pattern using Loop Playback with MIDI Merge enabled. This will allow you to build up your drum pattern in layers.

Preparing to Record

To get started, you will use the clip you just selected to set the range for recording. Then you will enable Loop Playback with MIDI Merge mode and record-enable the **MIDI Drums** track.

Make a selection and prepare to record:

1. Verify that your MIDI controller is connected to your system via an available USB port or MIDI port and that the controller is powered on.

2. Verify that the clip you chose on the **MIDI Drums** track is still selected.

3. From the **OPTIONS** menu, do each of the following:
   - Verify that **LOOP PLAYBACK** is enabled (checked).
   - Verify that **LOOP RECORD** is not selected (unchecked).

4. In the Transport window, click the **MIDI MERGE** button so that it becomes highlighted in blue.

   Figure 3.32 MIDI Merge button

5. Click the **TRACK RECORD ENABLE** button (**R**) on the **MIDI Drums** track to enable MIDI Merge recording on the track. The button will flash red.

Recording Additional Drum Parts

You are now ready to begin recording your additional drum parts. This portion of the exercise uses two separate record passes. Pass 1 is used to record hi-hat, and Pass 2 is used to record claps.

 The recording passes described below are intended to provide guidance only. Feel free to experiment with additional drum parts and record passes.

You can rehearse each record pass using Loop Playback, activating Record mode on the fly when you are ready to record. After each pass, deactivate Record mode to rehearse the next record pass. Deactivating Record mode between passes will allow you to undo the last take with no effect on the previous takes.

First Record Pass

For the first record pass, you will use the **F#1** key (Hi-Hat, closed) and **A#1** key (Hi-Hat, open) on the MIDI keyboard (or equivalent triggers on your available controller).

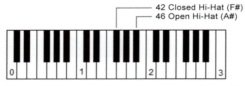

Figure 3.33 Notes for the hi-hat record pass shown on a standard MIDI keyboard

Record the first pass:

1. Press the **SPACEBAR** to begin Loop Playback.

2. While the selection plays, create a pattern and rehearse the timing for the hi-hat.

> **ℹ** If a noticeable latency occurs while recording, try lowering the Hardware Buffer Size (SETUP > PLAYBACK ENGINE). This will reduce latency, making it easier to keep time.

3. When ready, click the **RECORD ENABLE** button in the Transport window (or press **F12**) without stopping playback. MIDI Merge recording will begin on the MIDI Drums track.

4. Record your pattern on the next pass.

5. When finished, click the **RECORD ENABLE** button in the Transport window a second time (or press **F12**) to suspend MIDI Merge recording.

6. If you are satisfied with the recording, continue to the second record pass; otherwise, choose **EDIT > UNDO MIDI RECORDING** and try again.

> **ℹ** You can undo the last pass at any time without interrupting playback. This allows you to continue working without losing the creative feel between takes.

Second Record Pass

For the second pass, you will use the **D#1** key (Hand Claps) on the MIDI keyboard (or equivalent trigger on your available controller).

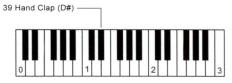

Figure 3.34 Notes for the Hand Claps record pass shown on a standard MIDI keyboard

Record the second pass:

1. With the selection continuing to play back, rehearse the timing for the hand claps.

2. When ready, click the **RECORD ENABLE** button in the Transport window without stopping playback. MIDI Merge recording will be reactivated.

3. Record your pattern on the next pass.

4. When finished, click the **RECORD ENABLE** button in the Transport window a second time to suspend MIDI Merge recording.

5. If you are satisfied with the recording, press the **SPACEBAR** to stop playback; otherwise, choose **EDIT > UNDO MIDI RECORDING** and try again.

Discussion Point #2

How is MIDI Merge recording with Loop Playback different from Loop Recording MIDI? What would be the result if you completed an additional Loop Record pass after completing the above steps?

Finishing Up

Before exiting Pro Tools, disarm the record track and listen to the session to verify the result. Also be sure to save the work you have done, as you will be reusing this session in later exercises.

Disable record and save the session:

1. When you're finished recording, disable **RECORD** on the MIDI Drums track and press **RETURN** (Mac) or **ENTER** (Windows) to return to the start of the session.

2. Press the **SPACEBAR** to listen to your recording. Undo and/or repeat any portion of the recording as needed.

3. When satisfied with the results, save and close the session. That completes this exercise.

Remember that you cannot close a Pro Tools session by closing its windows. You must choose CLOSE SESSION from the FILE menu.

LESSON 4

Working with MIDI & Virtual Instruments

When you start working with tempo changes, the concept of track timebases takes on renewed significance. This lesson covers the difference between sample-based and tick-based material and describes how each timebase affects different types of material on your tracks. The lesson also discusses the use of virtual instruments and reviews techniques for editing MIDI data.

GOALS

- Understand the difference between sample-based and tick-based tracks
- Understand how to render virtual instrument as audio
- Understand the different views available for working with MIDI data
- Recognize how various Pro Tools settings affect auditioning and playback of MIDI data
- Use various tools and techniques to edit your MIDI data

 Key topics from this lesson are included in the *Pro Tools 12 Essential Training: 110* course on Lynda.com, available here: alpp.us/PT110_Online.

In this lesson, we look at the differences in the way audio and MIDI information is referenced to the timeline on sample-based tracks as compared to tick-based tracks and discuss how these differences can affect the timing of a performance. We also look at the difference between stand-alone virtual instruments and plug-in virtual instruments, discuss methods of auditioning and playing back MIDI data, and review various techniques for editing MIDI data in Pro Tools.

Understanding Track Timebases

In the Pro Tools 101 course, you learned that Pro Tools uses two types of track timebases: sample-based and tick-based. Audio tracks are sample-based by default, while MIDI and Instrument tracks are tick-based by default. The differences between these timebases are important to understand, especially when working with sample-based data and tick-based data simultaneously. Material on sample-based tracks remains static and references an absolute Time Scale (Samples or Min:Sec), whereas material on tick-based tracks conforms to the session tempo and references a relative Time Scale (Bars|Beats).

Sample-Based Operation Versus Tick-Based Operation

Sample-based material, such as a vocal recording on an Audio track, references an absolute timeline. As the name suggests, the absolute timeline is unchanging. Every sub-division on the timeline has a specific duration of time regardless of the musical tempo of the session. Absolute Times Scales in Pro Tools include the following:

- Samples

- Mins:Secs

- Timecode

- Feet+Frames

By contrast, tick-based material, such as a MIDI recording on an Instrument track, references a relative timeline. Durations on a relative timeline change dynamically with the session tempo. Although a quarter note will always be a quarter note, its duration in time is completely dependent on the tempo of the session.

Pro Tools has one relative Time Scale:

- Bars|Beats

To demonstrate the distinction between sample-based operation and tick-based operation, consider a session with a MIDI drum loop on a tick-based Instrument track along with an audio recording of a bass line on a sample-based Audio track. For this example, at the default session tempo of 120 BPM both the MIDI and audio clips are 2 bars in length, equivalent to 4 seconds.

Figure 4.1 illustrates the following:

- Session Tempo: 120 BPM

- MIDI Drum Loop Clip Duration: 2 Bars (relative), 4 Seconds (absolute)

- Bass Line Clip Duration: 2 Bars (relative), 4 Seconds (absolute)

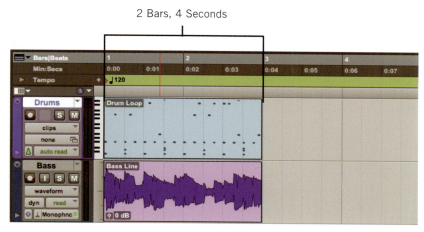

Figure 4.1 MIDI clip and audio clip are aligned at 120 BPM

If you now adjust the session tempo to 60 BPM, the two tracks will no longer match. The MIDI playback on the drum track will slow down to accommodate the new tempo. However, the audio recording of the bass line will be unaffected and will play back at its original speed. By changing the tempo, the MIDI and Audio tracks are no longer in sync, as shown in Figure 4.2.

In Lesson 5, we will look at how to address this issue using Elastic Audio.

Figure 4.2 illustrates the following:

- Session Tempo: 60 BPM
- MIDI Drum Loop Duration: 2 Bars (relative), 8 Seconds (absolute)
- Bass Line Duration: 1 Bar (relative), 4 Seconds (absolute)

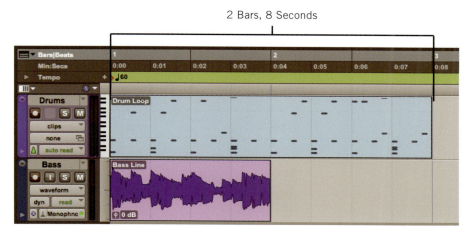

Figure 4.2 MIDI clip and audio clip are no longer aligned at 60 BPM

Track Timebases

Pro Tools uses different default timebases for Audio tracks versus MIDI or Instrument tracks; however, you can change any track timebase to either sample-based or tick-based at any time.

Audio Track Timebases

Audio in Pro Tools is *sample-based* by default. This means that audio clips and events are associated with specific sample locations on the timeline. The audio will remain fixed at its absolute location in time even when the session tempo is modified—though relative bar and beat locations will change.

If you make an Audio track tick-based, the start of the audio clips will become fixed to the Bars|Beats ruler, and the clips will move relative to the sample timeline when tempo and meter changes occur.

However, audio clips without Elastic Audio behave differently than MIDI clips do when using tick-based timing. MIDI clips change length as the tempo changes, while audio clips do not. Tempo changes affect only the start point of each audio clip in a tick-based track. Enabling Elastic Audio on the track applies real-time Time Compression and Expansion, allowing the audio clips to automatically conform to tempo changes.

MIDI and Instrument Track Timebases

MIDI data in Pro Tools is *tick-based* by default. This means that MIDI events are located at particular bar and beat locations in the session, and their timing adjusts based on the session tempo. MIDI events retain their bar|beat locations when the session tempo is modified—though their absolute locations in time will change.

If you make a MIDI track sample-based, all MIDI clips and events in the track will become fixed to absolute locations on the timeline. MIDI data will remain fixed at the corresponding sample locations, regardless of any tempo or meter changes in the session.

 You can select whether a track is sample-based or tick-based when you create it, or you can change the track timebase at a later point.

Tick-Based Timing and Note Values

Pro Tools has an internal MIDI resolution of 960,000 pulses per quarter note (ppq). When working with the Bars|Beats timescale, the counter display resolution in Pro Tools is tick-based, with 960 ticks to a quarter note.

The following table lists the number of ticks for various common note sizes. Notice the mathematical relationship between the tick value and the note duration. For example, an 1/8 note has half as many ticks as a 1/4 note, as its duration is half that of a 1/4 note. Similarly a dotted 1/8 note has 1.5 times as many ticks as a normal 1/8 note, as its duration is one and a half that of an 1/8 note.

Table 4.1 Tick Measurements for Common Note Values

Note Value	Normal	Dotted	Triplet
1/2 note	1920	2880	1280
1/4 note	960	1440	640
1/8 note	480	720	320
1/16 note	240	360	160

Virtual Instruments

Pro Tools' MIDI and Instrument tracks can be used to trigger external MIDI instruments, such as synthesizers or other sound modules, or they can use virtual instruments as sound sources. Virtual instruments are software applications that use the processing power of the computer to produce sounds or effects. Virtual instruments require no external hardware outside of your Pro Tools system or computer.

Virtual instruments typically reference the relative Time Scale in a session, and are usually driven by MIDI data from a MIDI or Instrument track or by the session's MIDI beat clock. A variety of virtual instrument plug-ins are included for use with Pro Tools, and many others are available as add-on components.

Using Plug-In Virtual Instruments

Plug-in virtual instruments run in real-time as inserts on tracks within a Pro Tools session. Plug-in virtual instruments are commonly placed on an Aux Input or Instrument track.

Processing Audio Tracks with Virtual Instruments

Certain plug-in virtual instruments can be used to directly process an Audio track when inserted directly on the track. An example of a virtual instrument plug-in that can process signals from an Audio track is the DB-33 virtual organ plug-in included with Pro Tools. This plug-in re-creates the sounds of classic tonewheel organs and rotary-speaker cabinets. The plug-in includes controls for using the preamp and rotating speaker simulation as an effect on an Audio track in Pro Tools.

Virtual MIDI Nodes

When using MIDI with virtual instrument plug-ins in Pro Tools, virtual MIDI nodes are created. These nodes act like MIDI ports and provide connections between Pro Tools and the plug-in. For example, when you instantiate a plug-in instrument such as Xpand!2 on a track, a new instance of the instrument becomes available in Pro Tools MIDI Output selectors at a unique virtual MIDI node.

Virtual instruments are also available in a stand-alone variety, utilizing software that runs independently from Pro Tools. This type of virtual instrument uses the ReWire protocol to connect to Pro Tools.

Rendering Virtual Instruments

When using MIDI routed through a virtual instrument, it can be useful at times to render the virtual instrument's output to an audio file. This can be done to enable audio processing options that are not available for MIDI or to conserve on processing resources.

Pro Tools provides several options for rendering the output of a virtual instrument to an audio file. Two of the simplest are (1) drag-and-drop a MIDI clip from an Instrument track to an Audio track and (2) activate the Track Freeze button on the track.

Using Drag-and-Drop Rendering

In order to use audio editing features such as fade-ins and outs or AudioSuite processing on a MIDI-based performance, you will need to first convert the MIDI performance into audio. This can be done easily by dragging the MIDI clip(s) from an Instrument track to an Audio track of the same format (mono or stereo). This process requires that the Instrument track have an active virtual instrument assigned.

To convert a MIDI performance to audio:

1. Create a new Audio track matching the format of the target Instrument track (mono or stereo).

2. Select one or more MIDI clips on the target Instrument track. (See Figure 4.3.)

Figure 4.3 MIDI Drums clip selected on the Drum VI track

3. Drag the clip(s) to the Audio track. Pro Tools will render the output from the Instrument track for the duration of the selected MIDI clip and place it on the Audio track.

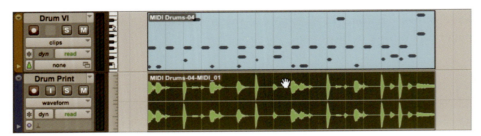

Figure 4.4 Audio Drums clip created on the Drum Print track

Using Track Freeze

Another option for rendering a MIDI performance as audio is the Track Freeze feature. This option will render the virtual instrument output as audio directly on the originating track. The resulting audio waveform will appear superimposed on the track's MIDI data.

The Track Freeze option is useful for conserving real-time processing resources. This can be important when using many processor-intensive virtual instruments or other Native plug-ins in a session or project. Track Freeze is also useful for sharing tracks with other Pro Tools users who may not have access to the same plug-ins you are using in a project or session, such as when using Avid's Cloud Collaboration features.

One consideration for using Track Freeze, however, is that you cannot edit the resulting audio waveforms on a frozen track. Any performance changes that are required must be made by unfreezing the track, editing the original performance, and then refreezing the track.

To use Track Freeze on an Instrument track, do one of the following:

- Click on the **TRACK FREEZE** button (snowflake icon) at the head of the target track.
- Right-click on the track nameplate and choose **FREEZE** from the pop-up menu.
- Select the target track and then choose **TRACK > FREEZE**.

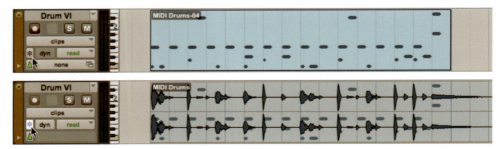

Figure 4.5 Using the Track Freeze button to render audio for the Drums VI track: before (top) and after (bottom)

When using any of the above options, the audio will instantly begin rendering across the entire track when you activate Track Freeze, and the track will be placed in a frozen state. To unfreeze a track, simply click the **Track Freeze** icon (snowflake) at the head of the track a second time.

 Track Freeze can also be used on Audio tracks and Aux Input tracks to render all real-time processing in order to conserve on processing resources or to prepare tracks for sharing and collaboration.

MIDI-Compatible Tracks and Track Views

As with Audio tracks, MIDI and Instrument tracks can display data in a variety of ways. Some available views include the following:

- **Clips View**—Displays MIDI data in clips for arranging and assembling
- **Notes View**—Displays MIDI notes as small individual segments in piano-roll style for editing
- **Velocity View**—Displays MIDI note attack velocities using velocity stalks
- **Volume, Pan, and Controller Graph Views**—Display automation playlists and continuous controller line graphs with a series of editable breakpoints

MIDI data can also be displayed in the MIDI Editor or Score Editor window. This section focuses on the views available in the main Edit window and the track controls available in the Mix window.

Viewing MIDI Data in the Edit Window

As discussed in the *Pro Tools 101* book, MIDI data appears in the Edit window arranged in track playlists, against the same timeline as audio. Common views for working with MIDI include Clips view (default), Notes view, and Velocity view. The following sections summarize each of these views.

 To toggle a track view between Notes and Clips, place the Edit cursor in the track and press **Control+Minus** (Mac) or **Start+Minus** (Windows) on the alphanumeric keyboard.

Clips View

The Clips view shows MIDI data grouped together as clips, in a manner similar to Waveform view for Audio tracks. You can think of MIDI clips as containers for MIDI data, including notes, continuous controller events, program changes, and System Exclusive events. While notes are visible in Clips view, they cannot be edited individually.

Figure 4.6 MIDI data in Clips view

MIDI clips generally have their start and end points aligned to bar boundaries by default. This allows you to arrange MIDI clips in a musically meaningful way, in whole-bar increments.

MIDI clips can be selected, copied, cut, and trimmed in the same way as audio clips, allowing you to quickly arrange song phrases or sections.

MIDI clips also appear in the Clip List (right side column in the Edit window), where they can be selected or dragged onto MIDI or Instrument tracks.

Notes View

The Notes view shows individual MIDI notes in a piano-roll format, with pitch represented on the vertical axis and duration represented on the horizontal axis. To view a MIDI or Instrument track in Notes view in the Edit window, choose **NOTES** from the Track View selector (Figure 4.7), or place the Edit cursor on the track and press **CONTROL+MINUS** (Mac) or **START+MINUS** (Windows).

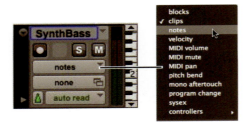

Figure 4.7 Changing a MIDI track display to Notes view from the Track View selector

The pitch range of MIDI notes displayed in Notes view depends on the track height and the current zoom value. When a track's notes do not fit within its current height, notes above or below the viewed area are shown as single-pixel lines at the very top or bottom of the track display. (See Figure 4.8.)

A mini-keyboard on the left-hand side of the track lets you audition, select, and scroll through the MIDI notes on a track.

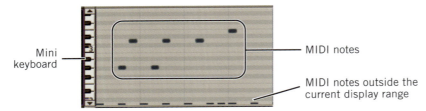

Figure 4.8 MIDI notes displayed in Notes view

You can click on any key in the mini-keyboard to audition the pitch or sound associated with the note value. If the note value you wish to see or audition is outside of the current display range, you can scroll the display up or down as needed.

To scroll the Notes display up or down on a MIDI-compatible track:

- Click the Up or Down scroll arrow on the mini-keyboard. Clicking the Up arrow will scroll to higher note ranges; clicking the Down arrow will scroll to lower note ranges.

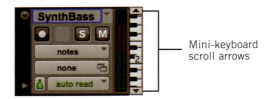

Figure 4.9 Scroll arrows on the mini-keyboard

Velocity View

The MIDI Velocity view shows the attack velocity of each note in the track with a vertical velocity stalk. Velocity stalks can be dragged up or down, individually or in groups, to change the velocities of their associated notes.

Figure 4.10 Velocity stalks displayed in the track playlist (Velocity view)

You can also display the velocity stalks using the track's Velocity controller lane. To show the Velocity controller lane, click the Show/Hide Lanes button (triangle) at the head of the track.

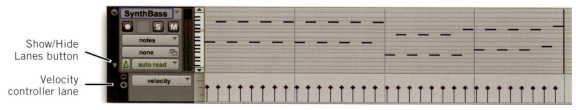

Figure 4.11 Velocity stalks displayed in the Velocity controller lane

MIDI-Compatible Tracks in the Pro Tools Mix Window

Each MIDI or Instrument track has its own set of controls in the Mix window for inputs, outputs, automation mode, volume, and so forth. The settings of these controls can affect the MIDI data recorded on the track.

The main Mix window controls for MIDI and Instrument tracks include the following:

- **MIDI INPUT SELECTOR**—The MIDI Input selector lets you choose which MIDI data the track will receive when recording. This selector is set to receive all MIDI channels from all connected devices by default.

 The MIDI Input and Output selectors for Instrument tracks are displayed in the Instruments view at the top of the Mix window. To display this view, choose VIEW > MIX WINDOW > INSTRUMENTS.

- **MIDI OUTPUT SELECTOR**—The MIDI Output selector allows you to select the output channels used for MIDI playback.

- **RECORD ENABLE**—The Record Enable button arms a MIDI or Instrument track for recording from the assigned MIDI input.

- **SOLO AND MUTE BUTTONS**—The Solo and Mute buttons on MIDI and Instrument tracks work in the same manner as on Audio tracks.

98 PT110: Pro Tools Fundamentals II

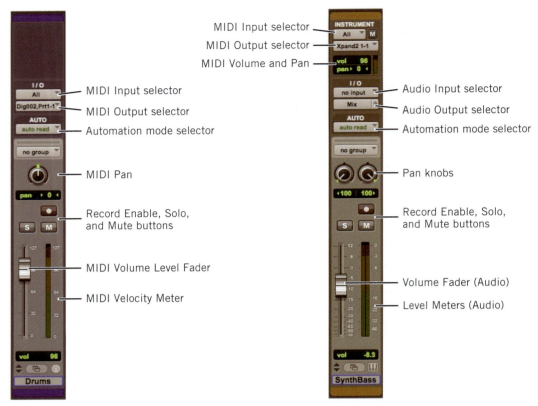

Figure 4.12 Track controls in the Pro Tools Mix window: MIDI track (left) and Instrument track (right)

- **PAN CONTROLS**—The main Pan Indicator and Pan knob(s) on Instrument tracks work in the same manner as on Audio tracks. MIDI pan is similar; however, the indicator shows MIDI pan values for data in the track, from < 64 (full left) to 63 > (full right), rather than audio pan.

- **VOLUME CONTROLS**—On MIDI tracks, the Volume Fader sets the MIDI volume for data in the track (with a range from 0 to 127). On Instrument tracks, the Volume Fader sets the audio volume level for the track. Instrument tracks also display MIDI Volume, in the Instruments view at the top of the track.

- **METER**—The meter on MIDI tracks shows MIDI velocity values (in a range from 0 to 127) for individual MIDI events on the track. The meter on Instrument tracks shows the audio volume produced by the virtual instrument on the track. Instrument tracks also have a MIDI meter (in the Instruments view), which shows MIDI velocity values.

Auditioning and Playing Back MIDI

Though working with MIDI data is similar to working with audio, some differences apply in the way that the tracks produce sound at the Pro Tools outputs. Certain options and preference settings in your session affect how you are able to monitor and audition MIDI data.

The following sections discuss audition and playback features that are specific to working with MIDI data.

MIDI Thru Option

The MIDI Thru option allows incoming MIDI data to pass through a track to its MIDI output. When MIDI Thru is enabled in the Options menu (the default), Pro Tools passes MIDI information from your controller through to the associated virtual instrument for a record-enabled MIDI or Instrument track. This lets you play MIDI instruments via Pro Tools and monitor them during recording.

Default Thru Instrument Option

MIDI clips in the Clip List can be previewed or auditioned through any virtual instrument plug-in in your session. Auditioned MIDI clips are played through Pro Tools using the Default Thru Instrument.

 Enabling a Default Thru Instrument can force all virtual instruments to operate in the low-latency domain. This may cause frequent errors when using smaller H/W Buffer Sizes.

Setting the Default Thru Instrument

Unlike a record-enabled MIDI or Instrument track, which has a dedicated input, the Default Thru Instrument must respond to all incoming MIDI data regardless of the port, device, or channel the signal is received from.

To set the Default Thru Instrument, do the following:

1. Choose **SETUP > PREFERENCES** and click the **MIDI** tab.

2. Click on the **DEFAULT THRU INSTRUMENT** pop-up menu and do one of the following:

   - Select a specific device to define a consistent preview sound source.
     – Or –
   - Select **FOLLOWS FIRST SELECTED MIDI TRACK** to route incoming MIDI through the first selected MIDI or Instrument track.

Figure 4.13 Selecting the Default Thru Instrument in the Preferences dialog box

To disable the Default Thru Instrument, select **NONE** from the Default Thru Instrument pop-up menu.

 To avoid playback errors, it is recommended to set the Default Thru Instrument to None when not required for auditioning MIDI clips or monitoring MIDI input.

Using the First Selected MIDI Track Option

The **FOLLOWS FIRST SELECTED MIDI TRACK** option allows you to change the Default Thru Instrument at any time by selecting the MIDI or Instrument track for the instrument you wish to hear. This enables you to play any of your instruments without having to put MIDI or Instrument tracks into record.

Troubleshooting the First Selected Track

When multiple MIDI or Instrument tracks are selected, previewing will use the top-selected MIDI or Instrument track in the Track List. When no MIDI or Instrument track is selected, previewing will use the top-listed MIDI or Instrument track in the Track List.

The Default Thru track from the Track List will be triggered regardless of whether that track is shown in the Mix and Edit windows. If you are getting no sound with the Default Thru Instrument set to FOLLOWS FIRST SELECTED MIDI TRACK, make sure that any unused Instrument tracks are moved to the *bottom* of the Track List. When the Default Thru track is inactive or muted (Instrument tracks only), it will not produce sound, effectively disabling the Default Thru Instrument. This can be especially difficult to identify when the track is hidden.

Auditioning from the Clip List

If you have enabled the Default Thru Instrument setting, you can use it to audition MIDI clips in the Clip List.

To audition a MIDI clip in the Clip List:

1. If the Default Thru Instrument is set to Follows First Selected, select the track you wish to use for the sound source.

2. OPTION-CLICK (Mac) or ALT-CLICK (Windows) on the MIDI clip in the Clip List. The clip will play back using the assigned Default Thru Instrument.

MIDI Thru Setting versus Default Thru Instrument Setting

The following table summarizes the MIDI-related options that can affect how MIDI is routed to a virtual instrument.

Table 4.2 MIDI Thru vs. Default Thru Instrument

Function	How Enabled	When Used
MIDI Thru	Options > MIDI Thru	When recording from a MIDI controller onto a MIDI or Instrument track or monitoring through a record-enabled MIDI or Instrument track
		– and –
		When monitoring with the Default Thru Instrument
Default Thru Instrument	Setup > Preferences	When monitoring a MIDI controller without a record-enabled MIDI or Instrument track
		– and –
		When auditioning a MIDI clip in the Clip List

Editing MIDI Data

Editing MIDI data is also similar to editing audio, though some important differences apply here as well. Some editing operations function differently when applied to MIDI data than when applied to audio waveforms. Additionally, MIDI notes and parameters can be modified in many ways that audio cannot.

Editing MIDI Clips

When working on MIDI or Instrument tracks, you'll find Clips view useful for editing and arranging song sections, clip by clip. Many of the operations available for working with MIDI clips match those available for working with audio clips (Copy, Cut, Paste, Clear, Trim, etc.).

While the essential functions are the same for MIDI and audio clips, some differences exist in the way that MIDI data is stored that affect how MIDI clips behave:

- When cutting or clearing a selection that includes a note's start point, the entire note is removed, regardless of whether the end of the note is selected. (See the MIDI note at the end of the selection in Figure 4.14.)

- When cutting or clearing a selection that includes a note's end point but not its start point, the note remains and overlaps the end of the clip. (See the note at the start of the selection in Figure 4.14.)

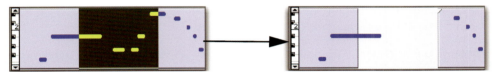

Figure 4.14 Cutting a selection from a MIDI clip with notes partially selected at the start and end

- Similarly, when trimming a MIDI clip's head beyond a note's start point, the entire note is removed. When trimming a clip's tail beyond a note's end point but not beyond its start point, the note remains and overhangs the end of the clip.

- When moving and placing MIDI clips with overhanging notes, the notes move with the clips. When placing a MIDI clip with overhanging notes next to or near another clip, the overhanging notes extend into the next clip on the track.

Editing MIDI Notes with the Pencil Tool

The Pencil tool allows for several types of MIDI editing. In many ways, the Pencil tool serves as a universal tool for editing MIDI.

Figure 4.15 Pencil tool

Smart Pencil Tool Functions

When editing in Notes view, the Pencil tool behaves like a Smart Tool. The Pencil becomes a Grabber when placed over the middle of a MIDI event, allowing you to move the event to a different note value (pitch) or time location (beat or sub-beat). (See Figure 4.16.)

Figure 4.16 The Pencil tool operating as a Grabber when placed over the middle of a note

The Pencil becomes a Trim tool when placed over either end of a MIDI event, allowing you to shorten or lengthen the note duration. (See Figure 4.17.)

Figure 4.17 The Pencil tool operating in Trim mode when placed near the end of a note

The function of the Pencil tool can also be temporarily changed by pressing certain modifier keys.

- Pressing **OPTION** (Mac) or **ALT** will temporarily change the Pencil to the Selector tool, Note Selector tool, or Eraser tool, depending on where the cursor is positioned.

- Pressing **CONTROL** (Mac) or **START** (Windows) will temporarily activate a Marquee Grabber (crosshair) tool for selecting note ranges.

- Pressing **COMMAND** (Mac) or **CTRL** (Windows) will activate the Velocity Trimmer when the Pencil tool is positioned over the middle of a MIDI note. This allows you to change a note's velocity by dragging up or down directly on the note.

Inserting MIDI Notes

The Pencil tool can be used to insert MIDI notes by drawing them on a MIDI or Instrument track.

To insert a MIDI note with the Pencil tool:

1. Click on the **TRACK VIEW SELECTOR** for the MIDI or Instrument track and set the view to **NOTES**, or place the Edit cursor on the track and press **CONTROL+MINUS** (Mac) or **START+MINUS** (Windows).

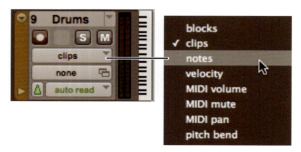

Figure 4.18 Changing an Instrument track to Notes view using the Track View selector

2. Select the **PENCIL** tool and make sure it is set to Freehand.

3. (Optional) Set the Main Time Scale to **BARS|BEATS**, set the Edit mode to **GRID**, and choose the Grid value. The Grid value will determine the duration of inserted notes when the Default Note Duration is set to Follow Grid. (See "Default Note Duration" below.)

4. Move the **PENCIL** into the playlist area for the MIDI track and locate the desired pitch and timeline location.

5. Click to insert a note with the default duration. (Alternatively, you can click and drag to insert a note of longer duration.)

> With Grid mode enabled, **COMMAND-DRAG** (Mac) or **CTRL-DRAG** (Windows) after clicking with the Pencil tool to temporarily suspend the Grid and create non-constrained note durations.

Default Note Duration

Unless otherwise specified, the current Grid value determines the default duration of a note inserted with the Pencil tool (even when Grid mode is not active). However, you can easily set the default note duration to a different value of your choosing.

To set the default note duration:

1. Click on the **DEFAULT NOTE DURATION** selector in the Edit window toolbar.

   Figure 4.19 Default Note Duration set to Follow Grid, with the Grid set at 1 bar

2. Select the desired note value from the pop-up menu.

   – Or –

   Select **FOLLOW GRID**, if not active, to have the Default Note Duration match the selected Grid value.

   Figure 4.20 Default Note Duration pop-up menu

   The Default Note Duration icon will change to display a note value of the selected duration.

   Figure 4.21 Default Note Duration set to an eighth note

3. To specify dotted or triplet note values, click the selector a second time (after selecting the base note value) and select the appropriate option to modify the base value.

   After setting the Default Note Duration, the new value will be used for any subsequent notes you insert.

   Figure 4.22 Changing the Default Note Duration allows note values that are different from the Grid value.

Editing Existing MIDI Notes

All aspects of a MIDI note can be edited in the Edit window (or in a MIDI Editor window), including start and end points, duration, pitch, and velocity. The Grabber, Selector, and Pencil tools can operate on individual notes or groups of notes.

Selecting MIDI Notes

Oftentimes, you will need to select multiple MIDI notes simultaneously, in order to copy them, move them, or change their velocity values, for example. Pro Tools provides a variety of methods for selecting multiple notes, either one at a time or in batches.

To select a group of MIDI notes, do one of the following:

- **SHIFT-CLICK** on each note with the **GRABBER** or **PENCIL** tool to add them to the selection one at a time.

- Click and drag a rectangle around a group of notes with the **GRABBER** tool to select several adjacent notes simultaneously. (The cursor will display a cross-hair icon when not positioned over a note.)

- Drag across a range of notes with the **SELECTOR** tool to select all notes in the track within the selected timeline range.

To select a single pitch for the entire length of a track:

- Click on a note in a MIDI or Instrument track's mini-keyboard with any tool. All notes of that pitch on the track will be selected.

Figure 4.23 Selecting a pitch by clicking a note on the mini-keyboard

> ### Example 4.1: Changing a MIDI Drum Performance
>
> After recording or programming a MIDI drum performance, you may want to experiment with the available drum sounds for the virtual drum instrument that you are using. If the current snare drum sound is not quite right for the song, for example, you can try using the same notes to trigger a different sound instead. This is easily done by selecting the notes with the mini-keyboard and transposing them up or down. Many virtual instrument drum patches have alternate drum sounds mapped to adjacent MIDI keys.
>
> By selecting all the notes for the snare and dragging them up or down, you may be able to replace an ill-fitting acoustic snare with a more suitable side stick, hand clap, or electric snare.

To select a range of pitches with the on-screen keyboard:

- Click on a key at one end of the range and **SHIFT-CLICK** on another key at the other end of the range, using the track's mini-keyboard.

  – Or –

- Click and drag across a range of keys on the track's mini-keyboard.

Transposing Notes

MIDI notes can be transposed by dragging up or down with the **Grabber** tool. If several notes are selected before dragging, the entire selection will be transposed.

To transpose a MIDI note with the Grabber tool:

1. Select the **Grabber** tool (or position the **Pencil** tool over the center of a note so it becomes a Grabber).

2. Click on a note or **Shift-click** on several notes to select them.

3. Drag the note(s) up or down. (Press **Shift** while dragging to preserve note start times.)

Figure 4.24 Dragging notes with the Grabber tool to transpose selected notes

 To transpose selected notes a half step at a time, hold Control (Mac) or Start (Windows) while pressing plus or minus on the numeric keypad.

 Option-drag (Mac) or **Alt-drag** (Windows) with the Grabber tool to duplicate selected notes while transposing them, leaving the originals unchanged.

Example 4.2: Creating a Parallel Harmony

After recording or programming a MIDI part for a melodic instrument such as a violin, you might decide to add a parallel harmony for part of the performance. To do so, you can simply select the MIDI notes that you want to harmonize; then drag the notes up or down while holding **Option** (Mac) or **Alt** (Windows) to duplicate them. As you drag, the virtual instrument will audition each pitch, helping you to select an appropriate interval for the harmony part by ear. After positioning the duplicated notes, you can lower their velocities to reduce the prominence of the harmony part.

Moving Notes

Like MIDI and audio clips, MIDI notes can be dragged earlier or later on the timeline with the Grabber tool to change their start points.

To move a MIDI note:

1. With the **Grabber** or **Pencil** tool, click on a note or **Shift-click** on several notes to select them.

2. Drag the note(s) left or right (hold **Shift** while dragging to constrain the pitch).

   As the note is dragged, the Current Cursor display indicates the new start point.

Trimming Note Start and End Times

Also like clips, start and end points for MIDI notes can be adjusted with the Trim tool or with the Trim command in the Edit menu. MIDI notes can also be separated with the Separate command.

To change the duration for a MIDI note or group of notes with the Trim tool:

1. Select each note that needs to be trimmed.

2. Select the standard **TRIM** tool (or move the **PENCIL** over the end of a note to access the the Trim tool).

3. Click and drag near the start or end of one of the selected notes and drag to shorten or lengthen the notes. All selected notes will trim simultaneously.

To trim MIDI notes with the Trim command:

1. Position the Edit cursor at the desired trim location in a note or across multiple notes.

2. Choose **EDIT > TRIM NOTES > START TO INSERTION** or **EDIT > TRIM NOTES > END TO INSERTION** to trim off the start or end of the note(s), respectively.

If you make a selection within a MIDI note or across multiple notes, you can trim the note(s) to the selection boundaries by choosing **EDIT > TRIM NOTES > TO SELECTION.**

To separate MIDI notes:

1. Position the Edit cursor or make a selection at the desired edit location in one or more notes.

2. Choose **EDIT > SEPARATE NOTES > AT SELECTION**. The notes will be separated (cut in two) at the Edit cursor or at the selection boundaries.

Editing Note Velocities

When a MIDI or Instrument track is set to Velocity view, each note's attack velocity is represented by a velocity stalk. The taller the velocity stalk, the higher the velocity value (1-127). Velocities can be edited by dragging individual velocity stalks, by drawing with the Pencil tool, or by scaling up or down with the Trim tool.

To edit a velocity stalk:

1. Click on the **TRACK VIEW SELECTOR** for the MIDI or Instrument track and set the view to **VELOCITY**.

   – Or –

   Click the track's **SHOW/HIDE LANES** button (triangle in the lower left at the head of the track) to display the velocity stalks using the track's Velocity controller lane.

2. Select the **GRABBER** or **PENCIL** tool.

3. Drag the diamond at the top of the velocity stalk up or down to increase or decrease the velocity value. As you drag, the velocity value will display at the top left of the playlist.

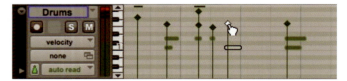

Figure 4.25 Dragging a velocity stalk

You can also change a note's velocity by **COMMAND-CLICKING** *(Mac) or* **CTRL-CLICKING** *(Windows) on the note in Notes view with the Pencil tool (activates the Velocity Trimmer) and dragging up or down with the mouse.*

To draw velocity values:

1. Select the **PENCIL** tool. Use the Freehand shape to draw a freehand velocity curve or select another option to draw using shapes (the Line Pencil, for example, lets you draw velocity ramps, up or down).

2. Click at the beginning of the note range and drag to draw velocity values. (To create a fade-in, click near the bottom of the velocity range, and drag up and to the right.)

Figure 4.26 Changing velocities with the Line Pencil

To scale velocities with the Trim tool:

1. Display the velocity stalks on the track or in the Velocity controller lane.

2. Using either the **SELECTOR** tool or the **GRABBER** tool, select the range of notes to be edited.

3. With the **TRIM** tool, click near the range of selected notes and drag up or down. Dragging up boosts the velocities for all selected notes, dragging down reduces them.

 In Velocity view, the Trim tool can also be used to trim note durations, in addition to changing velocities, by clicking near the end point of one of the selected notes.

Deleting MIDI Notes

MIDI notes can be deleted individually or in groups. To delete MIDI notes without separating the clip, you must be in Notes or Velocity view.

To delete a MIDI note or group of notes with the Clear command:

1. With the **GRABBER** tool or **SELECTOR** tool, select the note or notes to be deleted.

2. Choose **EDIT > CLEAR** or press the **DELETE** key. The notes will be removed from the track.

To delete a single MIDI note with the Pencil tool:

1. With the track in Notes view, select the **PENCIL** tool.

2. Hold **OPTION** (Mac) or **ALT** (Windows). When placed over a note, the Pencil tool will become an Eraser.

3. With the Eraser active (upside down pencil), click on a note to delete it.

Figure 4.27 Deleting a note with the Pencil tool

 You can also delete notes by double-clicking on them with either the Grabber or the Pencil tool.

Review/Discussion

1. What timebase do Audio tracks default to? MIDI tracks? Instrument tracks? (See "Understanding Track Timebases" beginning on page 90.)

2. Which Pro Tools timescales are absolute? Which are relative? What is the difference between absolute and relative timescales? (See "Sample-Based Operation Versus Tick-Based Operation" beginning on page 90.)

3. How do audio clips respond to tempo changes on a sample-based track? How do they respond if you change the track to tick-based (without using Elastic Audio)? (See "Audio Track Timebases" beginning on page 92.)

4. Pro Tools provides 960 ticks per quarter note; how many ticks does it provide per half note? How many per eighth note? (See "Tick-Based Timing and Note Values" beginning on page 92.)

5. Why might you want to render a MIDI performance as audio? What are some available options for rendering a virtual instrument's output to an audio file? (See "Rendering Virtual Instruments" on page 93.)

6. What are some of the different options available for viewing data on MIDI and Instrument tracks in the Edit window? What kinds of operations can you perform in each view? (See "MIDI-Compatible Tracks and Track Views" beginning on page 95.)

7. Where are the MIDI input and output controls located for MIDI tracks in the Mix window? Where are they located for Instrument tracks? (See "MIDI-Compatible Tracks in the Pro Tools Mix Window" beginning on page 97.)

8. What does the MIDI Thru option do? How is it enabled? (See "MIDI Thru Option" beginning on page 98.)

9. What is the Default Thru Instrument setting used for? How can you change the Default Thru Instrument setting? (See "Default Thru Instrument Option" beginning on page 99.)

10. What keyboard modifier would you use when clicking on a MIDI clip in the Clip List to audition it? What is required for this process to play sound? (See "Auditioning from the Clip List" beginning on page 100.)

11. How is editing MIDI data different from editing audio? How are MIDI notes affected when deleting a selection or trimming a clip compared to how audio waveforms are affected? (See "Editing MIDI Clips" beginning on page 100.)

12. What are some of the functions of the Pencil tool when editing MIDI notes? (See "Editing MIDI Notes with the Pencil Tool" beginning on page 101.)

13. What setting normally determines the Default Note Duration when adding notes with the Pencil tool? How can this setting be changed? (See "Default Note Duration" beginning on page 103.)

14. How can you select a range of MIDI notes using the on-screen keyboard? (See "Selecting MIDI Notes" beginning on page 104.)

15. What process can be used to transpose MIDI notes? What modifier can you use to preserve the note start times when transposing? (See "Transposing Notes" beginning on page 105.)

16. Describe some different ways of deleting notes on a MIDI or Instrument track. What track views allow you to delete notes? (See "Deleting MIDI Notes" beginning on page 107.)

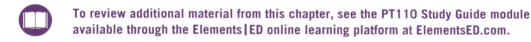

To review additional material from this chapter, see the PT110 Study Guide module available through the Elements|ED online learning platform at ElementsED.com.

EXERCISE 4

Using Virtual Instruments

Virtual instruments have become indispensable tools for many computer musicians, sound designers, and creative professionals. In this exercise, you will use the Xpand!2 virtual instrument plug-in, assign presets from the plug-in window, create an Aux Input track to use for the Vacuum virtual instrument, and route playback from a MIDI track to a virtual instrument on an Aux Input track.

Duration: 20 Minutes

Getting Started

To get started with this exercise, you will open the session you worked on in Exercise 3. If that session is not available, you can use the *Waiting Here.ptxt* session template to create a new session.

1. Locate and open the 110 Exercise 3 [Your Initials].ptx session file that you created previously. The session will open to show the Edit window.

If your Exercise 3 session is not available, open the *Waiting Here.ptxt* session template [PT110 Exercise Media (v12.8) > 03 Waiting Here > Waiting Here.ptxt] to create a new session.

Name the new session 110 Exercise 4 [Your Initials] and save it to the class files location for your course. Then skip to the next section.

---

2. Choose FILE > SAVE AS.

3. Navigate to the class files location for your course and create a new folder named 110 Exercise 4 [Your Initials].

4. Save the session in the newly created folder as 110 Exercise 4 [Your Initials].

Using Instrument Tracks

For this part of the exercise, you will display the Inserts view in the Edit window, add virtual instruments to two existing Instrument tracks, and choose appropriate plug-in presets for each track.

Display inserts and add a plug-in to the MIDI Loops track:

1. Choose VIEW > EDIT WINDOW VIEWS > INSERTS A-E to display the first five insert positions in the Edit window.

2. Locate the MIDI Loops track in the Edit window and click on INSERT SELECTOR A. (See Figure 4.28.)

Exercise 4 ■ Using Virtual Instruments   111

Figure 4.28 Clicking an Insert selector on the MIDI Loops track

3. For Insert A, choose **multichannel plug-in > Instrument > Xpand!2 (stereo)** to instantiate Xpand!2. The Xpand!2 plug-in window will open on screen.

4. Click on the Xpand!2 Librarian menu at the top of the plug-in window.

Figure 4.29 Xpand!2 Librarian menu

5. Choose the **28 Loops > 005 Click Beats** preset for the plug-in. Close the plug-in window when finished.

Figure 4.30 Presets in the Xpand!2 Librarian menu

Discussion Point #1

What is the advantage of showing the Inserts A-E view in the Edit window? How could you do this without using the View menu?

Add a plug-in to the MIDI Piano track:

1. Locate the MIDI Piano track in the Edit window and click on **INSERT SELECTOR A**.

2. Choose **MULTICHANNEL PLUG-IN > INSTRUMENT > XPAND!2 (STEREO)** to instantiate a second instance of Xpand!2. The Xpand!2 plug-in window will open.

3. From the Librarian menu, choose **13 ACOUSTIC PIANO > 06 NATURAL PIANO + STRINGS**.

4. Close the Xpand!2 plug-in window to reduce on-screen clutter.

5. Press **RETURN** or **ENTER** to return to the start; then play back the session to listen to the instruments.

Using an Auxiliary Input

Rather than using an Instrument track, you can place a virtual instrument on an Aux Input. In this section, you will configure an Aux Input track with the Vacuum plug-in and trigger it from an existing MIDI track.

Create an Aux Input and add the Vacuum plug-in:

1. Click on the **MIDI Beats** track in the Track List to select it.

2. Create a stereo Aux Input track and name it **Vacuum Aux**.

3. Click **INSERT SELECTOR A** on the Vacuum Aux track and choose **MULTICHANNEL PLUG-IN > INSTRUMENT > VACUUM (STEREO)** to instantiate the plug-in. The Vacuum plug-in window will open.

4. From the Librarian menu, choose **1 LEADS > 12 DIRTY RESO LEAD**.

Figure 4.31 Preset selected in the Vacuum Librarian menu

5. Close the plug-in window when finished to reduce on-screen clutter.

Route the MIDI Beats output to the Vacuum Aux track:

1. Choose **VIEW > EDIT WINDOW VIEWS > I/O** to display the I/O column in the Edit window.

2. Locate the MIDI Beats MIDI track and click on the **MIDI OUTPUT SELECTOR**.

Figure 4.32 MIDI Output selector in the Edit window I/O view

3. Choose **VACUUM 1 - CHANNEL-1** from the **MIDI OUTPUT SELECTOR** to route the track's signal to the plug-in you instantiated on the Vacuum Aux track.

4. Play back the session to listen to the instrument.

> **Discussion Point #2**
>
> What is the purpose of using an Aux Input track in this section? What options are available from the MIDI Output selector on the MIDI Beats track? What do the other destinations represent?

Finishing Up

Before exiting Pro Tools, turn off the Inserts view and I/O view in the Edit window. Also be sure to save the work you have done, as you will be reusing this session in later exercises.

Hide the Inserts and I/O views and save the session:

1. **OPTION-CLICK** (Mac) or **ALT-CLICK** (Windows) on both the Inserts A-E label and the I/O label at the top of Edit window view columns to hide both columns.

2. Press **RETURN** (Mac) or **ENTER** (Windows) to return to the session start.

3. Save and close the session. That concludes this exercise.

Remember that you cannot close a Pro Tools session by closing its windows. You must choose CLOSE SESSION from the FILE menu.

LESSON 5

Working with Elastic Audio

The Elastic Audio capabilities in Pro Tools have changed the way that the world works with audio. Having the ability to warp and conform an audio clip to match a tempo map or to correct the timing of a performance can save countless hours of work. The time-manipulation functions available through Elastic Audio unleash limitless creative possibilities. On top of that, the Elastic Audio pitch transposition features provide an entire other dimension for audio editing and manipulation.

This lesson describes how to enable Elastic Audio and how to use it to warp and conform audio. It also discusses Elastic Audio pitch transposition and describes how it can be used for melodic manipulation.

GOALS

- Enable Elastic Audio on an Audio track
- Select from the available Elastic Audio processors and recognize how they work
- View and manipulate Elastic Audio Event markers
- Work with Elastic Audio Warp markers to manipulate audio clips
- Use Elastic Audio pitch transposition to transpose audio clips on Elastic Audio–enabled tracks

Key topics from this lesson are included in the *Pro Tools 12 Essential Training: 110* course on Lynda.com, available here: alpp.us/PT110_Online.

In this lesson, we examine the world of Elastic Audio. By enabling Elastic Audio on a track, you will have the ability to conform audio clips on the track to the session tempo, manually adjust or warp the timing of any portion of the audio on the track, quantize performances to a grid or groove template, and more.

Elastic Audio Basics

Elastic Audio provides track-based Time Compression and Expansion (TCE) processing, enabling you to quickly and easily manipulate the timing of audio events or beat-match an audio performance to follow the session's Tempo ruler. Elastic Audio can be applied using real-time or rendered TCE processing.

Pro Tools' Elastic Audio processors use high-quality transient detection algorithms, combined with beat and tempo analysis, to calculate a file's native tempo and determine the file's duration in bars and beats. This analysis involves examining the audio content of the file to identify rhythmically significant audio events.

Enabling Elastic Audio on a Track

The first order of business when preparing to use Elastic Audio is to enable an Elastic Audio processor on the target track. Any Audio track in a Pro Tools session can be Elastic Audio–enabled using the track's Elastic Audio Plug-in selector in the Edit window.

 Elastic Audio processing is provided by special plug-in processors that are available in the Edit window only.

After applying an Elastic Audio processor, you can choose whether to apply changes in real-time or switch to rendered processing mode. All but one of Pro Tools' Elastic Audio processors use real-time processing by default.

Real-time Elastic Audio processing is immediate, so you can hear the results right away, but it can demand significant system resources when used on multiple tracks. Rendered Elastic Audio processing is non-real-time—meaning that you may have to wait for the results to render to disk prior to playback. The benefit of rendered mode is that it is less demanding on resources. This can be useful for large or complex sessions. If your system cannot keep up with the demands of real-time Elastic Audio processing, Pro Tools will display a message suggesting that you switch to rendered mode.

To enable Elastic Audio on a track:

1. Create a new Audio track or choose an existing Audio track.

2. Click the track's **Elastic Audio Plug-in selector** in the Edit window and select the appropriate Elastic Audio plug-in from the pop-up menu.

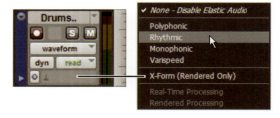

Figure 5.1 Selecting the Rhythmic Elastic Audio plug-in for a drum track

Any audio clips on the track will temporarily go offline while Elastic Audio analysis is performed. The waveforms will appear grayed out while files are offline.

3. (Optional) Click the track's **Elastic Audio Plug-in selector** a second time to change from Real-Time Processing to Rendered Processing, if desired.

Basic Elastic Audio Processors

Pro Tools provides four basic Elastic Audio processors. The option you select will determine how the audio on the track is processed. Each of the available processors uses a different TCE algorithm to produce its results, each tailored to a different type of audio material. It is important to select the plug-in whose algorithm best matches the material on the track you want to process.

 Though commonly referred to as Elastic Audio plug-ins, these processors are available in the Edit window only. You cannot use Elastic Audio plug-ins on track inserts (as you do with Native or DSP plug-ins).

Pro Tools' four basic Elastic Audio plug-ins can be used for either real-time or rendered processing. Each of the plug-ins is designed for a specific type of audio program material:

- **POLYPHONIC.** The Polyphonic processor is a general, all-purpose algorithm that is effective with a wide range of material. This is the default processor that Pro Tools uses for previewing and importing from Workspace browsers. It works well for complex loops and multi-instrument mixes.

- **RHYTHMIC.** The Rhythmic processor is best suited to material with clear attack transients and rapid decays, such as drums and percussion.

- **MONOPHONIC.** The Monophonic processor is best suited to monophonic material that needs formant relationships kept intact, such as vocals. The Monophonic processor is also well suited to monophonic instrumental lines, such as a bass track.

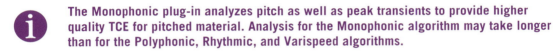 **The Monophonic plug-in analyzes pitch as well as peak transients to provide higher quality TCE for pitched material. Analysis for the Monophonic algorithm may take longer than for the Polyphonic, Rhythmic, and Varispeed algorithms.**

- **VARISPEED.** The Varispeed processor links time and pitch changes for tape-like speed-change effects and post-production sound effect uses.

The X-Form Processor (Advanced Processing)

The X-Form processor provides advanced TCE processing and operates in rendered mode only—it cannot process audio in real time. The X-Form Elastic Audio plug-in is a modified version of the standalone X-Form AudioSuite processing plug-in, which is a paid add-on for Pro Tools. The X-Form Elastic Audio processor comes with Pro Tools and provides much higher quality TCE algorithms than the basic Elastic Audio processors. X-Form is well suited for professional music production, sound design, and audio loop applications.

 To save time, use a real-time Elastic Audio processor while experimenting and fine-tuning your tempo map. Later, you can switch to X-Form to obtain the best TCE quality possible, once your tempo manipulations are complete.

The X-Form processor includes parameters for Quality and Formant options. (The formant shape of a voice or instrument gives the audio its overall characteristic sound or timbre.) X-Form lets you preserve the formant shape of audio when applying TCE processing, helping protect it from the undesirable artifacts that often accompany pitch shifting.

Auto-Enabling Elastic Audio for New Tracks

If you frequently work with Elastic Audio, you can have tracks automatically enabled for Elastic Audio, rather than having to manually enable each track. To have Pro Tools enable tracks for Elastic Audio as they are created, do one or more of the following:

- Choose the **ENABLE ELASTIC AUDIO ON NEW TRACKS** option in Preferences (**SETUP > PREFERENCES > PROCESSING** tab) and select a default plug-in processor from the pop-up menu.

    Any new tracks you create will be Elastic Audio–enabled using the selected processor.

    Figure 5.2 Setting the preference to enable Elastic Audio on all new tracks

- Enable the **ALL FILES** option in Preferences (Processing tab) for conforming files imported from the desktop. (See Figure 5.4.) Files dragged to the Track List or to empty space in the Edit window will be placed on new tick-based, Elastic Audio–enabled tracks.

    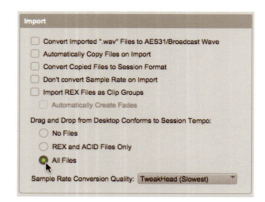

    Figure 5.4 Preference setting for enabling Elastic Audio for files dragged in from the desktop

- Enable the **AUDIO FILES CONFORM TO SESSION TEMPO** option (metronome) in a Workspace browser. Any audio files you drag to the Track List or to empty space in the Edit window will be placed on new tick-based, Elastic Audio–enabled tracks.

    Figure 5.3 Enabling the Audio Files Conform to Session Tempo function in a Workspace browser

The free Pro Tools I First software has Elastic Audio auto-enabled for all Audio tracks and does not include Preference settings for enabling or disabling this function.

Understanding Elastic Audio Analysis

When you enable Elastic Audio on a track, Pro Tools automatically analyzes the audio on the track for transient events. The waveforms temporarily appear grayed out as clips go offline during Elastic Audio analysis. Once the analysis is complete, the audio will come back online and the waveforms will appear normal again.

Elastic Audio analysis is file-based, meaning that when you work with a clip, the entire underlying audio file is analyzed. For clips from large files, this can take a while. As a result, small sub-set clips may be offline longer than expected due to the processing time required to analyze the underlying parent files.

Transient Detection

Elastic Audio analysis detects transient events in each audio file and uses them to identify rhythmic events and patterns. Detected transients are tagged in the file and indicated by Event markers. You can view and edit Event markers using Analysis view, discussed later in this lesson.

Tempo Detection

Using the detected transients, Elastic Audio analysis attempts to identify a tempo for the analyzed audio. Audio files containing a regular periodic rhythm can be successfully analyzed for tempo. If the tempo is determined successfully, then Pro Tools will also calculate the file's duration in bars and beats.

Analyzed files in which a tempo has been detected are treated as tick-based files, meaning that they contain timing information referenced to bars and beats. Tick-based files can be auditioned at the session tempo from a Workspace browser, as discussed in Lesson 3. They can also be conformed to the session tempo map when imported or placed on an Elastic Audio-enabled track.

Analyzed files in which no tempo has been detected are treated as sample-based files. Files with only a single transient (such as with a single snare hit) will have no tempo detected. Also, files that contain tempo changes or rubato (rushing or slowing of the tempo), or without regular periodic rhythmic patterns, will probably not have a detected tempo and will be treated as sample-based files.

Conforming Clips to the Session Tempo Map

After enabling Elastic Audio on a track, you might want to conform the audio on the track to follow the session tempo. This is useful for adjusting the tempo of an imported file or loop so that it conforms to the tempo map of your session, including any tempo changes that occur on the Tempo ruler.

> ### Example 5.1: Adding Audio to a Performance with an Accelerando
>
> In music production, it is common to record to a click. For a song that has an accelerando at the end, you would likely generate the desired tempo ramp on the Tempo ruler prior to tracking. This will ensure that the band plays a uniform tempo increase across the target bars at the end of the performance.
>
> In a later stage of song production, you may decide to add an instrument at the end, across the area containing the accelerando, using material that was previously tracked in an area of the song with a fixed tempo. For example, you may have an 8-bar section of rhythm guitar from an earlier chorus, recorded at a tempo of 125 BPM, which you would like to reuse at the end.

> After making a copy of the clip at the desired location, you can enable Elastic Audio on the track; then use the CLIP > CONFORM TO TEMPO command to automatically match the clip to the tempo map. The tempo of the rhythm guitar clip will change to follow the programmed tempo ramp, creating an accelerando that matches the other tracks.

To conform the tempo of a clip to your session tempo map:

1. After enabling Elastic Audio on a track, select the target clip on the track by clicking on it with the GRABBER tool or by double-clicking it with the SELECTOR tool.

2. Choose CLIP > CONFORM TO TEMPO. The clip will contract or expand as needed to conform to the session tempo and any tempo changes that occur within the clip boundaries.

> *You can also conform a clip on an Elastic Audio track by right-clicking on the clip and selecting CONFORM TO TEMPO from the pop-up menu.*

> *The results of conforming to the session tempo can be affected by the placement of Event markers in the analyzed files. When conforming to a complex tempo map, you may need to first modify or correct the detected Event markers, as discussed later in this lesson.*

Clips that have been conformed to the session tempo will include Warp markers corresponding to any tempo change events that occur within the clip boundaries. You can view and edit Warp markers using the Warp track view, discussed later in this lesson.

Warp Indicators

Clips that have been conformed to the session tempo or otherwise manipulated by Elastic Audio processing will display a Warp indicator in their upper right-hand corner. Since unmodified clips can reside on Elastic Audio–enabled tracks, not all clips on Elastic Audio tracks will display Warp indicators. (See Figure 5.5.) The Warp indicator will be present only when Elastic Audio processing has been applied to a clip.

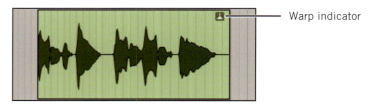

Figure 5.5 Warp indicator in Waveform view

The Warp indicator for Elastic Audio clips can be displayed or hidden in the Edit window.

To toggle the display of the Warp indicator in Elastic Audio clips:

- Select or deselect VIEW > CLIP > PROCESSING STATE.

Removing Clip Warping

If you have applied any Elastic Audio processing, or *warping*, that you are not satisfied with, you can remove the warping and revert the clip to its original state using the Remove Warp command. Warp markers are not deleted by the Remove Warp command, but any warping that has been applied is undone.

To remove clip warping:

1. Select the clip for which you want to remove warping.

2. Do one of the following:

    - Choose **CLIP > REMOVE WARP**.

    – Or –

    - With any Edit tool, right-click the clip and select **REMOVE WARP** from the pop-up menu.

Remove Warp can be applied to clips but not to clip groups. To unwarp clip groups, you must ungroup the clips, apply Remove Warp to the underlying clips, and then regroup the clips.

Elastic Audio Track Views

Pro Tools provides two track views for Elastic Audio–enabled tracks: Analysis view and Warp view.

- **ANALYSIS VIEW.** This view lets you edit detected Event markers. When you are working with audio that has clear, clean transients, you will ordinarily not need to use Analysis view. However, when working with material that does not have clear transients or material that contains transients for non-rhythmic events, you can use Analysis view to improve the results for certain types of TCE processing. Analysis view lets you add, move, or delete Event markers as needed.

 Cleaning up the Event markers can be useful to achieve better quality results from Elastic Audio processing and greater accuracy when conforming to a tempo map or quantizing with Elastic Audio.

- **WARP VIEW.** This view lets you manually "warp" audio to adjust the timing of audio events. In Warp view you can create and edit Warp markers. Warp view is designed for using Elastic Audio to correct the timing of a performance or to achieve special effects.

After applying an Elastic Audio processor to a track, you can change the track view to Analysis view or Warp view at any time to edit the associated markers.

To select an Elastic Audio view:

1. Click the Elastic Audio–enabled track's **TRACK VIEW SELECTOR**.

2. Select **ANALYSIS** or **WARP** from the Track View selector pop-up menu. (See Figure 5.6.)

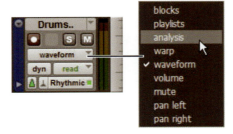

Figure 5.6 Selecting Analysis view from the Track View selector on a drum track

Elastic Audio Markers

Pro Tools provides three types of Elastic Audio markers: Event markers, Warp markers, and Tempo Event–generated Warp markers. All three types are visible in Warp view; only Event markers are visible in Analysis view.

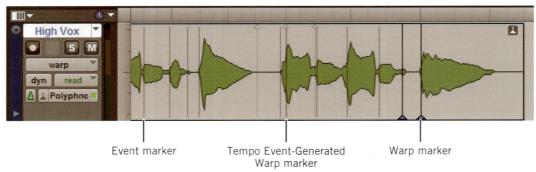

Figure 5.7 Elastic Audio markers in Warp view

In Analysis view, you can add, delete, and reposition Event markers. In Warp view, you can add, delete, and reposition Warp markers and use them as control points for applying Elastic Audio processing.

Tempo Event–generated Warp markers, if present, are displayed in Warp view only; however, you cannot directly move or edit Tempo Event-generated Warp markers on a track.

Event Markers

Event markers indicate detected audio events. Event markers are displayed as solid black lines in Analysis view and as gray lines in Warp view. Unlike Warp markers, Event markers do not fully extend to the top and bottom of the track.

Event markers can be modified in Analysis view, if needed, to improve results when processing with Elastic Audio. You can use the Grabber tool to reposition Event markers that have been added at the wrong place, or to add missing Event markers or delete extraneous ones. You can add, delete, or move Event markers in Analysis view only. Details on editing Event markers are provided later in this lesson.

 Event markers may not display when audio is zoomed out too far; to see Event markers, make sure that you are zoomed in sufficiently.

Warp Markers

Warp markers anchor the audio to the Timeline and are displayed in Warp view only. Warp markers appear as thick black vertical lines with a triangle at their base and function similar to push pins, attaching the audio waveform to points on a timebase ruler. You can use Warp markers to anchor (or pin) a point within an Elastic Audio clip to a fixed point on the Timeline.

When you pin one or more points to the ruler (Timeline), you can use subsequent Warp markers or Event markers to stretch or compress ranges of audio relative to those fixed points.

Warp markers can be added and modified in Warp view. Existing Warp markers can also be moved in Warp view to apply Elastic Audio processing, warping the audio to which the marker has been attached.

Tempo Event–Generated Warp Markers

Tempo Event–generated Warp markers are gray vertical lines with a diamond at the top that indicate where Elastic Audio processing has been applied to automatically conform audio to tempo events. They appear on tick-based tracks only and are not editable.

If you change the track timebase from ticks to samples, any Tempo Event–generated Warp markers will convert to regular, editable Warp markers, as the audio will no longer automatically conform to the tempo map.

Warping Sound with Elastic Audio

One very common application of Elastic Audio is to manually warp audio on one track to match another track or to align with specific timeline locations. Oftentimes you will need to warp a track to align with events on another audio track or with onscreen action in a video track. In these cases, you can manually warp an audio clip to speed it up, slow it down, or adjust the timing of audio events within the clip.

Using Warp View

To manually warp audio on a track, you will first need to set the display of the target track to Warp view. For certain types of warping, you will also need to manually add Warp markers to your clips.

To display Warp view:

1. Click the Elastic Audio–enabled track's **TRACK VIEW SELECTOR**.

2. Select **WARP** from the Track View pop-up menu. (See Figure 5.8.)

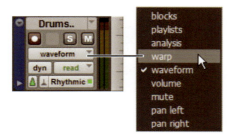

Figure 5.8 Selecting Warp view

Adding Warp Markers

To apply warping relative to fixed points in the waveform, you will need to add one or more Warp markers to the target clips. As discussed earlier in this lesson, Warp markers anchor points in the audio waveform to specific points on the Timeline. Warp markers give you detailed control over warping for audio clips and events.

To add a Warp marker to a clip, do one of the following:

- With the **PENCIL** tool, click anywhere in the clip. If you click on an Event marker, the Event marker will be converted to a Warp marker.

- With the **GRABBER** tool, **CONTROL-CLICK** (Mac) or **START-CLICK** (Windows) anywhere in the clip. If you click on an Event marker, the Event marker will be converted to a Warp marker.

- With the **GRABBER** tool, click an Event marker between existing Warp markers or double-click on an Event marker that is not between Warp markers. The Event marker will be converted to a Warp marker.

 You can also add Warp markers with the Grabber tool by double-clicking anywhere in a clip in Warp view. However, this method can result in the clip becoming selected, which can cause you to inadvertently move the clip when trying to drag a Warp marker.

To add Warp markers at the boundaries of a selection:

1. Make an Edit selection within a clip or across one or more clips.

2. Use any Edit tool to right-click within the selection and choose **Add Warp Marker** from the pop-up menu. Warp markers will be added at the selection start and end.

Correcting Warp Markers

Adding Warp markers to clips can be an imprecise operation, especially if you are not able to use existing Event markers as warp locations. If you end up with a Warp marker at the wrong spot, you can reposition it without warping the audio in the associated clip to fine-tune its location relative to the audio waveform.

To reposition a Warp marker (without applying warping), do one of the following:

- With the **Pencil** tool, click on a Warp marker and drag it to a new location.
- With the **Grabber** tool, **Control-click** (Mac) or **Start-click** (Windows) on a Warp marker and drag it to a new location.

Deleting Warp Markers

If you have added a Warp marker that you don't need, you can easily remove it from the clip by deleting it. If the Warp marker has been used as a control point for warping, deleting it will release the warping applied at that point.

To delete a Warp marker, do one of the following:

- With the **Grabber** tool, double-click on a Warp marker.
- With the **Grabber** or **Pencil** tool, **Option-click** (Mac) or **Alt-click** (Windows) on a Warp marker.

You can also select a range of Warp markers to delete multiple markers at once.

To delete all Warp markers within a selection:

1. In Warp view, make an Edit selection that includes the Warp markers you want to delete.
2. Do one of the following:
   - Press **Delete** or **Backspace** on your computer keyboard.
   - Or –
   - Right-click within the Edit selection and select **Remove Warp Marker** from the pop-up menu.

All Warp markers in the selected range will be deleted.

Types of Manual Warping

You can manually warp audio in one of three specific ways: Telescoping Warp, Accordion Warp, and Range Warp. Telescoping Warp and Accordion Warp are used to speed up or slow down an entire clip, whereas Range Warp is used to adjust the timing of events within a clip.

Applying a Telescoping Warp

A Telescoping Warp can be applied to any audio waveform that does not contain Warp markers. Telescoping Warps can be applied to clips on both sample-based and tick-based tracks.

 Telescoping Warps can also be applied to the start or end of clips that are bordered by a Warp marker on only one side.

The Telescoping Warp technique lets you click and drag an Event marker in Warp view to stretch or compress the entire waveform of a clip relative to its start or end point. (See Figure 5.9.)

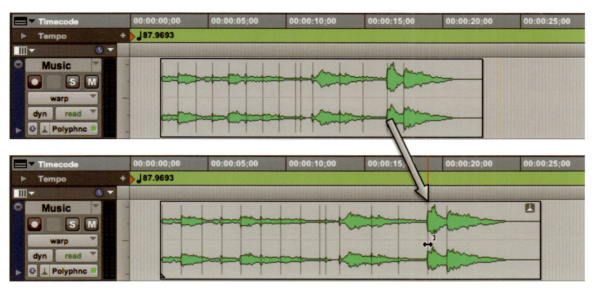

Figure 5.9 Applying a Telescoping Warp with a fixed clip start point

To apply a Telescoping Warp to a clip in Warp view, do one of the following:

- With the **Grabber** tool, drag any Event marker in a clip that has no Warp markers. A Warp marker will be created at the clip start, anchoring its position, and the waveform for the entire clip will telescope in or out relative to the clip start location.

- With the **Grabber** tool, **Option-click** (Mac) or **Alt-click** (Windows) and drag any Event marker in a clip that has no Warp markers. A Warp marker will be created at the clip end, anchoring its position, and the waveform for the entire clip will telescope in or out relative to the clip end location.

> ### Example 5.2: Stretching a Music Bed to Match a Video Cut
>
> In video post-production work, you often need to manipulate the timing of a music track to match or reinforce the onscreen action. Sometimes it is useful to have a music cue or event align with a scene change or a cut to a different camera angle.
>
> After importing a music clip, for example, you may need to slow it down to last for the proper duration. In the process, you can align a musical event near the end of the clip to a camera cut near the end of the scene. To do so, enable Elastic Audio on the track and put the track in Warp view. Then use the Grabber tool to drag the Event marker associated with the target music event to the right while keeping an eye on the Video window. The video track will scrub with your cursor position, allowing you to align the Event marker with the video cut, synchronizing the music with the onscreen change.

Applying an Accordion Warp

An Accordion Warp applies Elastic Audio processing on both sides of a single Warp marker in a clip. This lets you expand or compress the audio equally on both sides of a fixed point. (See Figure 5.10.)

The Accordion Warp technique is useful for audio files that have a downbeat in the middle of the clip.

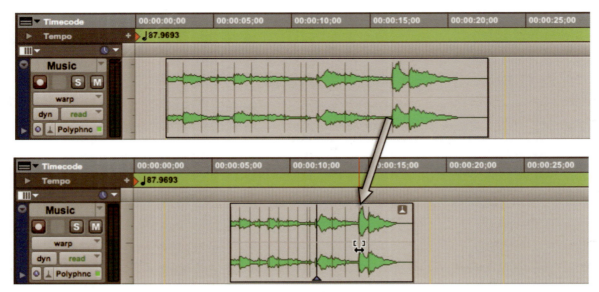

Figure 5.10 Applying an Accordion Warping a clip around a fixed point

To apply Accordion Warp to a clip:

1. In Warp view, add a single Warp marker at the point in the clip that you want to remain fixed on the Timeline.

2. With the **Grabber** tool, drag any Event marker on either side of the Warp marker. The waveform for the clip will expand/contract on both sides, anchored on the Warp marker.

Applying a Range Warp

Range Warps apply Elastic Audio processing between two fixed points in a clip. To apply a Range Warp, you must have at least two Warp markers present in the clip. Applying a Range Warp allows you to adjust the timing of audio events relative to one another.

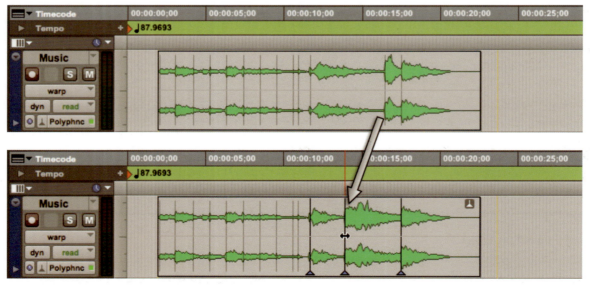

Figure 5.11 Applying a Range Warp between two fixed points in a waveform

To apply Range Warp within a clip:

1. In Warp view, add a Warp marker at the start point that you want to fix to the Timeline.

2. Add a second Warp marker to the end point that you want to fix to the Timeline.

3. Create a third Warp marker between the first two Warp markers and drag it to warp the underlying audio. The waveform will compress or expand on either side of the middle Warp marker while the audio outside the bounding markers remains unaffected.

To automatically create Warp markers from three adjacent Event markers, Shift-click on the middle Event marker with the Grabber tool. All three Event markers will convert to Warp markers, allowing you to easily apply a Range Warp with the middle marker.

Example 5.3: Correcting the Timing of a Note or Note Range

A common situation that Range Warping is particularly well suited for is correcting a portion of a performance where a musician has temporarily drifted off of the beat. In the situation where the bass player loses the groove following a complex drum fill, for example, one or more bass notes may be slightly late starting on the downbeat. Typically, the notes leading up to the problem area will be in time, as will the notes shortly after the area, where the musician locks back into the tempo.

In such cases, you can add Warp markers on either side of the missed downbeat to protect the unaffected areas. Adding another Warp marker on the first missed note will let you drag the note into position, either by visually referencing the drum tracks or by aligning the note to the beat in Grid mode.

Correcting the first note will also have an effect on the other unprotected notes in the compromised area and may be enough to bring them into time. If more precision is required, you can add Warp markers on each of the other notes and individually correct their timing.

Using Elastic Audio to Tighten a Rhythmic Performance

As an alternative to using Range Warping to manually correct the timing of individual notes in a music performance, you can use Elastic Audio to correct audio en masse within a selection by applying a Quantize operation. The Quantize functions, detailed in Lesson 6, let you align musical events to bars, beats, and sub-beats based on the session tempo. Commonly used to tighten up MIDI performances, quantization can also be applied successfully to Elastic Audio clips that have sufficiently accurate Event markers.

How Quantizing Affects Elastic Audio Events

When you apply quantization to a selection on an Elastic Audio-enabled track, the Event markers within the selected range are used as control points for warping the audio. The Event markers that are closest to the specified quantize grid are promoted to Warp markers and are moved to the grid, based on the quantize settings. As a result, the audio is warped such that any transients associated with those Event markers are quantized to the grid, creating a more rhythmically accurate performance.

Quantizing is particularly successful for audio that has clear, distinct attack transients correlated to a rhythmic grid or groove, such as drums, piano, guitar, bass guitar, etc. Quantization is less successful for audio that lacks rhythmic transients, such as strings, pads, ambient textures, and soft, legato performances.

Improving the Quantization Results

Although quantizing Elastic Audio provides a very quick way to correct timing issues, the results can often be less than perfect, either falsely quantizing events that are not rhythmically correlated or degrading the quality of the resulting audio or both. The root cause of these issues is typically excessive or imprecise Event markers.

For better results, you will need to clean up the Event markers prior to applying quantization. This can be done by editing Event markers in Analysis view and by adjusting the Event Sensitivity setting in the Elastic Properties window. (See "Improving the Quality of Warped Audio" later in this lesson.)

> **Example 5.4: Removing Inaccurate Event Markers for a Guitar Performance**
>
> Guitar recordings frequently include characteristic instrument sounds that are not necessarily rhythmically correlated. For example, both acoustic and electric guitar recordings often contain string squeaks caused by the player's fingers when changing hand positions and pick/strum noises caused by the player's pick or hand striking the soundboard or pick guard. These sounds are represented in the waveform by transient events and are typically tagged by Elastic Audio analysis with Event markers.
>
> To prevent these noises from being quantized and sounding unnatural, you will need to remove the associated Event markers prior to applying quantization. You can manually remove the unwanted markers by deleting them individually in Analysis view; alternatively, you may be able to remove most or all unwanted markers throughout an entire clip by lowering the clip's Event Sensitivity setting in the Elastic Properties window.

Using Elastic Audio to Experiment with Tempo

Another, less common use of Elastic Audio is to modify the tempo of an entire recording by changing the session tempo or introducing new tempo changes. This can be used for subtle effects—increasing the tempo by a few beats per minute to give a song a bit more energy—or for radical alterations—transforming a slow or mid-tempo song to an up-tempo version for a dance remix.

Applying Tick-Based Timing to Elastic Audio-Enabled Tracks

An easy way to achieve these effects and experiment with tempo for a session is to first enable Elastic Audio on all of the Audio tracks and to then change the timebase of all Audio tracks from samples to ticks. Using tick-based timing will allow the tracks to update dynamically to match any tempo changes you make in the session.

To change a track timebase to ticks, do the following:

1. Click on the track's **Timebase selector**.

2. Select **Ticks** from the resulting pop-up menu. (See Figure 5.12.)

Figure 5.12 Selecting tick-based timing from a track's Timebase selector

Lesson 5 ■ Working with Elastic Audio 129

 To have new tracks default to tick-based, enable the NEW TRACKS DEFAULT TO TICK TIMEBASE option in the Editing Preferences page.

> **Sample-based Elastic Audio versus Tick-based Elastic Audio**
>
> Elastic Audio tracks can be either sample-based or tick-based. Sample-based Elastic Audio lets you apply real-time or rendered processing by editing in Warp view, applying quantization, and using the TCE Trim tool. Tick-based Elastic Audio tracks are necessary only when you want to automatically apply Elastic Audio processing based on changes to the session tempo or tempo map.

Applying Tempo Changes

After enabling Elastic Audio and tick-based timing on your Audio tracks, you can freely experiment with alternate tempos and tempo changes. You can try out different tempos in real time using the manual tempo control in the Transport window or apply tempo changes to the Tempo ruler using any of the techniques you've learned thus far.

 Refer to Lesson 3 in this book for information on adding tempo events and linear tempo changes on the Tempo ruler.

To audition alternate tempos in real time, do the following:

1. Display the Transport window, if not already shown.

2. Disable the Tempo ruler by clicking on the Tempo Ruler Enable button to toggle it off (gray). (See Figure 5.13.)

3. Click in the Tempo field and do one of the following:

    - Type in a new tempo value.

    - Scroll to a new tempo value using a scroll wheel or trackpad.

    - Increase or decrease the tempo value using the UP ARROW and DOWN ARROW keys.

    - Click and drag up or down to increase or decrease the tempo.

Figure 5.13 Tempo controls in the Transport window

Manual tempo changes can be applied during playback, allowing you to immediately hear the results.

Improving the Quality of Warped Audio

As discussed previously in this lesson, quantizing with Elastic Audio can produce undesirable results if the audio contains inaccurate Event markers. Other types of Elastic Audio processing (conforming, manual warping, and tempo changes) can also produce undesirable artifacts due to missing or unnecessary Event markers.

Editing the Event markers in a clip for accuracy can make a significant difference in the timing accuracy and the audio quality resulting from Elastic Audio processing. To improve the audio quality further, you can switch to X-Form processing after completing all of your Elastic Audio manipulations.

Editing Event Markers in Analysis View

In Analysis view, you can add, move, and delete Event markers to make corrections where Elastic Audio analysis has not accurately detected audio events or has detected unwanted audio events. This can be especially useful for adding or positioning Event markers in audio without clear transients, such as legato strings, melismatic vocals, or soft synth pads.

 Consider the example of a slow synth pad that does not have clear transients. After Elastic Audio analysis, Event markers may be incorrectly located or may be missing altogether. By switching to Analysis view, you can add Event markers at each chord change and remove any unnecessary markers.

To display Analysis view:

1. Click the Elastic Audio–enabled track's **TRACK VIEW SELECTOR**.

2. Select **ANALYSIS** from the Track View selector pop-up menu.

Figure 5.14 Selecting Analysis view from the Track View selector

 In Analysis view, all Edit tool functions apply to Event markers only. You cannot use Edit tools for clip editing in Analysis view.

Adding and Positioning Event Markers

You can use Analysis view to add missing Event markers to Elastic Audio–enabled tracks and to reposition Event markers relative to the underlying audio waveform.

To add an Event marker:

1. Set the track to Analysis view.

2. Do one of the following:

    - With the **PENCIL** tool, click at the location where you want to add an Event marker.

    - With the **GRABBER** tool, double-click at the location where you want to add an Event marker.

    - With the **GRABBER** tool, **CONTROL-CLICK** (Mac) or **START-CLICK** (Windows) at the location where you want to add an Event marker.

 You can also add an Event marker using any Edit tool by right-clicking at the target location and selecting ADD EVENT MARKER from the pop-up menu.

To reposition an Event marker:

1. Set the track to Analysis view.

2. Using the **Pencil** tool or **Grabber** tool, drag the Event marker to a new location. The Event marker will be repositioned without affecting the underlying audio.

Deleting Event Markers

Analysis view can also be used to delete unwanted or erroneous Event markers on Elastic Audio–enabled tracks. Eliminating unnecessary Event markers can improve the quality of Elastic Audio processing.

To delete Event markers:

1. Set the track to Analysis view.

2. Do one of the following:

   - Using the **Pencil** tool or **Grabber** tool, **Option-click** (Mac) or **Alt-click** (Windows) on the Event marker you want to delete.

   - With the **Selector** tool, make an Edit selection that includes any Event markers you want to delete and press **Delete** or **Backspace** on your computer keyboard.

   - With the **Selector** tool, make an Edit selection that includes any Event markers you want to delete, right-click on the selection, and choose **Remove Event Marker** from the pop-up menu.

   The Event marker(s) will be deleted without affecting the underlying audio waveform.

If you notice a warbling or uneven sound during sustained notes or chords in a warped clip, switch the track to Analysis view and delete any Event markers that fall within the sustained areas. This will allow the TCE processing to be applied more smoothly and consistently across the sustained areas.

Do not delete Event markers at the start of notes, chords, or rhythmic hits. Doing so may cause the attack portions of the notes or hits to sound distorted and unnatural.

Adjusting Event Sensitivity

Pro Tools uses very aggressive transient detection in order to detect every possible audio event. Consequently, for highly transient material it is possible to have erroneously detected events.

Each transient is detected with an identified confidence level. You can lower the Event Sensitivity to filter out erroneous events that have a low confidence level relative to more significant transients with a higher level of confidence.

Understanding Event Confidence

Each Event marker is assigned a confidence level based on the relative clarity of the associated transient. A drum loop that has clear, sharp transients will have Event markers with a high degree of confidence, whereas a legato violin melody that has softer transients will have Event markers with a lower degree of confidence. The confidence level for detected transients is based in part on the clarity of the transient. Loud accented notes will be analyzed with a higher degree of confidence than soft, unaccented notes.

> ### The Effects of Amplitude and Frequency on Event Confidence
>
> Peak amplitude is not the most important measure for event confidence. The clarity of transients is measured in part by the spectral transition from one moment to the next. This tends to result in higher event confidence for high-frequency content, since high-frequency content typically has sharper transients. Thus, lowering the Event Sensitivity for a drum loop often affects the kick drum hits more than the hi-hat and cymbal hits, even though the kick drum hits may have a higher peak amplitude.

Using the Elastic Properties Window

The Event Sensitivity setting in the Elastic Properties window lets you filter Event markers for a clip based on the marker's confidence level. The Event Sensitivity acts like a threshold for retaining only transient events that are detected with a high degree of confidence.

> ### Example 5.5: Eliminating False Event Markers for Bass Guitar
>
> Low-frequency audio such as a bass guitar can introduce erroneous Event markers, especially during the attack portions of a note, due to the large swing in the audio waveform. As a result, it is very common for bass guitar tracks to exhibit unnatural sounding artifacts when warped with Elastic Audio.
>
> This situation is easily corrected by lowering the Event Sensitivity setting for each clip on the track. Simply select all of the clips, open the Elastic Properties window, and bring the Event Sensitivity setting down by a few percentage points. (Settings between 98% and 95% are usually sufficient.)
>
> By using Analysis view to monitor the Event markers as you adjust Event Sensitivity, you can zero in on the best setting. You want to eliminate as many false markers as possible without losing the Event markers that occur at the start of each note.

To change the Event Sensitivity:

1. Select a clip on an Elastic Audio–enabled track. The track can be either sample-based or tick-based.

2. Choose **CLIP > ELASTIC PROPERTIES** (or right-click the clip and choose **ELASTIC PROPERTIES** from the pop-up menu).

   The Elastic Properties window will open.

   Figure 5.15 Elastic Properties window

3. Click in the **EVENT SENSITIVITY** field and adjust the value as needed. In Warp or Analysis view you will see the number of Event markers decrease or increase as you lower or raise the Event Sensitivity.

> **Optimizing Elastic Audio for Non-Rhythmic Audio**
>
> Reducing the number of Event markers often yields better-sounding results for non-rhythmic audio (such as legato strings). You can either manually remove Event markers in Analysis view or lower the Event Sensitivity setting for the clip you want to process.
>
> Because Pro Tools preserves detected transients when applying TCE in order to avoid flamming and granulation of the transients, false transients are also preserved, and the resulting sound quality can suffer. When working with audio that does not have clearly defined transients, you can lower the Event Sensitivity to obtain better-sounding results.

Using X-Form

After completing your work on an Elastic Audio track (including making corrections to Event markers), you can change the processor on the track to X-Form for better quality results. When switching to X-Form, the audio for the track will go offline while being rendered to disk. (X-Form provides rendered processing only.)

X-Form processing can be quite time-consuming, so it is recommended to apply the X-Form processor only after all warping, editing, and tempo manipulations are complete. Any changes you make after applying X-Form will cause the audio go offline again and re-render.

 Elastic Audio changes are always generated using the original audio files rather than previously rendered files, so no audio degradation will occur with multiple changes. However, re-rendering with X-Form is always time-consuming. It is therefore more efficient to work with one of the other processors until you are ready for final-stage rendering.

Using Elastic Audio for Pitch Changes

Elastic Audio can also be used change the pitch of audio clips without affecting playback speed. Any clip on an Elastic Audio–enabled track can be transposed by plus or minus 2 octaves. You can apply Elastic Audio pitch transposition using either the Elastic Properties window or the Transpose window.

 Elastic Audio pitch transposition is not supported with the Monophonic algorithm.

Elastic Audio pitch transposition is clip-based, meaning it cannot be applied to partial clips. To transpose only a selected portion of a performance, you must first separate the selection as an independent clip.

Pitch Shifting with the Elastic Properties Window

The Elastic Properties window is useful for applying a pitch shift across selected audio clips in a session. In this window, you can apply pitch shifting in semitones or cents, up to 2-octaves up or down. This can be useful for modifying melodies, transposing performances, or retuning performances.

> **Example 5.6: Creating a Vocal Harmony**
>
> Elastic Audio pitch transposition can be used as a quick way to create a basic harmony to supplement a lead vocal. To do so, you can place a copy of the vocal line that you want to harmonize on each of two new tracks and enable the Polyphonic Elastic Audio processor on the tracks. Then use the Pitch Shift setting in the Elastic Properties window to transpose the clips on each track.

> For example, you might transpose the duplicate clip on the first track up by +4 semitones to create a harmony that is a major third above the original. To create a 3-part harmony, you could transpose the clip on the second track up by +7 semitones (a perfect fifth above the original). To blend the parts, lower the faders on the new tracks by 6 to 9 dB and offset their pan controls to the left and right.

To transpose the pitch of an audio clip in the Elastic Properties window, do the following:

1. Make sure the clip or clips you want to transpose are on Elastic Audio–enabled tracks.

2. With the **GRABBER** or **SELECTOR** tool, select the audio clip you want to transpose. Only clips that are completely selected will be affected.

3. Open the Elastic Properties window by choosing **CLIP > ELASTIC PROPERTIES** or by Right-clicking the selected clip and choosing **ELASTIC PROPERTIES** from the pop-up menu.

 You can also press OPTION+[5] (Mac) or ALT+[5] (Windows) on the numeric keypad to open the Elastic Properties window.

4. Adjust the **PITCH SHIFT** settings at the bottom by the desired amount (semitones and/or cents).

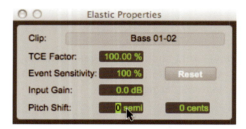

Figure 5.16 Selecting the Pitch Shift settings in the Elastic Properties window

Pitch Shifting with the Transpose Window

As an alternative to using the Elastic Properties window, pitch shifting can be applied using the **EVENT OPERATIONS > TRANSPOSE** window. This process is useful when you need to create a transposition across multiple tracks that include pitched MIDI performances, since the Transpose window affects selected MIDI data as well as selected Elastic Audio clips.

> ### Example 5.7: Creating a Key Change
>
> The Transpose window can be used to create a key change across all tracks in a recording. To modulate up a whole step for the final chorus of a song, for example, you can use the controls in this window.
>
> In the case of a song with Audio tracks for vocals, guitar, bass, and drums and an Instrument track for MIDI piano, you would start by enabling the Polyphonic processor on the vocal, guitar, and bass tracks (leaving off the drum tracks, since drums are not pitched and should not be transposed).
>
> Next, you would place the Edit cursor across each of these tracks at the start of the final chorus and use the Edit > Separate Clip > At Selection command to create independent clips for the section to be transposed. Then make a selection across all tracks in the session, extending from the start of the final chorus to the end of the session. Finally, open the Transpose window, set it to transpose up by 2 semitones, and click the Apply button.

To transpose pitch in the Transpose window, do the following:

1. Make sure the audio clip or clips that you want to transpose are on Elastic Audio–enabled tracks.

2. With the GRABBER or SELECTOR tool, select the material that you want to transpose. Only audio clips that are completely selected will be affected. (Selected MIDI data does not need to include entire clips.)

3. Choose EVENT > EVENT OPERATIONS > TRANSPOSE. The Transpose page of the Event Operations window will open. (See Figure 5.17.)

Figure 5.17 Transpose page of the Event Operations window

4. Do one of the following:

   - Adjust the TRANSPOSE BY settings by the desired amount (octaves and semitones).
   - Adjust the TRANSPOSE FROM and TO settings by the desired amount in relative note values.

 The TRANSPOSE ALL NOTES TO and TRANSPOSE IN KEY settings apply only to MIDI notes. When audio clips are selected, these options are unavailable.

5. Click APPLY. The selected material will transpose by the specified amount, applying Elastic Audio processing as needed.

Changing and Undoing Pitch Transposition

Since pitch transposition is an Elastic Audio property, it can be changed at any time without having a detrimental effect on audio quality. Changing the pitch shift values in the Elastic Properties window will render a new result based on the original, unprocessed file.

To change or undo pitch transposition, do the following:

1. Select a clip or clips that have been transposed on Elastic Audio–enabled tracks.

2. Open the Elastic Properties window by choosing CLIP > ELASTIC PROPERTIES or by right-clicking a selected clip and choosing ELASTIC PROPERTIES from the pop-up menu.

3. Adjust the settings in the Pitch Shift fields (semitones and cents) to change the amount of transposition being applied, or reset the fields to 0 (zero) to remove all transposition from the clip(s).

Review/Discussion

1. How would you go about enabling Elastic Audio on a track? (See "Enabling Elastic Audio on a Track" beginning on page 116.)

2. Which real-time Elastic Audio processor typically works best for drums? Which typically works best for vocals? (See "Basic Elastic Audio Processors" beginning on page 117.)

3. Which Elastic Audio plug-in provides only Rendered processing? When/why would you want to use Rendered processing? (See "The X-Form Processor" beginning on page 117.)

4. What can the Elastic Audio analysis' tempo detection determine about an audio file? What are some conditions that will cause no tempo to be detected? (See "Understanding Elastic Audio Analysis" beginning on page 119.)

5. Where are Warp Indicators displayed? What are they used for? (See "Warp Indicators" beginning on page 120.)

6. What views are available for working with Elastic Audio–enabled tracks? What is each view used for? (See "Elastic Audio Track Views" beginning on page 121.)

7. Name the three types of Elastic Audio markers. What are the differences between them? (See "Elastic Audio Markers" beginning on page 121.)

8. What are some ways to add Warp markers to a clip? List at least three. (See "Adding Warp Markers" beginning on page 123.)

9. What is a Telescoping Warp? How does it differ from an Accordion Warp? From a Range Warp? (See "Types of Manual Warping" beginning on page 124.)

10. What is the effect of quantizing a selection on an Elastic Audio-enabled track? What happens to the Event markers within the selection? (See "How Quantizing Affects Elastic Audio Events" beginning on page 127.)

11. Why is it important to have accurate Event markers in your clips when applying Quantize operations on Elastic Audio-enabled tracks? (See "Improving the Quantization Results" beginning on page 128.)

12. After enabling a track for Elastic Audio, how would you enable the track to update dynamically to match any subsequent tempo changes you make in the session? (See "Applying Tick-Based Timing to Elastic Audio-Enabled Tracks" beginning on page 128.)

Lesson 5 ■ Working with Elastic Audio   137

13. What are some ways to improve the quality of audio that has been warped with Elastic Audio processing? (See "Improving the Quality of Warped Audio" beginning on page 129.)

14. What is meant by Event Confidence? How can Event Confidence be used to eliminate false transients when applying TCE processing on Elastic Audio–enabled tracks? (See "Adjusting Event Sensitivity" beginning on page 131.)

15. What are two ways to apply Elastic Audio pitch transposition? What are some applications for using each option? (See "Using Elastic Audio for Pitch Changes" beginning on page 133.)

  To review additional material from this chapter, see the PT110 Study Guide module available through the Elements|ED online learning platform at ElementsED.com.

EXERCISE 5

Using Elastic Audio for Dialog

The powerful editing capabilities that Pro Tools provides are ideal for making corrections when mixing to picture. Being able to work non-destructively and non-linearly on dialog, effects, and backgrounds makes working with Pro Tools fast and flexible.

Elastic Audio can be used as a means of aligning audio, allowing you to easily correct material that is out of sync. In this exercise, you will activate Elastic Audio on a dialog track, use Warp markers and range warping to correct the timing of the dialog, and align Event markers to timecode in Grid mode.

Duration: 20 Minutes

Getting Started

For this exercise, you will work with an automobile commercial, replacing and correcting the dialog to create a new version of the ad for a different market. To get started, you will create a session from a template file and save it to the class files location specified by your instructor.

Open the template and save the session:

1. Launch Pro Tools and choose FILE > OPEN SESSION (or choose OPEN FROM DISK from the Dashboard).

2. Navigate to the Exercise Media folder and open the *Ugly Duckling.ptxt* template file [PT110 Exercise Media (v12.8) > 04 Ugly Duckling > Ugly Duckling.ptxt].

   A dialog box will open displaying default parameters based on the template.

3. Name the session 110 Exercise 5 [Your Initials] and select the PROMPT FOR LOCATION option near the bottom of the dialog box.

4. Click CREATE to proceed. A second dialog box will open, prompting you to choose a save location.

5. Navigate to an appropriate location and click SAVE. The session will open with the Edit window displayed.

Preparing the Replacement Dialog

For the first part of this exercise, you will be working with a new dialog track that has been recorded for a British version of the commercial. The script is identical to the original; however, some parts of the recording are out of sync with the video and don't pace correctly for the ad.

Activating the New Dialog Track

The replacement dialog track is currently hidden in the session and muted so that it is not audible during playback. To begin work on the new dialog, you will need to display and unmute the track.

Display, unmute, and play back the new dialog:

1. Click on the **TRACK SHOW/HIDE** symbol (light-gray dot) to the left of the **WORKING DIALOG** track in the Track List. (See Figure 5.18.)

   The symbol will turn solid black, and the Working Dialog track will display in the Edit window.

   Figure 5.18 Click the Track Show/Hide symbol to toggle the track display.

2. Click the **MUTE (M)** button on screen for the Working Dialog track to deactivate the mute.

3. Press **RETURN** (Mac) or **ENTER** (Windows) to return to the start of the session.

4. If needed, select **WINDOW > VIDEO** to display the Video window.

5. Press the **SPACEBAR** to begin playback. During playback, note that a portion of the new dialog is out of sync with the original and does not match well with the video.

6. When finished, press the **SPACEBAR** a second time to stop playback.

Preparing the Session

Before you get started, you may need to change the main timescale for the session, set the Edit mode, and configure selection options for the session.

Enable the Timecode ruler:

- If not already displayed, choose **VIEW > RULERS > TIMECODE**. The Timecode ruler will appear in the Timeline Display area of the Edit window. (See Figure 5.19.)

Figure 5.19 Timecode ruler displayed in the Edit window

Set the Main Timescale to Timecode

1. Click the **MAIN COUNTER SELECTOR** in the toolbar area at the top of the Edit window.

Figure 5.20 Main Counter selector in the Edit window

2. Choose **TIMECODE** from the pop-up menu. The Main Counter will change to show time in the format 00:00:00;00, representing time code in hours: minutes: seconds; frames.

Set the Edit mode and selection options:

1. Click the **GRID** button in the top left of the Edit window or press **F4** to activate Grid mode.

2. Enable **OPTIONS > LINK TRACK AND EDIT SELECTION**, if not already selected (checked).

Correcting the Timing

For this portion of the exercise, you will activate Elastic Audio on the Working Dialog track and perform range warping to align the start of various words to specific timecode locations in Grid mode.

Make a selection on the Working Dialog track:

1. Click on **ZOOM PRESET 2** to zoom in; then locate the two clips in the Dialog track that correspond to the out-of-sync area of the Working Dialog track.

    The target clips are "It's making a sound like rah rah" and "No rah."

2. Use the **GRABBER** tool to select the first of the two clips in the Dialog track. (The track will also become selected.)

3. Hold down the **SHIFT** key and click on the second clip. The Edit selection will extend across both clips, as shown below.

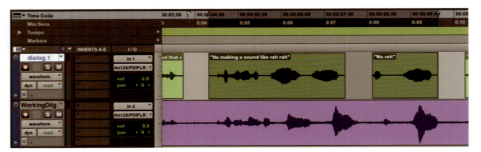

Figure 5.21 Select the first clip; then use Shift to extend the selection to the second clip.

4. Click on the track nameplate for the Working Dialog track so that it becomes selected. With the Working Dialog track selected, the Edit selection will move down to this track.

> **Discussion Point #1**
>
> What is the purpose of holding the Shift key in Step 3 above? What would happen if you clicked on the second clip without holding Shift?
>
> Why did the Edit selection move to the Working Dialog track when you selected the track in Step 4?

Activate Elastic Audio and review the selection:

1. Click on the **ELASTIC AUDIO PLUG-IN SELECTOR** at the head of the Working Dialog track and select **POLYPHONIC**. (See Figure 5.22.)

    The clips will go offline temporarily while they are being analyzed.

Figure 5.22 Elastic Audio plug-in selector on the Working Dialog track

2. Click on the **TRACK VIEW SELECTOR** and switch from **WAVEFORM** view to **WARP** view.

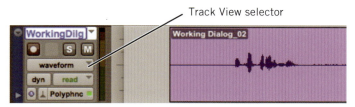

Figure 5.23 Track view selector for the Working dialog track

3. With the selection still active, right-click anywhere within the selection and choose **ADD WARP MARKER** from the right-click menu. Warp markers will be added at either end of the selection.

4. Zoom in a couple of levels to get a better view of the waveform (or click **ZOOM PRESET 3**).

5. Play back the selection a few times to get familiar with how the waveform corresponds to each of the words on the Working Dialog track.

> ### Discussion Point #2
>
> Why was it necessary to switch to Warp view in Step 2 above? Could you have switched to Analysis view instead? What do you think would have been the result in Step 3 if you had been in Analysis view?

Warp the timing for specific words:

1. With the **GRABBER** tool, click on the Event marker (vertical gray line) at the start of the second occurrence of the word "Rah" on the Working Dialog track. The Event marker will convert to a Warp marker.

Figure 5.24 Warp marker at the start of the second "Rah"

2. **OPTION-CLICK** (Mac) or **ALT-CLICK** (Windows) on the track nameplate for the Working Dialog track to deselect it and remove the Edit selection from the track.

3. Drag the Warp marker for the word "Rah" to the left so that it aligns with the corresponding part of the waveform on the Dialog track, around 00:00:06;22.

    Hint: The **CURSOR** display in the Edit window toolbar shows your current Timecode location as you drag. (See Figure 5.25.)

Figure 5.25 Cursor display in the Edit window toolbar

4. Click on the Event marker at the start of the word "No" on the **Working Dialog** track and drag it to the right slightly so that it aligns with the corresponding part of the waveform on the **Dialog** track, around 00:00:08;05.

5. Click on the Event marker at the start of the final "Rah" on the **Working Dialog** track and drag it to the left so that it aligns with the corresponding part of the waveform on the **Dialog** track, around 00:00:08;28.

6. Press the **SPACEBAR** to audition the changes. Note that the Working Dialog track now syncs with the original and matches well with the video.

Wrap Up

Now that you have corrected the vocals, you will need to make the original dialog track inactive so that it does not interfere with the session playback or other editing and mixing work.

Disable and hide the unused dialog track:

1. Click on the **Dialog** track nameplate in the Edit window to select the track.

Figure 5.26 Selecting the original dialog track

2. Choose **TRACK > MAKE INACTIVE** to disable the selected track. The track will become grayed out on screen.

3. Click on the **TRACK SHOW/HIDE** symbol to the left of the **Dialog** track in the Track List to hide the track.

Review the changes:

1. Press **RETURN** (Mac) or **ENTER** (Windows) on your keyboard to return to the start of the timeline.

2. Press the **SPACEBAR** to play back the session and review the changes you've made.

3. When finished, stop playback and save and close the session. That concludes this exercise.

 Remember that you cannot close a Pro Tools session by closing its windows. You must choose CLOSE SESSION from the FILE menu.

LESSON 6

Editing and Fine-Tuning a Performance

Pro Tools includes powerful tools for working with audio and MIDI data, enabling you to record, edit, and manipulate performances with ease. Using the right tool for the job can dramatically enhance your efficiency, and Pro Tools makes it easy to access the right tool when you need it. When using Elastic Audio or MIDI Real-Time Properties, Pro Tools also enables powerful workflows for conforming and time-correcting performances. This lesson covers techniques for editing, arranging, and quantizing MIDI data and audio in Pro Tools.

GOALS

- Use the Smart Tool to quickly access commonly used tools and functions
- Use advanced options to preview, create, and edit fades
- Quantize MIDI data, audio clips, and Elastic Audio events to the Grid
- Use Real-Time Properties to dynamically change a MIDI performance

Key topics from this lesson are included in the *Pro Tools 12 Essential Training: 110* course on Lynda.com, available here: alpp.us/PT110_Online.

This lesson introduces various tools and options available when working with audio and MIDI data as well as techniques for time-correcting MIDI and audio performances. It also covers advanced uses of the Fades dialog box and fade editing techniques.

Using the Smart Tool

As discussed in the *Pro Tools 101* course book, the Smart Tool is active when the Trim, Selector, and Grabber tools are all selected (highlighted) in the Edit Window Toolbar. The Smart Tool provides instant access to each of the member tools and also makes it easy to add fades and crossfades.

When active, the position of the cursor in relation to a clip or note or within an automation playlist determines how the Smart Tool functions.

Figure 6.1 Smart Tool when active (blue)

To enable the Smart Tool, do one of the following:

- Click the **SMART TOOL** button (bar over the Trim, Selector, and Grabber tools).
- Press any two of the three keys **F6** through **F8** simultaneously.

The Trim, Selector, and Grabber tools will illuminate along with the Smart Tool.

Activating the Primary Smart Tool Functions

When the Smart Tool is active, the cursor changes to indicate the currently available tool mode, based on the cursor position within a clip. The tool mode changes automatically according to the following rules:

- **SELECTOR TOOL:** When the cursor is positioned in the upper half of a clip, and not near a clip boundary, the Smart Tool will function in Selector mode and display the Selector I-beam cursor.

     To temporarily switch to the Scrubber, place the cursor over the clip so that the Selector tool is enabled, then press CONTROL (Mac) or START (Windows).

- **TRIM TOOL:** When the cursor is positioned near the center of a clip horizontally and within 12 pixels of a clip boundary, the Smart Tool will function in Trim mode and display the Trim icon. The display of a clip must be at least 36 pixels wide for Trim mode to be available. At smaller display sizes, the resolution is too low to trim accurately.

- **GRABBER TOOL:** When the cursor is positioned in the lower half of a clip and not near a clip boundary, the Smart Tool will function in Grabber mode and display the Grabber hand cursor.

     When you access any of these three tools with the Smart Tool enabled, all of the corresponding tools and tool-related keyboard shortcuts will also be available.

To disable the Smart Tool:

- Activate any other Edit tool via a toolbar button or the appropriate function key.

Creating Fades Using the Smart Tool

When the Smart Tool is active and the cursor is in the top quarter of a clip, the tool will change to Fade mode when you approach a clip boundary (within 12 pixels). As with Trim mode, the clip display must be at least 36 pixels wide for this mode to be available. You can zoom in to increase the horizontal display of the clip, if needed.

To create a fade using the Smart Tool:

- **Fade In:** Place the cursor near a clip start boundary, close to the top of the clip, and drag right. A fade in will be drawn from the start of the clip to the position where you release the mouse.

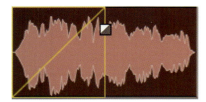

Figure 6.2 Creating a Fade In using the Smart Tool

- **Fade Out:** Place the cursor near a clip end boundary, close to the top of the clip, and drag left. A fade out will be drawn from the end of the clip to the position where you release the mouse.

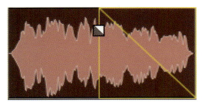

Figure 6.3 Creating a Fade Out using the Smart Tool

- **Crossfade:** Place the cursor near a clip boundary, close to the bottom of two adjacent clips, and drag left or right. A centered crossfade will be drawn from the clip boundary to the position where you release the mouse.

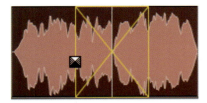

Figure 6.4 Creating a Crossfade using the Smart Tool

Smart Tool Fade Settings

The settings specified in the Editing Preference page will be used for all corresponding fade ins, fade outs, and crossfades created with the Smart Tool.

To change fade setting, do the following:

1. Choose **SETUP > PREFERENCES** and click on the **EDITING** tab.

2. Click on the corresponding button in the Fades section, under **DEFAULT FADE SETTINGS**. A Fades dialog box will open.

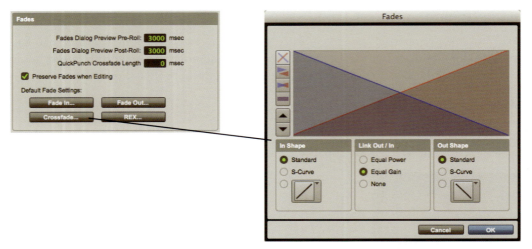

Figure 6.5 Fade settings in the Editing tab of Preferences (left) and the corresponding Fades dialog box (right)

3. Choose the desired fade curve and settings, and click **OK**.

 Smart Tool functions are also available in the free Pro Tools|First software; however, Pro Tools|First does not include Preference settings for specifying default fade curves.

The Fades that you can create using Smart Tool also follow these rules:

- If a fade or crossfade already exists on a clip boundary, Fade mode will not be available for that clip boundary when using the Smart Tool.
- All fades you create will be graphically drawn on the screen and rendered in real time.
- You can modify fades you create using the Smart Tool in various ways, as discussed below.

Working with Fades

Fade settings can be selected or modified at any time using the Fade In, Fade Out, and Crossfade dialog boxes. Fades can also be adjusted in various ways by editing them on a track playlist. Here, we discuss some of the options available for fine-tuning fades and crossfades.

Using the Fades Dialog Boxes

As discussed in the *Pro Tools 101* book, you can open a Fades dialog box by making a selection in the Edit window across a clip boundary and then choosing **EDIT > FADES > CREATE** or pressing **COMMAND+F** (Mac) or **CTRL+F** (Windows). You can also access the associated Fades dialog box at any time by double-clicking on an existing fade shape with the Grabber tool.

The Fades dialog boxes let you select, view, and audition fade settings and edit the curves used to perform a fade-in, fade-out, or crossfade. These dialog boxes also provide auditioning tools that you can use to preview your fade selections.

Lesson 6 ■ Editing and Fine-Tuning a Performance   147

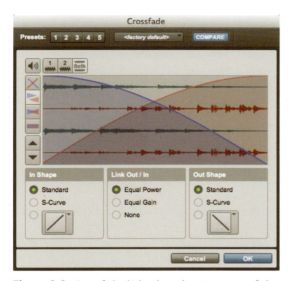

Figure 6.6 Crossfade dialog box showing a crossfade on a stereo track

Audition and Preview Controls

Figure 6.7 shows the controls available for auditioning and previewing fades in the Crossfade dialog box. The buttons arranged across the top provide options for displaying waveforms prior to applying them. The waveform display buttons are available only when the fade selection includes multiple tracks or channels.

The buttons arranged vertically down the left side of the Fades dialog box can be used to audition and preview fade settings in different ways on screen.

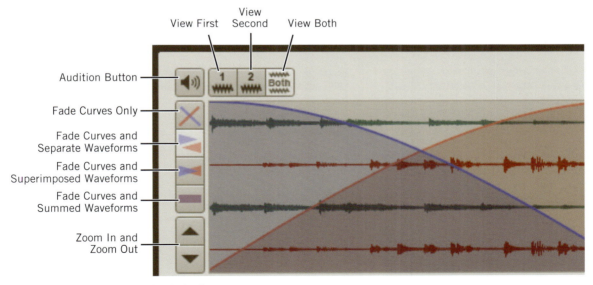

Figure 6.7 Controls in the Fades dialog box

AUDITION CONTROLS. The following controls are available at the top of the dialog box:

- The AUDITION button can be used to play the current fade settings through the Pro Tools hardware.

  Auditioning can also be toggled on or off by pressing the SPACEBAR.

- The VIEW FIRST TRACK/LEFT CHANNEL button is available when fading across more than one track or on a stereo track; select this button to view and audition only the audio on the first track or left channel.

- The **VIEW SECOND TRACK/RIGHT CHANNEL** button can be used to view and audition only the audio on the second track or right channel.

- The **VIEW BOTH TRACKS/CHANNELS** button can be used to audition the audio on the first and second tracks (or left and right channels) simultaneously.

 The two audition tracks are always the first two tracks included in a selection, starting from the top of the Edit window.

PREVIEW CONTROLS. The following controls are available on the left side of the Fades dialog box:

- The **FADE CURVES ONLY** button displays the fade curves without showing the actual audio waveforms.

- The **FADE CURVES AND SEPARATE WAVEFORMS** button displays the fade curves along with separate views of the fade-in and fade-out waveforms.

- The **FADE CURVES WITH SUPERIMPOSED WAVEFORMS** button displays the fade curves along with color-coded views of the fade-in and fade-out waveforms superimposed on one another.

- The **FADE CURVES AND SUMMED WAVEFORM** button displays the fade curves along with a single waveform representing the summation of the crossfaded audio.

- The **ZOOM IN** and **ZOOM OUT** buttons scale the waveform amplitude up or down, respectively.

Choosing Fade Settings

The Fades dialog boxes display fade-in shapes in red and fade-out shapes in blue. Either shape can be changed by choosing one of the two editable fade shapes (Standard or S-Curve) or by selecting from among the available presets in the shape drop-down selectors. The shape of each curve determines how the amplitude of a clip changes during the course of the fade.

 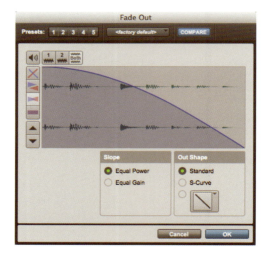

Figure 6.8 Fade-In dialog box (left) and Fade-Out dialog box (right).

To specify the fade settings, first select the desired fade shape(s) from the In Shape and/or Out Shape sections of the Fades dialog box. Then specify the fade slope option in the Link section (for crossfades) or Slope section (for fade-ins and fade-outs).

Fade Shape Settings

The In Shape and Out Shape sections allow you to choose the shape to use for a fade-in or fade-out, respectively. Both sections offer the same selections for their fade types.

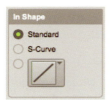 

Figure 6.9 Fade Shape setting options

- **Standard:** This option creates a single continuous general-purpose fade curve, which can be edited by dragging the curve in the Curve Editor.

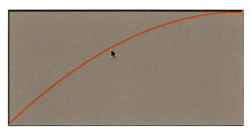 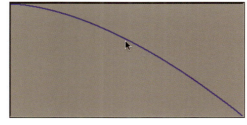

Figure 6.10 Standard Fade-In curve (left) and Fade-Out curve (right)

- **S-Curve:** This option selects an S-shaped curve. This fades faster at the curve's start and end and slower through its middle. S-shaped curves are particularly useful with material that is difficult to fade effectively. You can also edit S-curves by dragging in the Curve Editor.

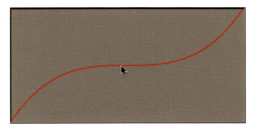 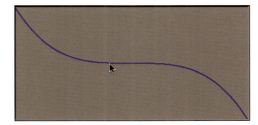

Figure 6.11 S-Curve Fade-Out (left) and S-Curve Fade-In (right)

- **Preset Curves:** Various preset curves are available under the pop-up menus. These can also be edited in the Curve Editor. Each fade curve offers a different fade rate, from fades that start slowly and then speed up at the end to fades that start quickly and then slow down toward the end.

Slope/Link Settings

When working with simple fade-ins and fade-outs, the Fades dialog boxes display a Slope section, providing both Equal Power and Equal Gain options. For crossfades, the dialog box displays the same options in a Link Out/In section, along with the additional **None** option.

Fades with Equal Power slopes retain more of their amplitude for a greater portion of the fade, in comparison to Equal Gain fades. The options for each type of fade are shown in Figure 6.12.

Figure 6.12 Fade Slope and Link Out/In setting options

The Link setting links the fade-out and fade-in curves together. If you adjust one curve, the corresponding curve also adjusts. This ensures that the crossfade maintains the proper amplitude at midpoint for an Equal Power or Equal Gain crossfade, as selected.

The Equal Power setting works best for crossfades between two different types of material, while the Equal Gain setting works best for crossfades between two identical (near phase-coherent) clips/instruments. Selecting None disables linking between the fade-out and fade-in curves, letting you adjust the curve shapes and start and end points separately.

> ### Example 6.2: Crossfading an Edit in a Guitar Solo
>
> After recording multiple takes of a difficult solo, it is common to end up with various edit points from different punch-ins and composited pieces. The quickest way to smooth out these edits is to apply short crossfades across each edit boundary. Because the targeted audio on either side is from the same instrument playing the same material, the waveforms are likely to be closely correlated at the edit point.
>
> In a guitar solo, for example, you may have a punch-in location in the middle of the last sustained note in order to capture a better release. Because the edit occurs on material that is very similar in the original and punched takes, the audio may be nearly phase coherent. Such material tends to be louder at the mid-point of the crossfade than non-correlated material. For this reason, the Equal Gain option is likely to provide more consistent results than Equal Power, which boosts the center of the crossfade.

Using Fade Presets

The top of the Fades dialog box includes five Fade Preset buttons. The Fade Presets are preconfigured for each Fades dialog box; however you can store your own fade settings in any numbered fade preset slot.

To recall a numbered fade preset, do one of the following:

- Click on the Fade Preset number that you wish to use.

Figure 6.13 Clicking on Fade Preset 1

- Hold **Control** (Mac) or **Start** (Windows) and type the Fade Preset number that you wish to use.

To store a fade setting as a numbered fade preset:

1. Configure the fade settings and shape(s) as desired.

2. **Command-click** (Mac) or **Ctrl-click** (Windows) on the Fade Preset number where you wish to store the settings. The Preset number will flash blue to confirm the save.

You can also save fade settings as a named preset, making them available under the Librarian menu.

To save fade settings as a named preset:

1. Configure the fade settings and shapes as desired.

2. Click on the Librarian menu (displaying <factory default>) and select SAVE SETTINGS AS. A Save dialog box will display.

3. Enter a name for your preset and click OK. The settings will be saved and the preset name will display in the Librarian menu.

Figure 6.14 The Save Preset dialog box

4. Click OK to apply the settings and close the Fades dialog box. The fade curve will be rendered in real time during playback, and a fade graphic will appear on the clip in the track playlist.

You will be able to recall and reuse your saved presets whenever using the associated Fades dialog box in the future. To recall a named preset, simply select it from the Librarian menu at the top of the dialog box.

 Refer to the *Pro Tools 101* book for information on creating fades with the Fade-In, Fade-Out, and Crossfade dialog boxes.

Editing Existing Fades

After creating fades in a session or project, you have several options for modifying or editing the fades to get them sounding exactly the way you want. You can modify the fade attributes and settings to change the fade shape and slope or you can edit the fade position or length.

Modifying Fade Attributes

You can modify the fade curves and shapes in a variety of different ways.

To change an existing fade to different fade settings using the Fades dialog box:

1. Double-click on the fade graphic on a track with the GRABBER tool. The Fades dialog box will open.

2. Select a new fade shape, slope, or Fade Preset.

3. Click OK. The original fade curve will be replaced by the new settings you've chosen.

To change an existing fade to a different fade curve from the Right-click menu:

1. Right-click on a fade graphic with any Edit tool.

2. Select Fades from the pop-up menu to access the fade options submenu.

3. Select the desired fade shape (Standard or S-Curve) or slope (Equal Power or Equal Gain) from the submenu. (See Figure 6.15.)

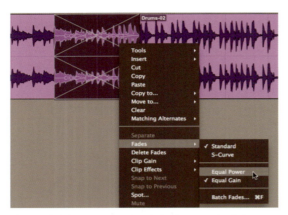

Figure 6.15 Changing the fade slope in the fade options submenu

To change a fade shape using keyboard commands:

1. Select the fade graphic by clicking on it with the **Grabber** tool or double-clicking on it with the **Selector** tool.

2. Press **Option+Control+Left/Right Arrow** (Mac) or **Alt+Start+Left/Right Arrow** (Windows) to change to the previous or next fade shape.

To change a fade curve using the Smart Tool:

1. With the Smart Tool active, position the mouse cursor over the fade graphic at the point where the Fade icon appears (half-shaded square for fade-ins and fade-outs or X-shaded square for crossfades).

2. Click and drag left/right on the fade curve. The fade graphic will be replaced with a yellow preview curve while you drag.

Figure 6.16 Positioning the Smart Tool on a fade (left) and adjusting the fade curve using the Smart Tool (right)

3. Release the mouse when the preview represents the desired shape.

 To access the fade adjustment functionality with the Selector tool, hold Command (Mac) or Control (Windows) while positioning the mouse cursor over a fade graphic.

Editing Fade Position and Duration

Aside from modifying an existing fade's shape and slope, you can also edit the fade in various ways to adjust its placement and duration. You can also easily remove fades you no longer want.

To reposition a fade, do one of the following:

- Click on a fade graphic with the **Grabber** tool and drag it to a new position.

- Select a fade graphic with the **Grabber** or **Selector** tool and nudge it forward or backward using the plus and minus keys on the numeric keypad.

    The underlying audio will trim to accommodate the new fade position.

To change the length of a fade, do one of the following:

- Place the **TRIM** tool at the beginning or ending of a fade graphic that you wish to adjust, and then click and drag with the mouse. The fade length will adjust accordingly.

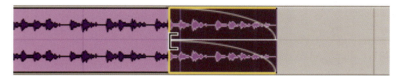

Figure 6.17 Trimming a fade

- Place the **SMART TOOL** at the beginning or ending of a fade graphic at the top or bottom of the clip (the Trim icon will display), and then click and drag with the mouse.

 Trimming fades in Shuffle mode will affect the sync and position of other clips on the track, just as normal trimming in Shuffle mode does.

To delete a single fade:

1. Click on a fade graphic with the **GRABBER** tool to select it.

Figure 6.18 Selecting a fade with the Grabber tool

2. Press **DELETE** on the keyboard. The selected fade will be deleted, leaving the original clip unchanged.

To delete one or more fades simultaneously:

1. Select the clip or range of clips that contain fades with the **SELECTOR** or **GRABBER** tool.

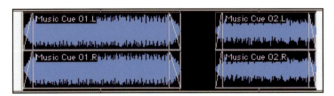

Figure 6.19 Multiple clips with fades selected

2. Choose **EDIT > FADES > DELETE**.

   All fades included in the selection will be deleted, leaving the original clips unchanged.

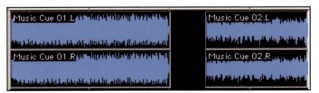

Figure 6.20 Clips after deleting fades

Creating Rhythmic Changes for Audio and MIDI Data

Pro Tools makes it easy to correct or modify the timing of rhythmic material by quantizing recordings and selections. Quantizing is the process of aligning musical events to a specified timing grid in order to provide a more beat-accurate timing for a performance. Pro Tools provides multiple methods for applying quantization.

In the Pro Tools 101 course, you learned about the Input Quantize function, which automatically aligns incoming MIDI notes to a timing grid as they are recorded. You can also quantize existing material with the Quantize command. This command can be applied to both MIDI and audio.

A third quantizing option exists for MIDI data: quantizing with MIDI Real-Time Properties. As discussed in the "MIDI Real-Time Properties" section later in this lesson, this function lets you modify MIDI notes in real time during playback without affecting the underlying MIDI data recorded on the track.

Using Input Quantize

As described in the *Pro Tools 101* book, the Input Quantize page of the Event Operations window allows you to enforce a timing pattern by quantizing incoming MIDI notes while recording.

To enable Input Quantize:

1. Choose **EVENT > EVENT OPERATIONS > INPUT QUANTIZE**. The Input Quantize page of the Event Operations window will open.

   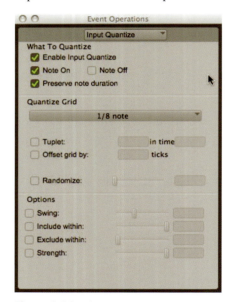

   Figure 6.21 The Input Quantize page in the Event Operations window

2. In the Input Quantize page, select the **ENABLE INPUT QUANTIZE** option.

3. Configure the options and parameter settings as desired. (See "**Error! Reference source not found.**" later in this lesson.)

4. Close the Event Operations window (optional) and record the MIDI performance.

 Be sure to disable Input Quantize when you are finished with the target recording. Once enabled in a session, Input Quantize will remain active for subsequent MIDI recording until you disable it in the Event Operations window.

Quantizing Existing Material

The standard Quantize function is commonly used to adjust existing MIDI notes to improve timing or to achieve a particular rhythmic feel, in the same way that Input Quantize works on incoming MIDI notes. However, the Quantize function can also be used to quantize audio clips and Elastic Audio events.

For audio clips, quantization adjusts the start times (or Sync Points) of the clips. For Elastic Audio, quantization adjusts the location of detected transient events and applies Elastic Audio processing accordingly.

> ### Creating Evenly Spaced Sound Effects
>
> Although quantizing is typically used for music production purposes, it can also be used to create timing effects for repetitive sounds in post production, sound design, and related applications.
>
> For example, quantizing the sound of a dripping faucet, a ticking clock, or a series of footsteps can create evenly spaced events that occur at a defined speed. These events can be synchronized with a music soundtrack by referencing a common tempo, if desired. Similarly, the timing of the events can be sped up or slowed down across a scene by quantizing to tempo changes or a tempo map.

Quantizing MIDI Data

You can use the Quantize command to adjust the timing of a MIDI performance relative to the grid by choosing a note value in the Quantize Grid pop-up menu.

To quantize existing MIDI data:

1. Make a selection on a MIDI or Instrument track.

2. Choose **EVENT > EVENT OPERATIONS > QUANTIZE** to display the Quantize page of the Event Operations window. (See Figure 6.22.)

    You can also press OPTION+0 [zero] (Mac) or ALT+0 [zero] (Windows) to display the Event Operations > Quantize page.

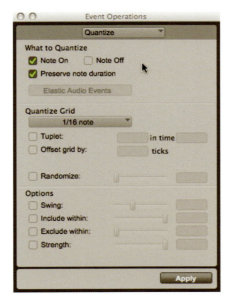

Figure 6.22 The Quantize page in the Event Operations window

3. In the **WHAT TO QUANTIZE** section of the window, choose the MIDI note attributes to quantize, and configure the remaining options and parameters as desired. (See "**Error! Reference source not found.**" later in this lesson.)

4. Click **APPLY** to quantize the selection. The MIDI notes will adjust according to the specified settings.

Quantizing Audio Clips

Quantization can be applied to clip start times (or Sync Points) on all Audio tracks, regardless of whether they are Elastic Audio–enabled, sample-based, or tick-based. This lets you quickly quantize audio clips without applying TCE processing, and is especially useful when working with "one-shot" (single-event) clips, such as drum samples or sound effects.

> ### Example 6.1: Creating Rhythm with Sound Effects
>
> A common technique when using sound effects in a song is to align the sounds with the rhythm or groove of the song. After importing a sound effect such as a telephone beep or church bell and placing several copies at approximate locations, you can use the Quantize function to align the clips with the groove of the song.
>
> In the case of a song that has a swung 1/8 note feel, for example, you would set the Quantize window to apply to audio clips, select an 1/8 note quantize grid, and enable the Swing option. With the sound effect clips selected, you could apply and audition quantization at successively increasing swing percentages until you hear the sound effects lock into the groove.

To quantize audio clips:

1. Select the audio clips you want to quantize on a track in the Edit window.

    Quantizing a clip group will adjust only the start location of the clip group (or its Sync Point). To quantize underlying sliced clips in a clip group, you must first ungroup, then quantize, and then regroup the clips.

2. Choose **EVENTS > EVENT OPERATIONS > QUANTIZE**, or press **OPTION+0** [zero] (Mac) or **ALT+0** [zero] (Windows).

3. In the Quantize window, select **AUDIO CLIPS** from the pop-up menu at the top.

Figure 6.23 Selecting the option for quantizing audio clips

4. Configure the remaining options and parameter settings as desired. (See "**Error! Reference source not found.**" later in this lesson.)

5. Click **APPLY**. The clip start times (or Sync Points, if present) will be quantized according to the specified quantize settings.

 Sync Points are discussed in the *Pro Tools 201* course book.

Quantizing Elastic Audio

As mentioned in Lesson 5, you can apply quantization to Elastic Audio events much as you would to MIDI notes. Quantizing can be applied to Event markers and Warp markers on Elastic Audio–enabled tracks, regardless of whether the tracks are sample-based or tick-based. When quantizing, Event markers closest to the quantize grid are promoted to Warp markers, and quantization is applied based on the selected Quantize settings.

To quantize Elastic Audio events:

1. Select the audio you want to quantize on Elastic Audio–enabled tracks. (Audio on tracks without Elastic Audio will not be quantized.)

2. Choose **EVENTS > EVENT OPERATIONS > QUANTIZE**, or press **OPTION+0** [zero] (Mac) or **ALT+0** [zero] (Windows).

3. In the Quantize window, select **ELASTIC AUDIO EVENTS** from the pop-up menu at the top.

Figure 6.24 Selecting the option for quantizing Elastic Audio events

4. Configure the remaining options and parameter settings as desired. (See "**Error! Reference source not found.**" below.)

5. Click **APPLY**. The Warp markers and Event markers closest to the Quantize Grid will be quantized according to the specified settings. TCE processing will be applied between quantized markers, and all other markers will maintain their position relative to the Quantize Grid.

Adjusting the Groove and Feel

The options and parameters in the Event Operations > Quantize window allow you to control how events are affected when quantization is applied. These settings can have a dramatic impact on the resulting feel of the quantized performance.

Quantizing MIDI Note Attributes

The options in the **What to Quantize** section allow you to choose how MIDI note attributes are quantized. These settings affect MIDI note positions and durations. (They have no effect on audio clips or Elastic Audio events.)

- **Note On:** Aligns note start points to the nearest grid value.

- **Note Off:** Aligns note end points to the nearest grid value.

- **Preserve Note Duration:** Preserves note durations by moving end points with start points. When deselected, note start and end points can move independently, changing note durations.

If the options for both Note On and Note Off are selected, the Preserve Note Duration option becomes inactive. The most common setting is to enable Note On and Preserve Note Duration, to affect when MIDI notes are played without changing how long they are held.

Setting Quantize Grid Options

The parameters in the Quantize Grid section allow you to set the options for how MIDI notes, audio clips, or Elastic Audio events are aligned to the grid.

- **Quantize Grid Pop-Up Menu:** As discussed above, this menu allows you to choose the grid increment used for quantizing.

- **Tuplet:** This option allows you to quantize using irregular note groupings like triplets or quintuplets.

- **Offset Grid By:** This option allows you to offset the Quantize Grid forward or backward in time by a specified number of ticks. Use this option to achieve a pushed feel (positive values) or laid-back feel (negative values).

- **Randomize:** This option moves notes randomly forward or back in time (after the quantization occurs). The Randomize setting can also affect note durations.

Adjusting the Feel

The choices in the **Options** section allow you to set additional quantize options that affect the feel of the resulting performance. The choices in the Options section include the following:

- **Swing:** Shifts every other grid boundary by the specified amount to achieve a "swing" feel. A Swing value of 0% yields no swing, while 100% yields a triplet feel.

- **Include Within:** Quantizes only the events close to the Quantize Grid (within the specified range). This can help clean up downbeats without affecting notes that represent smaller subdivisions of the beat.

- **Exclude Within:** Quantizes only the events that are far from the Quantize Grid (outside the specified range). This helps preserve the feel of notes close to the beat while correcting others that are drastically away from the beat.

- **Strength:** Determines how far notes are moved toward the Quantize Grid. Low settings preserve the original feel of the material; higher settings align the material more tightly to the Grid.

The Options section provides entirely different settings when applying groove quantization.

Information on groove quantization and the available Options settings is provided in the Pro Tools 210M book.

MIDI Real-Time Properties

As mentioned above, MIDI Real-Time Properties provide another option for making adjustments to MIDI data. MIDI Real-Time Properties let you change certain properties on MIDI and Instrument tracks (or within MIDI clips) by imposing a change in real time (during playback). The settings used for MIDI Real-Time Properties can be modified at any time without affecting the original MIDI data and can be adjusted during playback, while you listen for the desired result.

Real-Time Properties can be set in the Real-Time Properties view in the Edit window or in the Real-Time Properties floating window. Both options provide access to the five types of MIDI Real-Time Properties: Quantize, Duration, Delay, Velocity, and Transpose.

Using the Real-Time Properties View

The Real-Time Properties view in the Edit window applies to whole tracks. To apply Real-Time Properties to individual clips, you must use the Real-Time Properties floating window.

To enable the Real-Time Properties View in the Edit window:

1. Select **VIEW > EDIT WINDOW VIEWS > REAL-TIME PROPERTIES** or click on the **EDIT WINDOW VIEW SELECTOR** and select **REAL-TIME PROPERTIES** from the pop-up menu. A column displaying Real-Time Properties will appear at the head of the tracks display in the Edit window.

2. Click on a Real-Time Property button at the head of a track to enable it on the track. The button will turn green when enabled, and the adjustable parameters will be displayed.

Figure 6.25 Real-Time Properties column in the Edit window with all properties enabled on the MIDI 1 track

At smaller track heights, the Real-Time Properties column displays only one or two properties. By default, any enabled properties are displayed first.

To select a different Real-Time Property in Micro, Mini, or Small view:

- **COMMAND-CLICK** (Mac) or **CTRL-CLICK** (Windows) on a displayed real-time property element to select a different element to view from the pop-up menu.

Using the Real-Time Properties Floating Window

Using the Real-Time Properties floating window, you can apply Real-Time Properties to selected tracks or to specific clips.

To open the Real-Time Properties floating window:

- Choose **Event > MIDI Real-Time Properties**.

Figure 6.26 Real-Time Properties floating window with properties enabled

Track-Based Properties Versus Clip-Based Properties

The Real-Time Properties window can be used to apply either track-based or clip-based Real-Time Properties by making either a Track selection or an Edit selection, respectively. If you have both a Track selection and an Edit selection, you can choose to apply the Real-Time Properties to either the selected clip(s) or the selected track(s) from the **Apply to** pop-up menu at the top of the window.

Expanded Real-Time Properties Window

In the Real-Time Properties floating window, Quantize, Duration, and Velocity each provide an expand/collapse triangle to show or hide additional settings. Clicking the triangle once expands the view; clicking a second time collapses the view.

Figure 6.27 Real-Time Properties window, expanded view

Enabling Real-Time Properties

You can enable Real-Time Properties using either the Real-Time Properties view in the Edit window or the Real-Time Properties floating window. The two sets of controls affect the same properties, so any track-level changes you make in one are automatically reflected in the other.

To enable Real-Time Properties:

1. Select a track or make an Edit selection.

 When using Real-Time Properties, you may find it helpful to enable Link Track and Edit Selection to make a track selection from an Edit selection.

2. In either the Real-Time Properties view or the Real-Time Properties floating window, select the desired Real-Time Properties by clicking the property name (Quantize, Duration, Delay, Velocity, or Transpose). Enabled Real-Time Properties are highlighted in green and display their settings.

3. If using the Real-Time Properties window, select the track or clip to affect from the APPLY TO pop-up menu.

4. Configure the Real-Time Properties settings as desired.

   Enabled Real-Time Properties will be heard on playback for the selected tracks and clips.

Quantizing with Real-Time Properties

As is the case with the Quantize function in the Event Operations window, the Real-Time Quantize function can quantize to a selected grid size and can include tuplet and grid offset settings. You can also set a strength amount, an "include" range, and a randomize amount.

 This section focuses only on the Quantize Real-Time Property. Other Real-Time Properties are covered in detail in the 210M course.

Basic Quantize Options

The basic Quantize options are available in both the Real-Time Properties view (Edit window) and the Real-Time Properties window. The basic options let you select a note value for the quantize grid and specify a swing percentage, as needed.

- **Quantize Grid Menu:** Determines the beat boundaries to which notes are aligned.

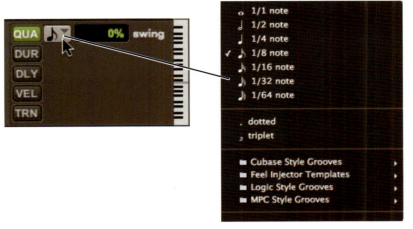

Figure 6.28 Selecting a grid size from the Quantize pop-up menu in the Edit window (Real-Time Properties view)

- **Swing Percent:** Shifts every other grid boundary by the specified percentage value. Any value between 0 and 300% can be selected.

Expanded Quantize Options

Expanded Quantize options are available only in the Real-Time Properties floating window. The following options are available by clicking the Quantize expand/collapse triangle to expand the window:

- **Tuplet:** Quantizes irregular note groupings like triplets or quintuplets. Enable the Tuplet checkbox and enter the ratio for the tuplet, such as 3 to 2 or 5 to 4.

- **Offset:** Offsets the Quantize Grid forward or backward in time by a specified number of ticks. Enable the Offset checkbox and enter a value between –2000 and 2000 to achieve a pushed or laid-back feel.

- **Strength:** Moves notes toward the Quantize Grid. Enable the Strength checkbox and enter the amount as a percentage between 0 and 100%. Low values preserve the original feel; higher values align notes more closely to the grid.

- **Include:** Quantizes only those notes that fall within the specified range of the Quantize Grid. Enable the Include checkbox and enter range start and end values between 0 and 100%.

- **Random:** Causes notes to be moved randomly forward or back in time (after the Quantize occurs). Enable the Random checkbox and enter a percentage between 0 and 100%.

Review/Discussion

1. What are the functions available with the Smart Tool? How can you access the Selector with the Smart Tool active? How can you access the Grabber? (See "Using the Smart Tool" beginning on page 144.)

2. How can you create fades with the Smart Tool? How can you specify the types of fade curves that are used with the Smart Tool? (See "Creating Fades Using the Smart Tool" and "Smart Tool Fade Settings" beginning on page 145.)

3. What menu command would you choose to activate a Fades dialog box? What is the associated keyboard shortcut? (See "Using the Fades Dialog Boxes" beginning on page 146.)

4. What are some options for previewing crossfades in the Fades dialog box? (See "Audition and Preview Controls" beginning on page 147.)

5. What are some options for saving and recalling fade shapes or configurations in the Fades dialog boxes? (See "Using Fade Presets" beginning on page 150.)

6. What are some options for editing existing fades on a track playlist? (See "Editing Existing Fades" beginning on page 151.)

7. What is the purpose of the Quantize function in Pro Tools? What are some different ways to apply quantization? (See "Creating Rhythmic Changes for Audio and MIDI Data" beginning on page 154.)

8. What is the purpose of quantizing audio clips? How is this different from quantizing Elastic Audio? (See "Quantizing Audio Clips" and "Quantizing Elastic Audio" beginning on page 156.)

9. What feature lets you apply changes to a MIDI performance without permanently altering the underlying MIDI data on a track? (See "MIDI Real-Time Properties" beginning on page 159.)

10. What types of tracks and clips are affected by Real-Time Properties? (See "MIDI Real-Time Properties" beginning on page 159.)

11. What are some of the differences between the Real-Time Properties view in the Edit window and the Real-Time Properties floating window? Which allows you to apply clip-based Real-Time Properties? (See "Using the Real-Time Properties View" and "Using the Real-Time Properties Floating Window" beginning on page 159.)

 To review additional material from this chapter, see the PT110 Study Guide module available through the Elements|ED online learning platform at ElementsED.com.

EXERCISE 6

MIDI Real-Time Properties

MIDI Real-Time Properties allow you to make adjustments to your MIDI performances at any time, letting you experiment without committing changes permanently. In this exercise, you will use the Real-Time Properties view in the Edit window to quantize a performance and add a swing feel. Then you will use the Real-Time Properties floating window to fine-tune the performance.

Getting Started

For this exercise, you will work with a session containing various MIDI performances on Instrument tracks. To get started, you will create a session from a template file and save it to the location specified by your instructor.

Open the template and save the session:

1. Launch Pro Tools and choose **FILE > OPEN SESSION** (or choose **OPEN FROM DISK** from the Dashboard).

2. Navigate to the Exercise Media folder and open the *Trouble Trouble.ptxt* template file [PT110 Exercise Media (v12.8) > 05 Trouble Trouble > Trouble Trouble.ptxt].

    A dialog box will open displaying default parameters based on the template.

3. Name the session 110 Exercise 6 [Your Initials] and select the **PROMPT FOR LOCATION** option near the bottom of the dialog box.

4. Click **CREATE** to proceed. A second dialog box will open, prompting you to choose a save location.

5. Navigate to an appropriate location and click **SAVE**. The session will open with the Edit window displayed.

Getting Acquainted with the Session

For the first part of this exercise, you will listen to the basic tracks to familiarize yourself with the tune. Next, you will listen to the guitar track to identify problems with the performance.

Listen to the rhythm tracks:

1. Locate the MIDI Guitar track in the Edit window.

2. Click the **MUTE (M)** button on screen for the MIDI Guitar track to mute the track.

3. Press **RETURN** (Mac) or **ENTER** (Windows) to place the playback cursor at the start of the session.

4. Press the **SPACEBAR** to begin playback. Listen to the session to get a feel for the rhythmic performance. Listen through the intro, first verse, and first chorus (as indicated on the Markers ruler).

5. When finished, press the **SPACEBAR** to stop playback; then unmute the MIDI Guitar track.

Listen to the Guitar track:

1. Click the **Solo (S)** button on screen to solo the MIDI Guitar track.

2. Right-click on the Click track at the bottom of the Track List (left side column of the Edit window) and choose **Make Active** from the pop-up menu.

3. Play back the session to listen to the MIDI Guitar performance. The Click track will play along with the soloed MIDI Guitar track.

4. During playback, note that the timing of the MIDI Guitar performance is off, relative to the click.

5. When finished, stop playback and unsolo the MIDI Guitar track.

Correcting the Timing of the MIDI Guitar

In this part of the exercise, you will use MIDI Real-Time Properties to improve the timing of the MIDI guitar. To do so, you will display the Real-Time Properties view in the Edit window and activate the Quantize function.

Display and work with the Real-Time Properties view:

1. Click the **Edit Window View selector** above the Tracks Display in the Edit window and choose **Real-Time Properties** from the pop-up menu.

    The Real-Time Properties column will display at the head of the tracks.

    Figure 6.29 Clicking the Edit Window View selector

2. Click the **Quantize (Qua)** button in the Real-Time Properties view on the MIDI Guitar track and set the quantize grid to the **1/4 note** setting.

    Figure 6.30 Setting initial Quantize parameters

3. Play back the session to hear the results.

4. Experiment with different quantize settings during playback to hear how they affect the performance. Try auditioning successively smaller grid sizes, from **1/4 note** through **1/16 note**. The performance will update in real time during playback as you adjust the settings.

5. Next, set the grid to **1/8 NOTE** and experiment with different **SWING** settings. Try starting with a swing of 15%. Gradually increase the amount in increments of 10 to 15% until you're satisfied with the results. The performance will begin to match the feel of the session with a swing of around 70 to 90%.

6. Once finished, stop playback.

> ### Discussion Point #1
> What was the effect on the MIDI Guitar track when you applied quantizing with a 1/8-note setting? What effect did adding the Swing setting have?

Fine-Tuning the Performance

Quantizing MIDI often has the effect of making the performance sound too mechanical, resulting in a loss of realism. To fix this, you will use some advanced settings in the Real-Time Properties window.

Display and work with the Real-Time Properties window:

1. Click on the **MIDI Guitar** track to select the track, if not already selected.

2. Choose **EVENT > MIDI REAL-TIME PROPERTIES** to display the Real-Time Properties floating window.

Figure 6.31 MIDI Real-Time Properties floating window

3. Verify that the **APPLY TO:** selector at the top of the window is set to **TRACK "MIDI GUITAR"**.

4. Click the show/hide triangle next to the **QUANTIZE** button to expand the Quantize section of the window.

5. Click the checkbox next to the **STRENGTH** parameter to enable it. This setting allows you to adjust the degree to which the original performance is conformed to the grid.

Figure 6.32 Enabling the Strength parameter

6. Begin playback and gradually reduce the Strength percentage until you are satisfied with the results. Try a Strength setting between 75 and 90% for the MIDI Guitar.

7. Click the checkbox next to the **RANDOM** parameter to enable it. This setting allows you to apply a random variation to the timing of each note in the performance.

8. Gradually increase the Random percentage until you are satisfied with the results. Try a Random setting between 10 and 30% for the MIDI Guitar.

9. Once you are happy with the results, stop playback and close the Real-Time Properties window.

> **Discussion Point #2**
>
> Why do you need to use the Real-Time Properties floating window for this section? What is the effect of applying the Random parameter? When would you not want to use this parameter?

Wrap Up

To wrap up, make the Click track inactive again so that it does not interfere with session playback or editing and mixing. Also be sure to save the work you have done, as you will be reusing this session in later exercises.

Disable the click track and review the changes:

1. Right-click on the **Click** track in the Track List and choose **MAKE INACTIVE** from the pop-up menu.

2. Press **RETURN** (Mac) or **ENTER** (Windows) on your keyboard to return to the start of the timeline.

3. Press the **SPACEBAR** to play back the session and review the changes you've made.

4. When finished, stop playback and save and close the session. That concludes this exercise.

Remember that you cannot close a Pro Tools session by closing its windows. You must choose **CLOSE SESSION** from the **FILE** menu.

LESSON 7

Additional Editing and Media Management

Pro Tools provides multiple ways of working with media files that allow you to match your workflow to your preferences and the special needs of your projects. This lesson covers various techniques and workflows that you can use to edit, arrange, and process your audio files. It also discusses techniques for working with files in the Clip List and exporting files to a sound library.

GOALS

- Use clip looping to quickly repeat a selection for a set duration or number of iterations
- Use Grid mode to edit material while conforming to a specified timing grid
- Use AudioSuite plug-ins to process audio
- Manage files in the Clip List
- Use options for exporting audio clips and clip definitions

Key topics from this lesson are included in the *Pro Tools 12 Essential Training: 110* course on Lynda.com, available here: alpp.us/PT110_Online.

Over the years, the capabilities that Pro Tools provides for editing and arranging audio have steadily grown and become more robust. Today, it is common to compose music and sound effects from bits of audio and MIDI material that are looped, arranged into patterns, and aligned to a grid-based timing reference. Having techniques available for arranging and reprocessing audio can be essential to your success combining sonic components. Likewise, being able to locate the clips you need, for use within the current session or for export to a sound library, is a key element to an efficient sound production workflow.

Clip Looping

Looping is common in music production and can also be a useful technique for sound design and post production workflows. Audio clips, MIDI clips, and clip groups can all be looped using the **Clip > Loop** menu command. Creating a clip loop is an easy way to repeat a single clip on a track, or clips across multiple tracks, for composing and arranging. The Clip > Loop command is similar to the Repeat and Duplicate commands, but the results are more flexible and are easier to work with.

Working with Clip Loops

A clip loop consists of a source clip and one or more loop iterations that are combined together, similar to a clip group. The source clip is the original clip selected for looping. The loop iterations are copies of the source clip contained within the clip loop.

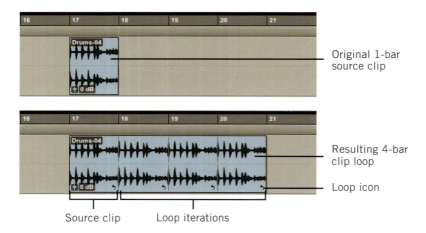

Figure 7.1 Source clip and resulting clip loop

When looping clips, you can specify the number of loop iterations to create, set a specific amount of time to fill with the loop, or allow the loop to repeat until the next clip or the end of the track. In cases where the loop duration doesn't equal a whole number of repetitions, the last loop iteration is truncated to fill to the end of the selection or the specified loop length.

Once created, a clip loop can be edited much like a clip group. For example, selecting and moving a clip loop selects and moves the source clip and all loop iterations together.

You can select clips across multiple tracks for looping.

Selecting and looping more than one clip on a track will loop only the first clip in the selection. To loop multiple clips, first group the clips, then loop the clip group.

Creating Clip Loops

Using the Clip Looping dialog box, you can specify a loop length for a selection of audio or MIDI data, or for a mixed selection across multiple tracks.

To loop a clip:

1. Select a single audio clip, MIDI clip, or clip group or select clips or clip groups across multiple tracks (no more than one clip/clip group per track).

2. Choose **CLIP > LOOP**. The Clip Looping dialog box will open.

Figure 7.2 Clip Looping dialog box

 You can also access the Clip Looping dialog box by pressing COMMAND+OPTION+L (Mac) or CTRL+ALT+L (Windows).

3. Do one of the following:

    - Select the **NUMBER OF LOOPS** option and enter the desired number of loop iterations.
    - Select the **LOOP LENGTH** option and enter the desired loop duration.
    - Select the **LOOP UNTIL END OF THE SESSION OR NEXT CLIP** option. The looped clip will repeat until it reaches the end of the session or the next clip on the track.

4. If desired, select the **ENABLE CROSSFADE** option. This will create crossfades at the loop points. To edit the loop crossfade settings, click the **SETTINGS** button. The Loop Crossfade dialog box will open.

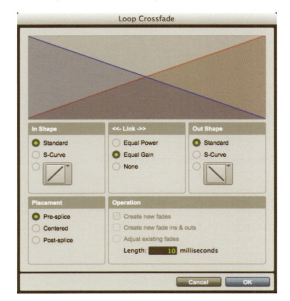

Figure 7.3 Loop Crossfade dialog box

5. If using crossfades, configure the **Loop Crossfade** parameters as desired, including the placement and length of the crossfades; then click **OK** to close the Loop Crossfade dialog box.

6. Click **OK** in the Clip Looping dialog box to create the clip loop. The source clip on each track will become a clip loop extending for the specified length or duration. Each loop iteration will display a Loop icon in its lower-right corner.

Figure 7.4 One-bar looped clip with Loop icon displayed in loop iterations

> ### Example 7.1: Extending Room Tone
> A common task in video post-production work is to add room tone to a scene. For an indoor scene with dialog between main characters, you may find yourself adding room tone between lines of dialog. Using a clip of room tone extracted from a field recording, you can easily fill any large gap between existing dialog clips with a clip loop. Simply paste the room tone at the start of the gap; then choose Clip > Loop and use the option to Loop Until End of the Session or Next Clip. To smooth out the transition between loops and create a seamless result, use the Enable Crossfades option.

Modifying Clip Loop Settings

Loop settings can be changed at any time after creating a clip loop by revisiting the Clip Looping dialog box.

To modify the loop settings for a looped clip, do one of the following:

- Select the looped clip and choose **Clip > Loop**, or press **Option+Command+L** (Mac) or **Ctrl+Alt+L** (Windows).
- Double-click on any **Loop** icon with the **Selector** tool.
- Select the looped clip, right-click with any Edit tool, and select **Loop** from the pop-up menu.

    The Clip Looping dialog box will open, allowing you to modify the loop settings.

Editing Clip Loops

A looped section behaves as a single clip, so clicking in it with the Grabber tool selects the whole clip loop. However, positioning the Grabber or Selector tools at the bottom right of the clip (over the Loop icon) will change the tool mode so that individual loops can be selected. With the Grabber tool, you can select a single loop; with the Selector tool, you can select a group of whole loop iterations by clicking and dragging.

You can also use the Trim tool on clip loops to edit them in different ways, depending on where you position the tool in the clip loop.

Using the Standard Trim Tool

The standard Trim tool can be used to trim looped clips. The Trim tool provides two trimming modes:

- If the tool is in the main part of the clip, the entire clip loop can be trimmed in or out, adding or removing loop iterations as needed.

 Hold CONTROL (Mac) or START (Windows) while trimming to trim in whole loop iterations.

- If the tool is in line with the Loop icon, the length of the loop iterations will be trimmed. For example, you can trim a loop iteration from 4 beats long down to 2 beats. The overall length of the looped clip will remain the same, with the number of iterations changing as needed.

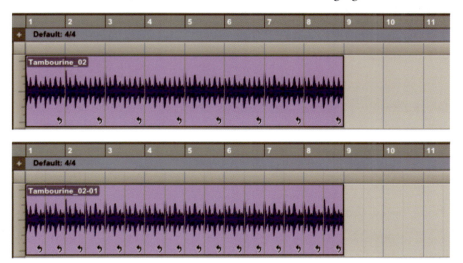

Figure 7.5 Original clip loop (top) and modified clip loop after trimming loop iterations to 2 beats (bottom)

Using the Loop Trim Tool

The Loop Trim tool is an alternate mode of the Trim tool, and is accessed by clicking and holding (or right-clicking) on the Trim tool button.

Figure 7.6 Selecting the Loop Trim tool

The Loop Trim tool functions in exactly the same manner as the Standard Trim tool except that it allows you to create clip loops from any clip, bypassing the **CLIP > LOOP** command and dialog box. When placed over the bottom half of a non-looped clip, the Loop Trim tool behaves like the Standard Trim tool, but when positioned over the top half, it creates loop iterations.

To create a clip loop from a non-looped clip using the Loop Trim tool:

1. Click and hold the **TRIM** tool button and select **LOOP** from the pop-up menu, or press **F6** as needed to toggle to the Loop Trim tool.

2. Place the cursor over either end of a clip in the top half of the track. The cursor icon will display a trim bracket with a loop arrow.

3. Click and drag in the top half of the clip. The existing clip boundaries will be maintained, but the clip will be repeated to create a clip loop.

The Loop Trim tool acts on existing clip loops in the same way as the standard Trim tool.

Considerations for Working with Clip Loops

Most of the time, working with clip loops is relatively straightforward. However, in certain situations, additional considerations may apply. Keep the following tips in mind to get the most out of your work with clip loops.

- Looping can be applied only to an entire source clip or clip group. To loop a selection that includes only a portion of a clip, you must trim the clip to the selection or separate the clip at the selection first.

- Looping cannot be applied to multiple clips on the same track. To loop a selection that includes multiple clips, first create a clip group from the selection.

- Creating a clip group to use for clip looping enables you to include areas outside of a clip within the loop, such as empty space (silence) at the beginning or ending of the clip. This can be useful to ensure that a clip used for looping begins and ends on the grid.

- Looping can be applied to multitrack clip groups and mixed clip groups in the same way that it is applied on a single track.

- When looping clips on multiple tracks, loops will be applied to the source clip on each track separately. If the source clips have different lengths, the loop locations will vary between tracks. To ensure that the loop point is identical between tracks, create a multitrack clip group from the selection before creating the clip loop.

- Looped clips can be combined with other clips into clip groups, which can then be looped again, effectively creating nested loops. However, you will only be able to edit the loop settings for the top level of loop iterations without unlooping/ungrouping.

Example 7.2: Keeping Imported Loops on the Grid

When composing with loops, it is common to import files from loop libraries and repeat them over long durations using a clip loop. Sometimes a clip loop from an imported file will gradually get out of time with the composition or the click track. In the case of an imported 1-bar tambourine loop, for example, the clip loop may sound fine through the first verse, but by the chorus or second verse the tambourine might be getting ahead of the beat, and by the last chorus it may be completely out of time.

This happens when the original tambourine clip is slightly short of a full bar in your session, even by just a few samples. When looped over a short distance, the discrepancy is not noticeable; but over a long duration, the imperfection compounds to the point that the loop is no longer on the grid.

To fix this problem, revert to the original clip; then make a 1-bar selection over the clip in Grid mode and create an exact 1-bar clip group. Now when you loop the clip group, it will stay in perfect time.

Unlooping Clips

Pro Tools provides two options for unlooping clips. You can choose to remove all loop iterations or to flatten all iterations into individual clips. You can also ungroup and flatten all nested clip loops and clip groups with a single command.

To unloop a looped clip:

1. Select the looped clip.

2. Choose **CLIP > UNLOOP**. The Unloop Clips dialog box will open.

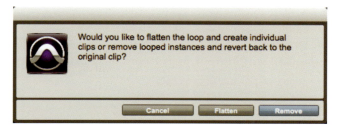

Figure 7.7 Unloop Clips dialog box

3. Select one of the following:

    * **REMOVE**—Unloops and removes all loop iterations, returning the source clip (first full loop iteration) to its original state.

    * **FLATTEN**—Unloops the clip and creates individual clips from each loop iteration.

 The **CLIP > UNGROUP** command functions on loops the same as using the Unloop command and choosing Flatten.

To unloop and ungroup a clip loop with nested material down to its individual clips:

1. Select a looped clip that contains one or more clip groups.

2. Choose **CLIP > UNGROUP ALL**. All loop iterations will be flattened and all clip groups will be ungrouped, down to the lowest nested level.

After ungrouping, you can edit the underlying clips and then choose **CLIP > REGROUP** to re-create the underlying clip groups. Any unedited loop iterations will also be re-created.

Editing Techniques

As you have learned previously, Pro Tools allows you to work against a timing grid, based on an interval of your choosing, to help align clips, notes, and events as you edit. In Pro Tools 12.6 and later, you also have the option of working in Layered Editing mode, which helps preserve underlying clips when overlapped by another, smaller clip.

Working with the Grid

The Grid settings affect edit operations when working in Grid mode and provide a visual reference for all edit modes. In Grid mode, selections and insertion points snap to Grid intervals, affecting cut, copy, and paste operations. Move and trim operations either align to the Grid or move in Grid increments relative to their origination point, depending on the option selected (Absolute Grid mode or Relative Grid mode).

Absolute Grid Mode

In Absolute Grid mode, moving any clip or MIDI note snaps the clip point to the Grid boundaries. If a start point falls between Grid boundaries, dragging the item will snap its start time to the nearest grid boundary.

Figure 7.8 Absolute Grid mode enabled

Relative Grid Mode

In Relative Grid mode, clips and MIDI notes can be moved by Grid units. If a start point falls between grid beats and the Grid is set to 1/4 notes, dragging the item will move it in 1/4 note increments, preserving its position relative to the nearest beat.

Figure 7.9 Relative Grid mode enabled

> #### Example 7.3: Moving a Volume Swell to a Different Bar
>
> A popular technique in music production is to have a volume swell that crescendos and peaks on the beat. This could be achieved with a reverse reverb effect on a vocal, a reverse cymbal crash, or a volume control on a guitar. Whatever the case, the start of the swell is likely not correlated to a beat or sub-beat. In cases like this the clip might not be easy to cut to the grid.
>
> An easy way to move a clip like this while keeping it in time is to move it in grid increments. For example, if a guitar swell peaks perfectly on the downbeat but you need to move it two bars later, you can do so by using Relative Grid mode with the Grid value set to 1 bar. When you drag the clip along the timeline in Relative Grid mode, the clip will move in whole-bar increments, keeping the peak aligned to the downbeat of each bar.

To access each of the grid modes:

1. Click and hold on the **GRID** button in the Edit window. The Grid Mode pop-up menu will appear.
2. Select the desired Grid mode from the menu.

Separating Clips on the Grid

The Separate Clip function can be used in conjunction with the timing grid to quickly create clips of a defined size. The **SEPARATE CLIP > ON GRID** command separates clips based on the current Grid value. You can also add padding to the start of each clip, if desired, to preserve any note attacks that are ahead of the beat.

To separate clips based on a grid interval:

1. Make the desired Edit selection.
2. Set the Grid interval using the **GRID VALUE POP-UP** menu.

3. Choose **EDIT > SEPARATE CLIP > ON GRID**. The Pre-Separate Amount dialog box will open.

Figure 7.10 The Pre-Separate Amount dialog box

4. Specify a Pre-Separate amount (handle) to pad the head of the newly separated clips. To separate clips precisely on the Grid, leave the Pre-Separate amount set to 0.

5. Click **OK**. The selected area will be separated into new clips at the Grid intervals.

> You can also separate clips at transients (**EDIT > SEPARATE CLIP > AT TRANSIENTS**). This feature separates clips at each detected transient using the same algorithm as the Tab to Transients feature.

> When used on clip loops, the Separate Clips commands (At Selection, On Grid, and At Transients) will automatically unloop and flatten the clips before separating them.

Using Layered Editing

The Layered Editing option can be enabled to preserve underlying clips when clips are overlapped. This can be especially useful for sound design applications, where you may be working with layered clips and adjusting the placement of clips relative to one another as you work. Layered Editing affects both audio and MIDI clips.

To toggle Layered Editing on/off, do one of the following:

- Choose **OPTIONS > LAYERED EDITING**.

- Click the Layered Editing button in the Edit window toolbar. Layered Editing is enabled when this button is lit blue.

Figure 7.11 Layered Editing mode enabled

With Layered Editing enabled, you can stack clips on top of one another while retaining the freedom to move, trim, or delete the top-most clips without losing the underlying material.

In the example below, several clips have been stacked up, with the **Vox 1** clip at the bottom, the **Vox 2** clip positioned on top of that, and the **Vox 3** clip positioned at the top.

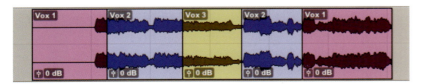

Figure 7.12 Clips stacked on one another

With Layered Editing enabled, the **Vox 3** clip can be trimmed, moved, or deleted without causing a separation in the **Vox 2** clip beneath it.

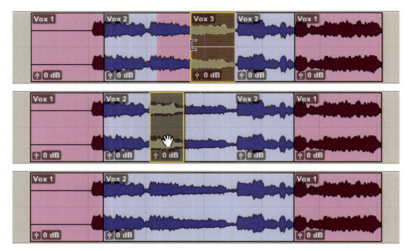

Figure 7.13 Editing the top clip while keeping the underlying clip intact: trim (top), move (middle), and delete (bottom)

The same operations can be performed on the **Vox 2** clip without disrupting the continuity of the **Vox 1** clip beneath it.

AudioSuite Overview

As you work with the audio on your tracks, you may want to apply processing to specific selections. AudioSuite plug-ins are designed for this purpose. As non-real-time processors, AudioSuite plug-ins require you either to create new audio source files or to alter the original source files. Many AudioSuite plug-ins are included with Pro Tools systems; others are available for purchase from Avid and third-party manufacturers.

AudioSuite versus Insert Processing

AudioSuite processing is file-based, meaning it renders its results to files on disk. Some AudioSuite plug-ins have corresponding real-time plug-in equivalents. Real-time plug-ins generally have the same control parameters as their AudioSuite counterparts; however, they process audio in real time during playback.

You can choose AudioSuite processing in order to conserve on real-time processing resources. AudioSuite processing can also be applied to only a selected portion of a track and can be written into a file for use outside of the session. Additionally, certain AudioSuite processes are not possible using real-time plug-ins.

AudioSuite Features

AudioSuite plug-ins provide the following basic features:

- **Floating plug-in window.** Once an AudioSuite plug-in is selected, its processing window remains on the screen until you close it, allowing you to process other clips with the same settings.

- **Destructive or non-destructive processing.** You can choose to permanently change selected clips/files (destructive) or to create new files that reflect the chosen process (non-destructive).

- **Playlist-based selection or Clip List–based processing.** AudioSuite processing can be set to affect an individual clip on a track or all occurrences of the clip in the session.

- **Preview with bypass.** Many AudioSuite plug-ins support a preview mode, allowing you to audition the effect before rendering, and a Bypass button for comparing the previewed audio to the original.

AudioSuite plug-ins also include the following advanced features:

- **Preservation of fades and metadata.** Depending on the processing mode selected, you can preserve any fades applied to clips as well as any metadata associated with the clips.

- **AudioSuite handles.** AudioSuite processing can be applied beyond the current Edit selection, up to the length of the entire underlying file referenced by the clip. This allows you to trim clips out past the rendered selection after processing.

- **Reverse option for Delay and Reverb.** A Reverse button in the AudioSuite plug-in window lets you render reverse delay and reverb effects with a single click.

Using AudioSuite Plug-Ins

Applying an AudioSuite plug-in involves five main steps:

1. Select the audio to be processed.
2. Choose an AudioSuite plug-in.
3. Configure the AudioSuite controls.
4. Configure the plug-in parameters.
5. Process (render) the audio.

Step 1: Selecting Audio to Be Processed

Clips can be selected for processing from Audio track playlists in the Edit window or from the Clip List. You can **Shift-click** to select multiple clips.

Pro Tools automatically selects the corresponding clips in the track playlists when clips are selected in the Clip List. Likewise, it automatically selects the corresponding clips in the Clip List when clips are selected in the track playlist. (These options can be changed in the **Editing** tab of the **Preferences** dialog box.)

Selecting Audio in a Playlist

AudioSuite plug-ins can be applied to whole clips, partial clips, or any combination, across one or more tracks in the Edit window.

In Figure 7.14, shown before processing, the selection contains whole and partial clips.

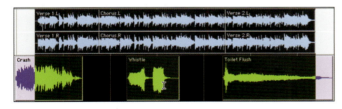

Figure 7.14 Audio selected in a track playlist

After processing, new clips appear for all processed clips, unprocessed clips, and partial clips. (See Figure 7.15.)

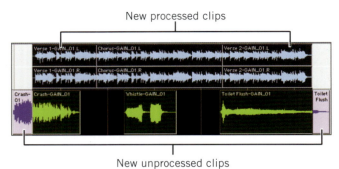

Figure 7.15 Processed audio in a track playlist

Only the selected audio is processed; any audio not included in the selection is separated and left unaffected by AudioSuite processing.

Selecting Audio in the Clip List

Alternatively, you can select audio clips for processing by clicking on them in the Clip List, as shown below.

Figure 7.16 Audio clips selected in the Clip List

Step 2: Choosing an AudioSuite Plug-In

Once your audio selection has been made, you are ready to choose a plug-in from the AudioSuite menu.

To choose an AudioSuite plug-in:

- Choose the plug-in you want to use from the main **AUDIOSUITE** menu.

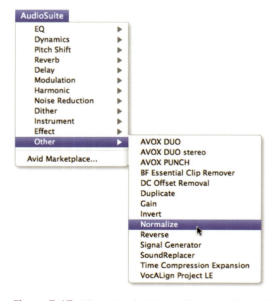

Figure 7.17 Choosing the Normalize AudioSuite plug-in

The AudioSuite plug-in window will open, displaying controls for the selected plug-in.

Figure 7.18 The Normalize AudioSuite plug-in window

Each AudioSuite plug-in provides standard controls at the top of the plug-in window. The bottom portion of the window provides controls that are specific to the selected plug-in.

 You can click in any plug-in window text field, type values directly in the field, then press RETURN (Mac) or ENTER (Windows) to accept the value.

Step 3: Configuring AudioSuite Controls

After choosing an AudioSuite plug-in, your next step is to set the AudioSuite control parameters, using the selectors and buttons at the top of the plug-in window.

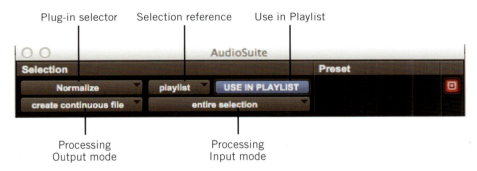

Figure 7.19 AudioSuite control parameters

The following AudioSuite controls are available:

- **Plug-In Selector.** The PLUG-IN SELECTOR button allows you to choose a different AudioSuite plug-in while retaining your audio selection.

- **Selection Reference.** The SELECTION REFERENCE button specifies whether the AudioSuite plug-in will affect only the selected copy of a clip or all instances of that clip in the session.

  - **Playlist.** To process only the selected occurrence of a clip, choose this setting.
  - **Clip List.** To process all occurrences of a clip in a session or project, choose this setting and enable the Use in Playlist button (see below).

 To process any selected partial clips, you must set the Selection Reference to Playlist.

- **Use in Playlist.** The Use in Playlist button controls whether the processed audio will replace your selection in the track playlist.

  - When deselected (gray), the newly processed audio will appear in the Clip List only and will not replace the selected audio on a track. Use this to create a processed copy of the clip for use elsewhere.

  - When selected (highlighted in blue), the newly processed audio will appear in both the Clip List and in track playlists. This is typically the desired behavior.

Figure 7.20 Use in Playlist deselected (left) and selected (highlighted in blue) (right)

- **Processing Output Mode.** This setting determines how the AudioSuite plug-in will output the processed file. One destructive mode and two non-destructive modes are available.

> **Destructive processing permanently overwrites the original audio stored on the hard drive. Non-destructive processing creates new, processed files on the hard drive instead.**

> **Not all AudioSuite plug-ins support destructive processing.**

  - **Overwrite files.** This option provides destructive processing. When selected, rendering will be applied to the parent sound file, permanently changing it. The new audio will replace the original audio in the file, and *all instances of the audio in the session will be changed*, regardless of the plug-in's Selection Reference or Use in Playlist settings.

    Because the result is irreversible, a dialog box appears prior to processing, allowing you to cancel the operation or select non-destructive processing instead.

Figure 7.21 Warning dialog box that appears when choosing to overwrite files with destructive processing

  - **Create individual files.** This non-destructive option processes the selected audio and outputs the result as separate, individual files matching the clips or partial clips in the original selection.

  - **Create continuous file.** This non-destructive option processes the selected audio and outputs the result as a single file. All clips and partial clips in the selection are merged into a single, continuous file.

- **Processing Input Mode.** This setting determines how the AudioSuite plug-in will analyze selections that contain multiple clips.

  - **Clip by Clip.** This setting analyzes each clip in a selection individually. This is helpful for processes like Normalization, where you want to maximize the effect for each individual clip, rather than process each clip relative to the entire selection.

  - **Entire Selection.** This setting analyzes an entire selection of clips, treating them as if they were one complete clip. Use this setting to apply continuous processing to all of the clips in the selection as a group, rather than processing each individual clip separately.

The images in Figures 7.22 through 7.24 below illustrate how these settings affect clips processed by the AudioSuite Normalize plug-in. This example uses three clips (Verse 1, Chorus, and Verse 2) recorded at different volumes on a single track.

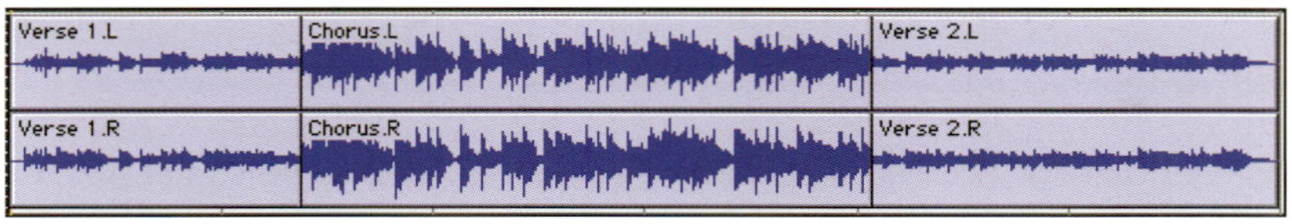

Figure 7.22 Original clips prior to AudioSuite processing

Clip by Clip Input Processing

When applying the Normalize process to the original clips using the Clip by Clip input mode, each clip has its amplitude normalized (maximized) individually, resulting in three clips with similar amplitude. (The peaks within each clip have been adjusted to the maximum amplitude, with the remainder of the waveform in each clip adjusted proportionally.)

Figure 7.23 Clips after normalizing with the Clip by Clip option

Entire Selection Input Processing

By contrast, applying the Normalize process to the original clips using the Entire Selection input mode causes the clips to be normalized (maximized) based on the peak volume for the entire selection. Since the amplitude of the chorus clip was already high, the overall amplitude of the selection does not change significantly.

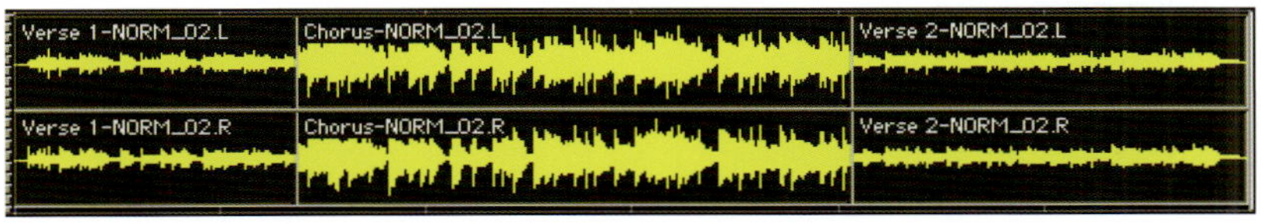

Figure 7.24 Clips after normalizing with the Entire Selection option

Step 4: Configuring Plug-In Parameters

The plug-in parameters allow you to configure the specific controls unique to a particular plug-in. For illustration purposes, this text covers the Normalize AudioSuite plug-in.

The Normalize plug-in increases the overall level of a clip or selection to optimize the audio's amplitude level. The audio's peak level is raised to the value set in the Level control. Gain is applied proportionally to the audio in the selection, thereby retaining the same relative volume levels throughout the selection.

> ### Example 7.4: Optimizing Sound Effects for a Video Game
>
> Sound design for video games can involve creating hundreds, thousands, and even tens of thousands of separate audio assets. Each of these assets needs to be exported from Pro Tools for implementation in the game via a gaming engine. Prior to exporting, the audio files must be optimized so that they have consistent levels that peak near full scale. This allows the game developers and programmers to set and control levels in the game engine with predictable results from one audio file to the next.

> In the case of developing sound effects for a first-person shooter, you may have explosion sounds, artillery, rockets, impacts, and other sounds that you have crafted as individual clips in Pro Tools. By applying Normalize to selected clips, and using Clip-by-Clip processing, you can render effects that all peak at the same level relative to full scale (say 97% of full volume).

Normalize Levels. The Level slider defaults to 100 percent (0.0 dB); this raises the peak signal to the maximum level possible before clipping. Files normalized at 100 percent can easily clip with subsequent gain-based processing (such as EQ) or when you create volume automation. You should generally set the Level control to an appropriate lower level prior to processing. (Note that if you apply processing and are not satisfied with the results, you can choose **Edit > Undo**, adjust the settings, and reprocess the selection.)

Other AudioSuite Controls. When processing multiple channels of audio (from a stereo track or across multiple tracks, for example), an additional pop-up menu is available, providing the following options:

- **Mono Mode.** This setting normalizes audio on a channel-by-channel basis, by analyzing the peak on each channel. This maximizes the effect for each selected audio channel.

- **Multi-Input Mode.** This setting normalizes audio across all channels in the selection at once. This preserves the relative levels of each selected audio channel.

Figure 7.25 Channel processing options menu

Step 5: Processing the Audio

After you have configured the plug-in controls and parameters, you are ready to render the processed audio.

To render AudioSuite processing:

1. At the bottom of the AudioSuite window, enter a Handle Length (default is 2.00 seconds) or click the **Whole File** button to apply the AudioSuite processing to the length of the entire underlying file.

Figure 7.26 Entering a Handle Length

 AudioSuite handles are available only when the Processing Output mode is set to Create Continuous File or when the Processing Input mode is set to Clip by Clip with the Output mode set to either Create Continuous File or Create Individual Files.

2. Click the **Render** button at the bottom of the plug-in window. The AudioSuite processing will be applied to the selected audio according to the specified settings.

Considerations for Handle Length and Whole File Settings

The **HANDLE LENGTH** and **WHOLE FILE** options are not available when the Processing Input mode is set to **ENTIRE SELECTION** or when the Processing Output mode is set to **OVERWRITE FILES**. In these cases, processing is applied only to the selected area.

Additionally, the **WHOLE FILE** option is not available when the Processing Output mode is set to **CREATE CONTINUOUS FILE**. In this case, processing is applied to the underlying audio beyond the selection boundaries for the duration of the Handle Length whenever the selection starts and ends within a clip or on a clip boundary. Whenever the selection start or end is outside of a clip boundary (in silence), the processing is applied only to the audio *within* the selected clip(s) at that boundary, not to any underlying audio.

So, for example, when applying reverb to a clip, selecting just the clip will cause the reverb tails from underlying audio before the clip to bleed into the start of the processed clip, based on the Handle Length setting. Similarly, trimming out the end of the clip to expose the reverb decay at the end would also expose any underlying audio (which also has the reverb processing applied). By contrast, extending the selection before applying reverb so that it starts and ends outside of the clip (assuming no other audio is immediately adjacent) would cause the reverb to affect only the audio contained in the clip. Trimming out the end would expose the reverb tail decaying into silence.

When the Processing Output mode is set to **CREATE INDIVIDUAL FILES** (and the Processing Input mode is set to **CLIP BY CLIP**), processing is always applied to the underlying audio for the duration of the Handle Length. This can impact the results when applying gain-based processing such as normalization and compression or time-based effects such as reverb and delay. In these cases, you may wish to change the Handle Length from its default of 2.00 seconds to a shorter value (or set it to 0.00).

AudioSuite File Naming

AudioSuite-rendered files are automatically named using a convention that appends characters to the original file name to identify the processing applied.

- **Playlist Processing.** New processed files are named using the original clip name followed by a hyphen, a four-letter abbreviation for the AudioSuite plug-in used, an underscore, and a two-digit edit number (starting at 01).

  As an example, a clip named Light Wind would have the new file name Light Wind-PiSh_01 after applying the Pitch Shift AudioSuite plug-in with playlist processing.

- **Clip List Processing.** New processed files are named using the original clip name followed by a hyphen, a four-letter abbreviation for the AudioSuite plug-in used, a second hyphen, and a two-digit edit number (starting at 00).

  As an example, a clip named Light Wind would have the new file name Light Wind-PiSh-00 after applying the Pitch Shift AudioSuite plug-in with Clip List processing selected.

 When processing audio non-destructively, the Pro Tools multi-level Undo and Redo commands let you undo and redo AudioSuite processes.

Working with the Clip List

The Pro Tools Clip List provides a convenient location for storing, identifying, auditioning, and selecting clips in your session. However, as you record and edit the media in your session, the Clip List will populate with many by-product subset clips, unused takes, and other detritus, which can make it difficult to locate a specific desired clip.

Pro Tools provides various Clip List–related commands that can help you find specific clips, select and remove unwanted clips, and export clips for use in other sessions.

Finding a Clip in the Clip List

The Clip List displays all audio, MIDI, and video clips, auto-created clips, and clip groups in a single, comprehensive list. All clips that are recorded, imported, or created by editing appear in this list.

By default, selecting a clip on a track will also select it in the Clip List and vice versa (subject to Preferences settings under the Editing page). Once selected in the Clip List, a clip can be processed, added to a new track location by drag and drop, or removed from your session.

Identifying a Clip by Auditioning

To help identify a clip you are looking for, you can audition any audio clip, MIDI clip, or clip group from the Clip List.

To audition a clip in the Clip List:

- **Option-click** (Mac) or **Alt-click** (Windows) on the clip. The clip will play back through the assigned audition path.

Locating a Clip Using the Find Command

At the top of the Clip List is the Clip List pop-up menu, which provides tools to search, select, sort, export, clear, and manage items in the Clip List. (See Figure 7.27.) To view the menu, click the **Clip List pop-up** selector, or right-click anywhere on the Clips bar at the top of the Clip List.

Figure 7.27 Clip List pop-up selector and menu

For precise searching, Pro Tools provides a Find command for filtering the clips shown in the Clip List. This command can be used to display relevant clips while temporarily hiding the others.

To display the Find Clips dialog box:

- Choose **Find** from the Clip List pop-up menu. The **Find Clips** dialog box will open.

Figure 7.28 The Find Clips dialog box

You can also access the Find Clips dialog box by pressing COMMAND+SHIFT+F (Mac) or CTRL+SHIFT+F (Windows).

Conducting a Search

The Find Clips dialog box offers two options: search for clips by name and show newly added clips. These options can be used separately or together to specify which items are displayed in the Clip List.

To find and display clips in the Clip List:

1. Display the Find Clips dialog box using the CLIP LIST POP-UP menu or the keyboard shortcut.

2. Do one of the following:

    - Select BY NAME and type a name or partial name for clips you want to find. The search string will appear [in brackets] at the top of the Clip List; only matching clips will be displayed in the Clip List.

    - Select INCLUDE SUBSEQUENTLY ADDED CLIPS to show newly added clips going forward. A plus (+) sign will appear at the top of the Clip List to indicate that this option is selected.

    - Select both options to start with a list of clips whose names include the search string and also include newly added clips going forward.

3. Click OK to complete the search. Any matching clips will be displayed in the Clip List.

When searching by name, the list updates dynamically while you type in the Find Clips dialog box. When you click OK, the search string becomes a live filter, displaying a real-time list of matching items. Any time you create, rename, or add a clip with a matching name, it will be shown in the Clip List.

When using the INCLUDE SUBSEQUENTLY ADDED CLIPS option, all new clips you create or add to the session will be shown in the Clip List, regardless of whether the name includes the search string.

When both options are selected, the Clip List will display a mix of results, including clips with names that match the search string and clips you've added or created since initiating the search.

Figure 7.29 Clip List filtered by name and subsequently added clips

Clearing a Search

You can clear a search to remove filtering from the Clip List. Clearing a search resets the Clip List to show all clips in the session according to the settings in effect prior to initiating the search.

To clear a search:

- Select CLEAR FIND from the Clip List pop-up menu. The Clip List will return to its prior display.

 You can also clear a search by pressing COMMAND+SHIFT+D (Mac) or CTRL+SHIFT+D (Windows).

The Find History

Text entered into the Find Clips dialog box is saved in a Find History, letting you quickly repeat previous searches with a minimum of retyping.

To repeat a previous search:

1. Display the Find Clips dialog box using the Clip List pop-up menu or the keyboard shortcut.
2. Select the **BY NAME** option, if not already active.
3. Click on the down arrow to the right of the text field and select a text string from the Find History pop-up menu.

Figure 7.30 Selecting a search string from the Find History

 If the Find History pop-up menu is disabled (down arrow grayed out), you can re-activate it by entering a space or other character in the text field.

The Find History is saved with the session. In addition to listing each text string previously entered, the Find History allows you to insert entries manually without having to perform a search.

You can add entries, remove entries, and clear the Find History using the Find History pop-up menu.

Figure 7.31 Adding an entry to the Find History

Cleaning Up the Clip List

As the Clip List grows in your session, you may choose to remove the clips that you no longer need, in order to minimize clutter. From the Clip List, you can select and remove any unused or unneeded clips.

Selecting Multiple Clips

Clips can be selected in the Clip List across a contiguous range or as a non-contiguous selection of individual clips. Clips can be added to or removed from the selection using modifier keys.

To select a contiguous range of clips in the Clip List:

1. Click the name of the first clip you wish to select in the Clip List.
2. Shift-click the name of the last clip you wish to select. All clips in the range between the first clip and the last clip will be selected.

You can also select a range of clips by moving the cursor to the left of the clip names until the pointer becomes a Marquee cursor (crosshairs); then click and drag the Marquee around the clips you want to select.

To select or deselect non-contiguously (individual clips or ranges):

1. Press and hold the **COMMAND** key (Mac) or the **CTRL** key (Windows).

2. Click on individual items to select or deselect them non-contiguously.

    – Or –

    Move the cursor to the left of the clip name until the Marquee cursor appears (crosshairs); then click and drag.

    - To add clips, the Marquee should be to the left of an *unhighlighted* clip name.

    - To remove clips, the Marquee should be to the left of a *highlighted* clip name.

Figure 7.32 Crosshair marquee cursor for adding/removing clips

Selecting Unused Clips

Oftentimes it will be convenient to select and remove all of the unused clips in your session. This can be done quickly using the Clip List pop-up menu.

Example 7.5: Cleaning Up After Tracking

After completing initial tracking and overdubs, it is common to have a Clip List full of unused takes. These can result from warm ups, false starts, mistakes, or unsuccessful experimentation. In some cases, you may use only partial takes; in other cases, you may wish to discard entire takes. Either way, you will have clips in the Clip List that are not needed in the session. These unwanted clips not only clutter the Clip List, but can also consume space on the hard drive and make session transfers slow.

By selecting all unused clips in the Clip List and purging them from your session, you can keep the session orderly, recover disk space, and speed up the process of transferring a session between drives or between studios. Choose **SELECT > UNUSED** from the Clip List pop-up menu; then return to the Clip List pop-up menu and choose **CLEAR**. In the resulting dialog box, select either **DELETE** or **MOVE TO TRASH**. You can also use the **COMPACT** command under the Clip List pop-up menu to remove the unneeded portions of parent audio files after removing any unused subset clips.

The **SELECT > UNUSED** command in the Clip List pop-up menu automatically selects all clips and files that are not currently used in a track playlist. Note that whole-file clips may be included in this selection even if the session uses derivative subset clips that are based on these parent files.

To automatically select all unused clips in your session:

1. From the Clip List pop-up menu, choose **Select**, then choose one of the following:

    - **Unused:** Use this option to select all Audio, MIDI, and Video clips, including whole-file clips, that are not currently used on any track playlists.

    - **Unused Audio Except Whole Files:** Use this option to select all Audio clips, excluding whole file clips, that are not currently used on any track playlists.

    - **Offline:** Use this option to select all clips that are reference offline media (i.e., files that cannot be located on a mounted volume).

Figure 7.33 Selecting unused clips from the Clip List pop-up menu

2. After the unused clips are selected, choose **Clear** from the Clip List pop-up menu to remove or delete the audio. The Clear Clips dialog box will open.

Figure 7.34 The Clear Clips dialog box

3. Click **Remove** to remove the unused clips from the session while leaving parent files in the Audio Files folder (or their current location), **Move To Trash** to remove the clips and move associated parent files to the trash, or **Delete** to remove the clips and permanently delete associated parent files from disk.

 Removing or Deleting files with the Clear command cannot be undone.

Removing Clips Versus Deleting Files

Pro Tools makes an important distinction between removing clips and moving or deleting clips:

- When you remove a clip from a session, the parent audio file remains on the hard drive and can be used elsewhere in the session (by subset clips) or in other sessions.

- When you move an audio file to the trash or delete it, all clips referencing that file are also removed from the session. Moved or deleted files are no longer available for the current session or any other sessions that reference the files.

Removing Clips

Since removing audio clips does not delete audio, it is the safer choice. Select this option when you are cleaning up your Clip List to ensure that you do not accidentally delete parent audio files that are still in use.

When you remove clips using the Clear Clips dialog box, Pro Tools checks whether the clip is used in the session or is referenced in the computer's RAM. If the clip is currently on a track, stored in the Clipboard, or referenced in the undo queue, a confirmation dialog box will appear.

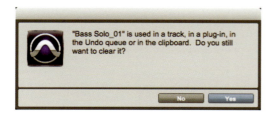

Figure 7.35 Clear Clips confirmation dialog box

- Click **YES** to clear the clip from the Clip List and the corresponding track, undo queue, or Clipboard.
- Click **NO** to cancel the Clear command.

Deleting Audio Files

Moving audio files to the trash or deleting them from the hard drive can reduce the overall storage requirements of your session. This is useful when creating an archive, session deliverable, or backup copy. However, this process requires a specific sequence of steps to safeguard against data loss. (See Lesson 10 for details on creating an archive).

As with removing clips, Pro Tools checks whether the clip is used in the session, on the Clipboard, or in the undo queue and prompts you with a confirmation dialog box, if needed. When deleting files, if no confirmation dialog box is needed, Pro Tools displays a warning dialog box before proceeding.

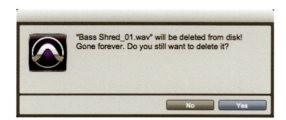

Figure 7.36 Delete Clips warning dialog box

- Click **YES** to permanently delete the audio file from your hard drive.
- Click **NO** to cancel the operation.

 The Delete option erases audio files from your hard drive, making them unavailable for the current session and all other sessions that reference the files. This action cannot be undone. Use this command with caution.

If you attempt to move to the trash or delete an audio file that is referenced by other clips in the session, a dialog box will appear, allowing you to remove the file instead.

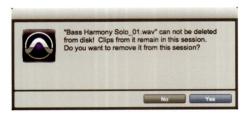

Figure 7.37 Dialog box that appears when unable to delete a file

- Click **Yes** to remove the file from the Clip List while leaving it on the hard drive.
- Click **No** to leave the file untouched in the Clip List.

 When clearing or deleting multiple files or clips, Option-click (Mac) or Alt-click (Windows) on the Yes or No button to stop multiple warnings from appearing.

Exporting Selections

From time to time, you may create audio selections or subset clips that you would like to make available outside of the current session. Examples might include an edited sound effect that you want to add to an FX library or a selected section of a drums track that you want to add to a loop library.

If the target clips or selections do not exist as parent files on disk, you'll have no immediate way to use them outside of the current session. Similarly, if the included audio contains fades or crossfades, these will not be represented in any disk files.

Fortunately, Pro Tools provides a variety of ways to make such clips and selections available externally. Two commonly used options are the Consolidate Clip command and the Export Clips as Files command.

Consolidating Clips

One of the most commonly used methods of rendering a clip or selection to disk as a parent file is the Consolidate Clip command. This command renders the Edit selection as a new audio file, including any selected empty space (silence) and fade effects. The resulting file is placed in your session's Audio Files folder.

To create an external file using the Consolidate Clip command:

1. Make a selection encompassing the target audio.
2. Choose **Edit > Consolidate Clip**. A new whole-file clip will be created from your selection, and the new clip will be selected in the Clip List.

 You can also press Option+Shift+3 (Mac) or Alt+Shift+3 (Windows) to consolidate a selection with the Consolidate Clip command.

3. (Optional) Right-click on the clip in the Clip List and choose **Reveal in Finder** (Mac) or **Reveal in Explorer** (Windows). The Audio Files folder will open with the newly created audio file selected.

   From here, you can copy the file to an FX library or other directory location, if desired.

Capturing and Exporting a Clip

The Consolidate Clip command replaces the original track selection with the new parent file. This can disturb an original, unedited clip by creating unwanted separations. If you don't wish to disturb your original audio playlist, a better option may be to use the Capture command followed by the Export Clips as Files command.

Using the Capture Command

This command lets you create a new subset clip in the Clip List without making a separation on the track.

 The Capture command is available only when the selection covers a continuous section of audio; you cannot capture selections that cross clip boundaries.

 To capture a clip from a selection that includes clip boundaries, fades, and/or areas of silence, you must first create a clip group from the source clips.

To capture a clip from a selection:

1. Make a selection encompassing the target audio.

2. Choose **CLIP > CAPTURE**. A dialog box will display, prompting you to name the clip.

Figure 7.38 The Name dialog box for a captured clip

3. Type the clip name and click **OK**. A new subset clip will be created and placed in the Clip List.

Exporting a Captured Clip

After capturing a clip, you can export it from your session as an audio file. Any whole-file or subset audio clips in the Clip List can be exported as files for use outside of the session.

> #### Example 7.6: Exporting Dialog for a Video Game
>
> After recording and processing lines of dialog for a character in a video game, you will need to export each line as a separate file. This allows the dialog to be implemented in the game engine for non-sequential playback in response to gameplay. In such cases, you may find yourself needing to export selected sections of longer audio files containing multiple takes or multiple separate lines of dialog.
>
> The fastest solution is to capture each line as a subset clip (choose **CLIP > CAPTURE**) and name the clips according to the filenames specified in the game script. Then select all of the subset clips in the Clip List and export them as files (choose **EXPORT CLIPS AS FILES** from the Clip List pop-up menu). The exported files will retain the names of the subset clips you created.

To export clips as files:

1. Select one or more audio clips in the Clip List.

2. From the Clip List pop-up menu, choose **EXPORT CLIPS AS FILES**. The Export Selected dialog box will display. (See Figure 7.39.)

3. Set the export parameters for the file(s) as desired.

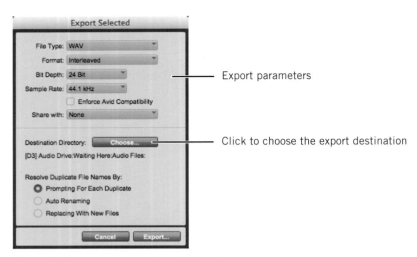

Figure 7.39 The Export Selected dialog box

4. (Optional) Click the **CHOOSE** button to select a destination for the exported file(s).

   - In the resulting dialog box, navigate to the desired library or other directory location.
   - Click **OPEN** to select the current location and dismiss the dialog box.

5. Click the **EXPORT** button to complete the file export. New audio files will be created at the selected destination.

Lesson 7 ■ Additional Editing and Media Management   **195**

Review/Discussion

1. Describe the process of creating a clip loop. What are some of the options available in the Clip Looping dialog box? (See "Creating Clip Loops" beginning on page 171.)

2. What are the two ways that the Trim tool can be used to edit a clip loop? (See "Using the Standard Trim Tool" beginning on page 173.)

3. How would you go about creating a loop from several separate clips on a track that you want to have repeat as a unit? (See "Considerations for Working with Clip Loops" beginning on page 174.)

4. What happens to clip loops when you choose the Clip > Ungroup All command? (See "Unlooping Clips" beginning on page 175.)

5. What is the difference between Absolute and Relative Grid modes? When would you use each? (See "Working with the Grid" beginning on page 175.)

6. What is the purpose of Layered Editing mode? How can Layered Editing be enabled or disabled? (See "Using Layered Editing" beginning on page 177.)

7. Do AudioSuite plug-ins provide real-time processing or non-real-time processing? When might you use AudioSuite processing instead of a plug-in insert? (See "AudioSuite Overview" beginning on page 178.)

8. What does the **USE IN PLAYLIST** button do in the AudioSuite plug-in window? How can you tell when this option is active? (See "Step 3: Configuring AudioSuite Controls" beginning on page 181.)

9. Explain the difference between applying AudioSuite processing as *Clip by Clip* versus *Entire Selection*. (See "Step 3: Configuring AudioSuite Controls" beginning on page 181.)

10. Why is it important to consider the Handle Length setting when processing with an AudioSuite plug-in? What types of processing might be affected by AudioSuite handles? (See "Considerations for Handle Length and Whole File Settings" beginning on page 185.)

11. What modifier key can you use to audition a clip in the Clip List? What kinds of clips can be auditioned? (See "Identifying a Clip by Auditioning" beginning on page 186.)

12. Suppose you open an existing session to do some additional recording and editing. How could you set the Clip List to display only the newly recorded and edited clips? (See "Conducting a Search" beginning on page 187.)

13. What are some options for selecting multiple clips in the Clip List? How can you select a range of contiguous clips? How can you select multiple non-contiguous clips? (See "Selecting Multiple Clips" beginning on page 188.)

14. What is the difference between removing clips versus moving to trash or deleting clips using the Clear command in the Clip List? (See "Removing Clips Versus Deleting Files" beginning on page 190.)

15. What are some options for making selections or subset clips available outside of the current session? What is the purpose of using the Capture command when exporting clips? (See "Exporting Selections" beginning on page 192.)

To review additional material from this chapter, see the PT110 Study Guide module available through the Elements|ED online learning platform at ElementsED.com.

EXERCISE 7

Working with Clip Loops and Editing on the Grid

Among the advantages of working with a proper tempo map is the ability to edit on the grid. By combining Grid mode with Pro Tools' clip looping capabilities, you can easily create repeating patterns that you can then copy, paste, and adjust to fit your song arrangement.

In this exercise, you will create a clip loop, create copies of the clip loop at the start of each chorus, extend the clip loop for the last chorus, and modify the loop iterations with the Trim tool for the final four bars. You will also use the Separate command to create separations on grid boundaries and edit individual drum hits.

Duration: 25 Minutes

Getting Started

To get started, you will open the session you created in Exercise 4. If that session is not available, you can use the *Waiting Here.ptxt* session template to create a new session.

1. Locate and open the 110 Exercise 4 [Your Initials].ptx session file that you created previously. The session will open to show the Edit window.

> If your Exercise 4 session is not available, open the *Waiting Here.ptxt* session template [PT110 Exercise Media (v12.8) > 03 Waiting Here > Waiting Here.ptxt] to create a new session.
>
> Name the new session 110 Exercise 7 [Your Initials] and save it to the class files location for your course. Then skip to the next section.

2. Choose FILE > SAVE AS.

3. Navigate to the class files location for your course and create a folder named 110 Exercise 7 [Your Initials].

4. Save the session in the newly created folder as 110 Exercise 7 [Your Initials].

Creating a Clip Loop

For this part of the exercise, you will loop the clip on the **Snare Dub** track to extend it for the length of the first chorus.

Select the clip and apply clip looping:

1. Click on ZOOM PRESET 2 to set an appropriate starting zoom level.

2. Locate the **Snare Dub** track in your session and select the **Snare_03** clip on the track.

3. Solo the track and press the **SPACEBAR** to audition the clip. Stop playback when finished.

4. With the **Snare_03** clip selected, choose **CLIP > LOOP** to open the Clip Looping dialog box.

5. In the Clip Looping dialog box, select the **LOOP LENGTH** option and set the value to 8 bars (8|0|000).

Figure 7.40 Loop Length set to 8 bars in the Clip Looping dialog box

6. Click **OK** to create the clip loop.

   The clip loop will display a looping arrow in the bottom-right corner of each loop iteration.

7. Press the **SPACEBAR** to listen to the results and confirm that the clip repeats smoothly.

   When finished, press the **SPACEBAR** again to stop playback.

Reusing the Clip Loop

In this part of the exercise you will copy the clip loop and reuse it for the other two choruses in the song.

Copy and paste the clip loop at Chorus 2:

1. Click on **ZOOM PRESET 1** to zoom out.

2. With the clip loop still selected, choose **EDIT > COPY** or press **COMMAND+C** (Mac) or **CTRL+C** (Windows). The clip loop will be copied to your computer's Clipboard.

3. Click on the Grid Value pop-up selector in the Edit window toolbar and set the grid to **1 BAR**. (See Figure 7.41.)

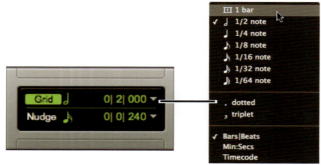

Figure 7.41 Setting the grid size

4. Using the **SELECTOR** tool, click at Bar 29 on the **Snare Dub** track to position the Edit cursor at the start of the second chorus. You may need to scroll the Edit window to get to Bar 29.

Refer to the Bars|Beats ruler above the tracks in the Edit window to identify the proper time location.

5. Choose **Edit > Paste** or press **Command+V** (Mac) or **Ctrl+V** (Windows) to paste a copy of the Snare_03 clip loop on the track for the second chorus.

Paste the another copy of the clip group at Chorus 3:

1. Click with the **Selector** tool at Bar 49 on the Snare Dub track to position the Edit cursor at the start of the third chorus.

2. Choose **Edit > Paste** or press **Command+V** (Mac) or **Ctrl+V** (Windows) to paste an additional copy of the Snare_03 clip loop on the track for the third chorus.

3. Click on **Zoom Preset 2** to zoom back in.

4. With the clip loop still selected, press the **Right arrow** key on your computer keyboard to scroll the end of the clip loop to the center of your screen.

Discussion Point #1

What is the effect of pressing the Right arrow key? What would happen if your selection included multiple clips and you pressed the Right arrow key? What do you expect would happen if you pressed the Left arrow key?

Modifying the Clip Loop

Because the third chorus in this song repeats, the clip loop is not long enough for the entire chorus. In this section of the exercise, you will use the Trim tool to extend the clip loop. Then you will modify the last 4 bars to change the rhythm at the end of the song. Lastly, you will separate the final bar on the grid and edit individual drum hits.

Extend the loop with the Trim tool:

1. Select the **Trim** tool and place it near the end of the last Snare_03 loop iteration on the track. The Trim tool will display the loop trim icon (bracket with a loop arrow).

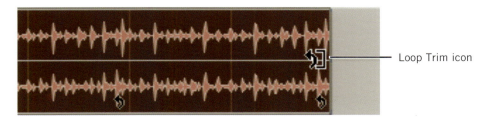 — Loop Trim icon

Figure 7.42 Loop Trim tool icon displayed at the end of the clip loop

2. Click inside the clip and drag to the right to extend the clip loop to Bar 65.

When you release the mouse, additional clip iterations will be added as needed to extend the clip loop.

Modify the last 4 bars of the loop:

1. Using the **Selector** tool, click inside the clip loop at Bar 61 to position the Edit cursor at that location.

2. Choose **Edit > Separate Clip > At Selection** or press **Command+E** (Mac) or **Ctrl+E** (Windows) to separate the clip loop at Bar 61.

   You will now have a separate 4-bar clip loop at the end of the track.

3. Click on the Grid Value pop-up selector in the toolbar and set the grid to **1/2 note** (0|2|000).

4. Reselect the **Trim** tool and position it over the looping arrow along the bottom of the clip at Bar 65. The Trim tool will display the standard trim icon (bracket with no loop arrow).

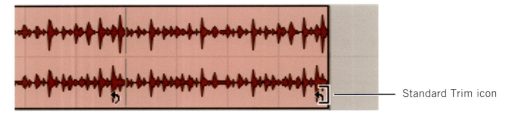

Figure 7.43 Standard Trim tool icon displayed over the looping arrow

5. Click inside the clip and drag to the left to shorten the loop iteration. Trim the loop iteration to a single ½ note in duration.

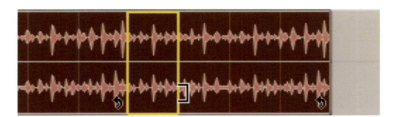

Figure 7.44 Trimming the loop iteration to a single ½-note duration

When you release the mouse, loop arrows will appear at every ½-note Grid boundary, but the overall length of the clip group will remain 4 bars.

6. Press the **spacebar** to listen to the results of the change.

Discussion Point #2

What was the purpose of separating the clip loop in Step 2 above? What would be the effect of trimming in Step 5 *without* first separating the clip?

Edit individual 1/8 notes:

1. Using the **Selector** tool, select just the last bar in the clip loop (64|1|000 to 65|1|000).

2. Click on the Grid Value pop-up selector in the toolbar and set the grid to **1/8 note** (0|0|480).

3. Choose **Edit > Separate Clip > On Grid**. The Pre-Separate Amount dialog box will appear. (See Figure 7.45.)

Figure 7.45 The Pre-Separate Amount dialog box

4. Enter a small pre-separation value (2 to 5 mSec) to allow for some padding and click **OK**. The selected audio will be separated into 1/8-note clips.

5. Click **ZOOM PRESET 3** to zoom in on the selected clips.

6. Double-click with the **SELECTOR** tool on the third 1/8-note clip to select just that clip.

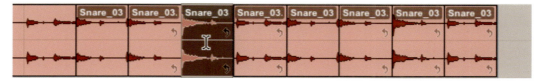

Figure 7.46 Clip selected on the Snare Dub track

7. Choose **EDIT > DUPLICATE** or press **COMMAND+D** (Mac) or **CTRL+D** (Windows) to duplicate the clip, placing the duplicate one 1/8 note later.

Discussion Point #3

What is the purpose of specifying a pre-separate amount when separating on the Grid? Why might this be important?

Duplicate the final snare hit:

1. Click on the Grid Value pop-up selector in the toolbar and set the grid to **1/16 NOTE** (0|0|240).

2. Make a 1/16-note selection on the track from **64|4|000** to **64|4|240** to select just the last snare hit.

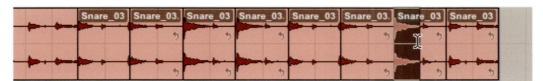

Figure 7.47 Last snare hit selected on the Snare Dub track

3. Duplicate the selection three times to create a snare fill at the end of the track.

Figure 7.48 Results of duplicating the snare hit

4. Click **Zoom Preset 2** to zoom out. Then scroll as needed to position the playback cursor at Bar 57.

5. Press the **spacebar** to listen to the changes you've made for the end of the final chorus.

> **Discussion Point #4**
>
> In Step 3 above, could you have achieved the same result with clip looping as you did by duplicating the selection? What considerations might apply in that case?

Finishing Up

To finish, you can listen to the results of your work in context before closing the session. Also, be sure to save the work you have done for future use or to submit for a grade.

Audition changes and save the session:

1. Press **Return** (Mac) or **Enter** (Windows) to return to the start of the session.

2. Unsolo the **Snare Dub** track and listen to the session with the completed changes.

3. When finished, stop playback.

4. Save and close the session. That concludes this exercise.

Remember that you cannot close a Pro Tools session by closing its windows. You must choose Close Session from the File menu.

LESSON 8

Basic Mixing and Signal Flow

The user-configurable, scalable, and modular nature of Pro Tools provides users with significant flexibility for customizing mixes. All the traditional attributes of an analog console are combined with hardware options and advanced Pro Tools software mixing capabilities. To begin harnessing this power, it is imperative to first understand some basic terminology and Pro Tools mixing concepts. As your skills develop, you can achieve higher levels of mixing competency and efficiency, allowing for experimentation and added creativity.

GOALS

- Use track color coding to help organize and identify material
- Use inserts and sends for effects processing
- Use Pro Tools mixer display options
- Understand real-time plug-in concepts
- Work with Aux Input tracks
- Work with Master Fader tracks

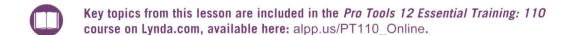

Key topics from this lesson are included in the *Pro Tools 12 Essential Training: 110* course on Lynda.com, available here: alpp.us/PT110_Online.

As you discovered in the Pro Tools 101 course, Pro Tools has a powerful built-in software mixer. This lesson will help you to prepare for your final mix by adding effects as inserts on tracks as well as by using them as a shared resource in send-and-return configurations. The lesson also discusses specific controls and functions available for sends and plug-ins.

Track Colors, Icons, and Status Indicators

Pro Tools provides several options for visually organizing and identifying tracks and quickly assessing their status. Track colors, Track Type icons, and track status indicators offer simple and effective visual feedback.

Track Color Coding

Pro Tools automatically assigns default colors to tracks and clips based on your Preference settings.

 Custom color-coding with the Color Palette is discussed in the *Pro Tools 201* book.

Color-coding can be especially helpful in sessions with large track counts. Color-coding affects tracks in the Mix and Edit windows. The assigned colors are displayed in color bars at the top and bottom of each channel strip in the Mix window and to the left of each track in the Edit window.

Figure 8.1 Track color bars: Mix window (left) and Edit window (right)

The options for track color-coding Preferences are as follows:

- **None.** Turns off color assignment for tracks.

- **Tracks and MIDI Channels.** Assigns a unique color to each track according to its voice assignment or the MIDI channel assignment made with the MIDI Output selector.

- **Tracks and MIDI Devices.** Assigns a unique color to each track according to its voice assignment or the MIDI device assignment made with the MIDI Output selector.

 In Standard Pro Tools, color-coding options that assign colors based on voice assignment will assign a unique color to each non-MIDI/Instrument track.

- **Groups.** Assigns a color to each track according to its Group ID. When groups are suspended using the Suspend Groups command, the track color bars are not shown.

- **Track Type.** Assigns a color to each track according to its type (Audio, MIDI, Instrument, Video, Aux Input, or Master Fader). This is the default track color setting.

To change the default track color-coding:

1. Choose **SETUP > PREFERENCES**.

2. Click on the **DISPLAY** tab.

3. In the Color Coding section, select an option under **DEFAULT TRACK COLOR CODING**.

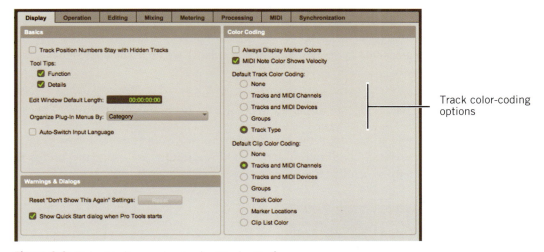

Figure 8.2 Color Coding section in the Display Preferences page

4. Click **DONE**.

To display track color bars in the Mix or Edit window, do one of the following:

- From the **VIEW** menu, select **MIX WINDOW VIEWS > TRACK COLOR** or **EDIT WINDOW VIEWS > TRACK COLOR**.

- Click the **MIX WINDOW VIEW SELECTOR** or **EDIT WINDOW VIEW SELECTOR** and select **TRACK COLOR** from the pop-up menu.

Track Type Icons

Track Type icons help you identify the types of tracks in a Pro Tools session. The track types available in standard Pro Tools include the following:

- Audio (disk tracks)

- Auxiliary Input

- MIDI

- Instrument

- Video

- Master Fader

Track Type icons are displayed for each of these track types in the Mix window. These icons are especially helpful to get familiar with a large session that came from another studio or to reorient yourself in a session that you haven't worked on for a while.

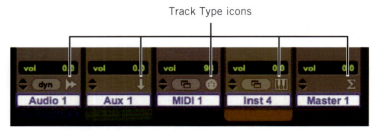

Figure 8.3 Track Type icons for various tracks in Pro Tools

 Video tracks are not represented in the Mix window since they have no associated signal flow for mixing purposes.

Track Status Indicators

Various visual indicators are available at the top of the Edit window for tracks in your session or project. These indicators light whenever the associated condition is active. The indicators are especially useful for large sessions where the affected tracks may be scrolled out of view.

Figure 8.4 Track status indictors: Task Manager, Freeze, Solo, and Mute (from left to right)

Task Manager Status Indicator

Whenever a background task is in progress, the Task Manager Status indicator will light and show a rotating animation. This indicator can light during Elastic Audio analysis or rendering and during certain other operations that require background processing or analysis.

Clicking on the Task Manager Status indicator will open the Task Manager window, where you can view, pause, or cancel background tasks.

 Details on using the Task Manager are covered in the *Pro Tools 201* course book.

Freeze Indicator

The Global Freeze Tracks icon will light blue when any track is frozen. When no tracks are frozen, the Global Freeze Tracks icon will appear dim green. When the Global Freeze Tracks icon is lit, **OPTION-CLICKING** (Mac) or **ALT-CLICKING** (Windows) on the icon will unfreeze all frozen tracks.

Solo Indicator

The Track Solo Indicator lights yellow when any track is soloed. When no tracks are soloed, the Track Solo indicator appears dim green. When the Track Solo indicator is lit, clicking it will clear all soloed tracks in the session.

Mute Indicator

The Track Mute Indicator lights orange when any track in the session is muted. When no tracks are muted, the Track Mute indicator appears dim green. Because Mute is an automatable mixing function, the Track Mute indicator *does not* clear mutes when clicked.

Using Inserts for Effects Processing

Pro Tools allows you to place up to 10 inserts on any Audio track, Instrument track, Aux Input, or Master Fader. Inserts are grouped into two sets of five: Inserts A–E and Inserts F–J. The two Inserts view areas provide access to the 10 Insert selectors. You can use inserts for either internal plug-in processing or external hardware processing of a track's signal.

Pro Tools processes inserts in series, adding each effect to the previous one on the track (from top to bottom). For this reason, you should arrange the individual processors on a track in a sequence that maximizes the desired effect for your signal chain.

Inserts on Audio Tracks and Aux Inputs

Inserts on Audio tracks and Aux Inputs are pre-fader, meaning they are applied before the fader section affects the signal level passing through the track. This ensures consistency in signal processing. However, on a high-amplitude track, a pre-fader insert that boosts signal gain can cause clipping or "overs" in your session. Be sure to listen to your tracks and use on-screen metering to avoid clipping.

Clips versus Overs

The clip indicators in Pro Tools distinguish between true clips (signals that will distort an input, output, or disk file) and overs (signals that exceed 0 dBFS en route to an internal destination). A true clip condition is shown by a red clip indicator in a track meter (Audio tracks and Master Faders). Non-clipping overages are shown by yellow clip indicators on a track or send meter.

Inserts on Master Faders

In contrast to inserts on Audio tracks and Aux Inputs, inserts on Master Faders are always post-fader, meaning the inserts are applied after the fader section affects the signal level. If clipping occurs as a result of a signal boost from an insert, it can be eliminated by adjusting the signal level with the Volume fader.

Plug-In Inserts

By choosing a plug-in insert, you can add a software signal processor directly into the signal path of a channel and adjust your processor settings from within Pro Tools. Additionally, most plug-in parameters can be enabled for automation using the **AUTO** button in the plug-in window. Plug-ins can easily be added to a track's signal path using an Insert selector in the Mix or Edit window.

To add EQ to a guitar track using a plug-in insert, for example, you could place an EQ III plug-in into the signal path using Insert selector A. The signal flow passes from the track playlist (the audio file on disk), through the inserted EQ, on through the remainder of the insert positions (B through J), and then on to the fader section in the mixer strip.

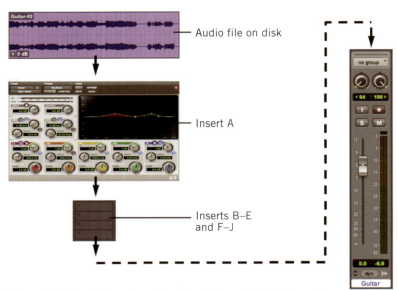

Figure 8.5 Signal flow through a plug-in insert (EQ III shown)

Hardware Inserts

You can use hardware inserts to route audio through an external device connected to parallel inputs and outputs of your audio interface (if it has sufficient I/O). By choosing a hardware insert, you can add an external signal processor directly into the signal path of a track.

Like software inserts, hardware inserts are added using Insert selectors in the Mix or Edit window. However, hardware inserts also require that you connect your audio interface to the input of the external device and connect the output of the device back to your audio interface.

To add an external EQ to a guitar track, for example, you could connect the device to your interface and route to the corresponding channel from an Insert selector, as shown in Figure 8.6. The signal will pass from the track playlist, out through the audio interface, through the external EQ, back in through the audio interface, through the remaining inserts, and finally on to the fader section in the mixer strip.

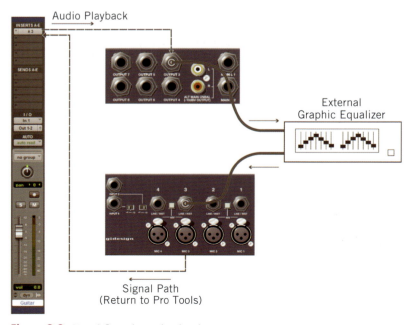

Figure 8.6 Signal flow through a hardware insert

Using Sends and Returns for Effects Processing

A *send* is a mix output of one or more tracks sent to another receiving device, such as an external reverb or digital delay. A send can be *pre-fader*, meaning the send level is unaffected by the channel fader level, or *post-fader*, meaning the send level changes with the channel fader level. Pro Tools allows you to place up to 10 sends on any Audio track, Instrument track, or Aux Input. There are no sends on Master Fader tracks.

Creating a Send

To create a send from a track, you can use any available Send selector. After creating the send, you will need to adjust the send level to achieve the desired effect.

A sent signal may pass through an external device for processing before returning to Pro Tools. Alternatively, the send can remain in Pro Tools and travel to its destination on an internal mix bus.

Choosing a Send Type

The type of send you choose will depend on how you plan to use the send signal. To add effects using an external device, use an Output send; to add effects using a plug-in, use a Bus send.

- **Output Send.** This type of send routes a signal out of your audio interface, through an external processor, and back into your audio interface to return the processed audio to Pro Tools.
- **Bus Send.** This type of send uses an internal mix bus to route a signal to an Aux Input in your session where it is processed by a plug-in.

Using Send Selectors

In Pro Tools you can create either an Output send or a Bus send from a Send selector. Both types are available in either mono or stereo.

To add a send to a track:

1. Make sure a Sends view is displayed in the Mix or Edit window.
2. Click an available Send selector, choose the desired send type (Output or Bus), and choose a mono or stereo send.

 You can also route a send directly to a track destination from the Send selector. Choose TRACK > TRACKNAME to create a Bus send to an existing track or choose NEW TRACK to add a destination track for your Bus send.

 See Lesson 10 for more information on routing to tracks.

- For an Output send, route to any of your available audio interface outputs.

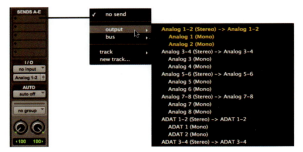

Figure 8.7 Routing a send to a hardware output

- For a Bus send, use any available internal mix bus.

Figure 8.8 Routing a send to an internal mix bus

 Pro Tools 12 provides unlimited internal mix busses. You can add busses to a session at any time using the I/O Setup dialog box (Setup > I/O).

3. Release the mouse button after selecting the desired send assignment. The name of the selected output or mix bus will display in the Send Assignment button, and the Send window will open.

After a send has been created, the send assignment will be displayed in the Send button next to the Send selector. In the Figure 8.9, a stereo send has been created on Send A using Bus 3-4.

Figure 8.9 Send A assigned to Bus 3-4

Setting the Send Level

By default, new sends are created with a volume setting of negative infinity. This precautionary measure helps prevent accidental overload to your system, allowing you to gradually increase the send level until the desired volume is reached.

To set the send level, use the Send level slider in the Send window.

 For more detail on the Send window, see "Using the Send Window" later in this lesson.

Changing the Default Send Level Preference

If you prefer to have new sends automatically default to unity gain (0 dB), you can configure this in Preferences. This will save you the extra step of having to manually raise the level of each new send.

To set the send default level preference:

1. Choose Setup > Preferences.

2. Click on the Mixing tab.

3. In the Setup section, enable/disable the option for Sends Default to "-INF" as desired. (See Figure 8.10.)

Lesson 8 ■ Basic Mixing and Signal Flow   211

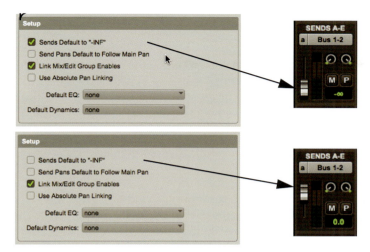

Figure 8.10 Sends Default to "-INF" preference enabled (top) and disabled (bottom)

Send Display Options

Each Audio track, Aux Input, and Instrument track provides 10 sends for routing audio to internal busses or hardware outputs. Master Faders have no sends, as Master Faders are destinations by definition. All 10 sends provide identical controls, routing options, and automation capabilities.

Sends View Areas

The ten sends available in Pro Tools are grouped into two sets of five: Sends A–E and Sends F–J. The View menu provides separate options for displaying these Sends views in the Mix and Edit windows.

The Sends view areas can be displayed differently in the Mix and Edit windows, allowing you to display Sends A–E in the Mix window, for example, while displaying Sends F–J in the Edit window.

Figure 8.11 Sends view in the Mix view showing the first five send positions

To display a Sends view:

■ Choose VIEW > MIX WINDOW VIEWS or VIEW > EDIT WINDOW VIEWS and select the desired Sends view from the submenu (SENDS A-E or SENDS F-J). The selected Sends view area will display in the corresponding window.

Expanded Sends View

Each send position can be configured to display its assignment in an expanded view across all tracks.

Figure 8.12 Send view options: standard view (left) and expanded view (right)

> **Example 8.1: Using Sends for Headphone Mixes**
>
> Although Sends are frequently used for effects processing and submixing, they are also convenient for setting up headphone mixes for artists to use while tracking. When recording an entire band, for example, you may need to set up several different headphone mixes so that each performer can hear a blend of the audio that is suitable to their individual needs and preferences.
>
> By adding a send across all tracks that are assigned to your main outputs, you can create an alternate "cue mix" output for headphones. To keep the headphone mix independent of the main mix as you work, you'll need to set the sends to Pre-fader mode.
>
> Putting each of the Sends that you are using for headphone mixes into expanded view gives you immediate access to the send controls and levels. This makes it easier to set up the mix and allows you to quickly respond to a musician's request for "a little more me" in their phones.

To toggle between the standard view and expanded view for a send position:

- Choose **VIEW > EXPANDED SENDS** and select the desired send position from the submenu. The corresponding send position will display in expanded view.

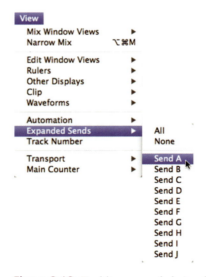

Figure 8.13 Enabling expanded view for Send A

 You can also toggle Expanded view on/off by COMMAND-CLICKING (Mac) or CTRL-CLICKING (Windows) on a Send selector.

Expanded sends provide access to the same controls that are available in a Send window. (See "Using the Send Window" later in this lesson.)

Creating a Return

The track type used to return the signal to the mix is typically an Aux Input. This return channel also has output assignments, with level and pan controls, allowing precise control over how the processed signal is re-introduced to the session and combined with other audio.

After creating a send for effects processing, you will need to create an Aux Input track to use as a return and, in the case of returning a Bus send, to apply the associated processing.

To create a return for a Send:

1. Choose **TRACK > NEW**.

2. In the **NEW TRACKS** dialog box, specify an Aux Input with the appropriate track format (mono or stereo).

Figure 8.14 New Tracks dialog box set for a stereo Aux Input

3. Click **CREATE**.

4. Double-click on the Aux Input track nameplate to give the track a meaningful name. (For example, you might name the return based on the processing it will apply, such as *Reverb*.)

5. Using the **AUDIO INPUT PATH SELECTOR** for the Aux Input, select one of the following:

   - **Interface:** Use this option if the track is being used to return an Output send to an external device.
   - **Bus:** Use this option if the track is being used to return a Bus send.

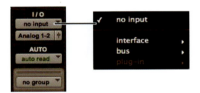

Figure 8.15 Setting the input for an Aux Input track

6. Click on the **AUDIO OUTPUT PATH SELECTOR** and set it to the desired main output mix, as needed.

Figure 8.16 The output selector for an Aux Input track set to analog outputs 1-2

Adding Internal Effects using Plug-Ins

Aux Input tracks used to return bus sends can use any available plug-in on your system to add internal software-based effects processing to the signal.

To add internal effects to a return track:

1. Click on an **INSERT SELECTOR** on the Aux Input track and choose a plug-in from the menu hierarchy.

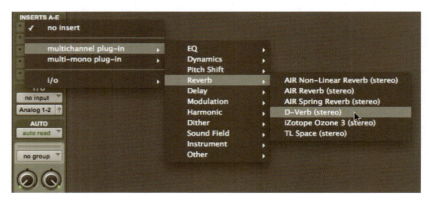

Figure 8.17 Selecting a plug-in for an insert position

2. In the resulting plug-in window, set the effect parameters as desired.

Figure 8.18 The D-Verb plug-in window

The Volume fader on the Aux Input track can be used to control how much of the wet (processed) signal is combined with the dry (unprocessed) tracks. In other words, this fader allows you to precisely mix the Aux Input track's signal with the rest of the tracks in the main mix of the session.

Using Solo Safe Mode

Pro Tools allows you to enable *Solo Safe* mode on any track to prevent that track from muting when you solo another track. This feature is useful for Aux Inputs that are being used for effects returns, allowing the effect to remain in a mix when Audio tracks that are feeding the effects track are soloed.

 You can also use Solo Safe mode on MIDI tracks so that their playback is not affected when you solo an Aux Input track that hosts a virtual instrument they are feeding.

> **Example 8.2: Keeping Effects in Place on a Vocal Mix**
>
> When mixing and editing a vocal with multiple layers (doubled parts and harmonies), if often helps to hear the vocal tracks isolated from the rest of the mix. This is easily accomplished by soloing all of the vocal tracks. However, soloing the vocal tracks will effectively mute all other tracks, including any return tracks used for effects processing on the vocals.
>
> In many cases, it is important to hear the contributions of effects such as reverb and delay while fine-tuning a vocal mix. To keep these effects active while soloing vocal tracks, you can "solo-safe" each of the Aux Input return tracks. This will avoid the need to solo each of the return tracks any time you solo one or more vocal tracks.

To enable Solo Safe mode on a track:

- **COMMAND-CLICK** (Mac) or **CTRL-CLICK** (Windows) on the **SOLO** button on a track. The Solo button will become dimmed to indicate that the track is in Solo Safe mode.

Tracks in Solo Safe mode can be soloed as normal, and they remain in Solo Safe mode when unsoloed.

To return a track from Solo Safe mode to normal mode:

- **COMMAND-CLICK** (Mac) or **CTRL-CLICK** (Windows) on the **SOLO** button of a track that is in Solo Safe mode. The Solo button will return to normal.

Figure 8.19 Solo Safe mode enabled (left) and disabled (right)

Working with Sends

Once you've created your sends, you may need to configure various send controls and options. You may also want to duplicate a send you've created onto another track or on the same track at a different send position. This section discusses these processes, as well as options for changing or removing unneeded sends.

Using the Send Window

The Send window provides access to all available send controls. The Send window appears whenever you assign a send or click on a Send Assignment button at a position where a send is currently assigned.

Send Window Types

Figure 8.20 shows the Send window types that are possible with mono and stereo tracks. A send can be either mono or stereo on any mono or stereo track, giving four possible send configurations in a stereo session: mono send on a mono track, mono send on a stereo track, stereo send on a mono track, or stereo send on a stereo track.

Figure 8.20 Send types, from left to right: mono send (mono track), mono send (stereo track), stereo send (mono track), and stereo send (stereo track)

Send Controls

You can use the controls in the Send window to adjust a send's volume, pan (stereo sends only), and mute settings. You can also use the top section of the Send window to access additional settings.

Figure 8.21 Send controls at the top of the send window (stereo send from a stereo track shown)

Most of the controls available in a Send window are also available in miniature when using Expanded Sends view on a track, as shown in Figure 8.22. (See "Send Display Options" earlier in this lesson for information on enabling Expanded Sends view.)

Figure 8.22 Send controls in Expanded Sends view

The Send controls include the following options:

- **Send Level Slider:** This slider sets the level for the send, up to +12 dB.

- **Pre Button:** The pre-fader button is active when highlighted in blue, making the send level independent of the track's output fader position. When the PRE button is not highlighted (default), the send is post-fader, and the track's output fader directly affects the send level.

- **Mute Button:** When highlighted, the MUTE button is active and prevents the track's audio from passing to the output of the send.

- **Pan Knob(s):** Available for stereo sends only, these knobs allow you to control the signal balance between the left and right outputs.

- **Path Selector:** This pop-up menu allows you to change or remove the send assignment.

 Any inserts on a track will also affect sends, regardless of whether the sends are pre- or post fader (inserts are always pre-fader, except on Master Fader tracks).

Send Panner Options

Stereo sends on stereo tracks have two panning controls, one for each side of the left/right pair. The Send window provides controls to enable various options for send panning:

- The **FMP** button (Follow Main Pan) links the Send pan to the Main pan for the track, allowing for fast setup of cue mixes or effects processing.

- The **LINK** button enables the left and right channel pan controls to be linked together for precise panning of stereo and multichannel tracks. When disabled, the left and right channel pans operate independently.

- The **INVERSE PAN** button can be used with panner linking to invert, or reverse, the panning between the left and right channels.

Figure 8.23 Panner options—left to right: FMP enabled, linking enabled, inverse linking enabled, linking disabled

To enable or disable Follow Main Pan:

- Click on the **FMP** button so that it becomes highlighted (enabled) or unhighlighted (disabled). When highlighted, the Send pan will follow the Main track pan, and the panning controls in the Send window will be disabled.

To enable or disable panner linking:

- Click the LINK icon to enable linking (highlighted) or disable linking (not highlighted). The panning controls will become linked together so that any pan settings you make on one control will be duplicated on the other control.

At times, you may want the left and right channels to pan in opposite directions. In Inverse Pan mode, sweeping one channel from left to right causes the opposite channel to simultaneously sweep from right to left.

To enable or disable inverse linking on a stereo send:

- To enable inverse panning, click both the LINK icon and the INVERSE PAN icon so that they both become highlighted. The panning controls will become inversely linked—any settings you make with one control will be reflected as a mirror image on the other.

- To disable Inverse linking and use standard link mode, click the INVERSE PAN icon so that it becomes unhighlighted while leaving the LINK icon enabled (highlighted).

- To disable all linking, click the LINK icon so that it becomes unhighlighted. (The Inverse Pan button has no effect when the Link button is disabled.)

> Panner linking options are also available for a track's main pan controls. To access the main panner link controls for a track, open the track's floating output window by clicking on the mini-fader icon on a track's Output selector.

Moving and Copying Sends

Sends can be moved and copied to other tracks, or to other positions on the same track, using conventional drag and drop. Sends can be dropped to create new sends at the destination, or they can be dropped onto existing send assignments to replace them.

To move a send:

- Click on a SEND ASSIGNMENT button and drag it to a new position in the original track or to the desired position in a different track. The selected send will be moved to the new location and removed from the old location.

To copy a send:

- OPTION-CLICK (Mac) or ALT-CLICK (Windows) on a SEND ASSIGNMENT button and drag it to a new position. The selected send will be copied to the new location.

Moving or copying a send maintains all related routing assignments, all compatible automation, and level/pan/mute settings, as well as the send output format.

The following conditions apply in special cases when moving or copying sends among tracks:

- When moving or copying a stereo send from a mono track to a stereo track, Send pan automation (if any) will be dropped without warning.

- When moving or copying a stereo send from a stereo track to a mono track, the left Send pan automation data is retained and the right side data is dropped. A warning dialog appears for you to confirm or cancel this destructive operation.

Lesson 8 ■ Basic Mixing and Signal Flow   **219**

■ When moving or copying a send and replacing an existing send, all automation on the existing send will be replaced. A warning dialog appears for you to confirm or cancel this destructive operation.

Changing and Removing Sends

At times, you might want to change a send assignment or remove the send completely.

To change or remove a send:

1. If the send you want to change is not visible in the Send window, do the following:

   • Choose the desired track using the **TRACK SELECTOR** in the Send window.

   • Using the **OUTPUT VIEW SELECTOR**, choose the send you wish to affect (A-J), if not currently displayed.

2. Use the Send's **OUTPUT PATH SELECTOR** to choose the new send path, or choose **NO SEND** to remove the send completely.

Using Native Plug-Ins

As you've learned previously, plug-ins are software programs that add functionality to Pro Tools. Plug-ins exist for a multitude of sound-processing applications—from synthesis to effects processing to sonic modeling.

Native plug-ins run on host-based Pro Tools systems using track inserts. When you add a Native plug-in to a track, it processes the audio in real time—you can instantly hear its effect on the track while playing back audio—without committing the effect permanently to that track.

Native plug-ins rely on the processing power of the host computer. The more powerful your computer, the greater the number and variety of Native plug-ins you can use simultaneously.

The types of audio processors available through plug-ins can be broken down into two main categories:

■ **Gain-Based Processors:** EQ, Compressor, Gate, Expander, etc.

■ **Time-Based Processors:** Reverb, Chorus, Delay, Echo, etc.

Using Gain-Based Processors

When adding EQ and other gain-based or dynamics processing to your mix, you will typically assign the plug-ins as inserts to each track individually. This type of processing is typically applied to the entire signal (100% wet), rather than being mixed together with a dry signal.

Gain-based processors can also be shared using a submaster, allowing you to add the effect to all tracks in the submix simultaneously, processing the combined signal as a group.

Using Time-Based Processors

While gain-based processors are commonly assigned to each track individually, time-based processors like reverb are often shared. Sharing effects is useful when you want a common effect for multiple tracks. This also makes more efficient use of your processing resources.

Shared time-based effects are typically added using a send and return setup. This allows you to add the effects at different levels by adjusting the send level for each track individually. By bussing the send to an Aux Input track, you can then set up shared effects for all tracks using that send path. Native plug-ins can be added as inserts on the Aux Input track, and you can control the overall wet-to-dry signal in the mix using the track's Volume fader.

Time-based effects can also be shared using a submaster, allowing you to add the effect to each track in the submix at the same level, using the plug-in controls to adjust the mix ratio.

Using the Plug-In Window

Whenever you add a plug-in insert, the plug-in window appears. This window allows you to enable, disable, change, or edit any insert on any track or Master Fader in your session.

Figure 8.24 below shows the plug-in window for a stereo 1-Band EQ III Native plug-in.

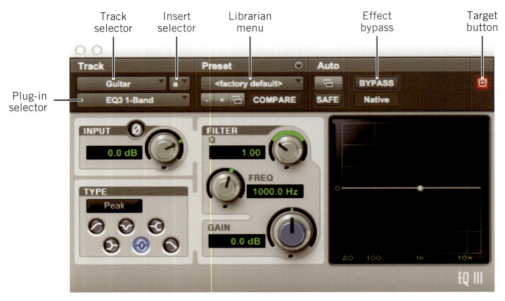

Figure 8.24 Plug-in window and controls

All plug-in windows include the following standard controls in their header section:

- **Track Selector:** Lets you select any track in your session that processes audio; the selected track can have a plug-in on any of its 10 inserts enabled, disabled, or changed.

- **Insert Selector:** Lets you access any insert position (A–J) on the current track. The pop-up menu shows any plug-ins present by the corresponding insert letter.

Figure 8.25 Insert selector menu in the plug-in window

- **Plug-in Selector:** Lets you access any installed plug-in or any hardware insert position available through your audio interface.

- **Librarian Menu:** Lets you select from available presets for the current plug-in. When a plug-in is assigned, it will have no preset selected and <Factory Default> will display in the Librarian menu.

- **Bypass Button:** Bypasses the currently selected plug-in, allowing you to monitor the track with and without the effect. When a plug-in is bypassed, the corresponding Insert Selector on the track will display in light blue (if the plug-in window is open) or dark blue (if the plug-in window is closed).

Lesson 8 ■ Basic Mixing and Signal Flow   221

 You can also toggle bypass on/off for a plug-in with the Plug-In window closed by COMMAND-CLICKING (Mac) or CTRL-CLICKING (Windows) directly on the insert.

- **Target Button:** Sets the current window as the target for computer keyboard commands. The Target button is enabled (lit red) by default. When you open a new plug-in window, it replaces the current window and becomes the new target. To open multiple plug-in windows, anchor the current window by toggling the Target button off (gray). Opening additional windows will not affect a non-targeted window.

 Multiple untargeted plug-in or Send windows can also be displayed by Shift-clicking on their associated insert or send positions.

Master Fader Tracks

Master Faders control the master levels of output and bus paths. Master Faders provide post-fader effects processing and master level control and can be used for a main mix, a headphone/cue mix, a submix, or other signal-routing application.

Unlike inserts on Audio tracks and Aux Inputs, Master Fader inserts are always *post-fader*. This lets you insert dither or a similar plug-in on your master mix and ensure that it is always applied at 100%.

 For information on applying dither with a Master Fader, see Lesson 10.

Master Faders provide up to 10 post-fader inserts and no sends. Also, Master Fader tracks do not have Pan controls or Mute and Solo buttons.

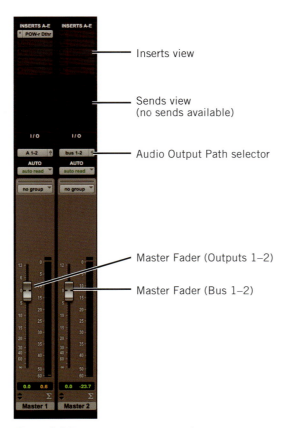

Figure 8.26 Master Faders assigned to main outputs 1–2 (left) and to an internal mix bus (right)

Uses of Master Faders

Master Faders can be used to do any of the following:

- Control and process output mixes
- Monitor and meter an output level (e.g., a bus or hardware output) to guard against clipping
- Control submix levels
- Control effects send levels
- Control levels on submasters (bussed tracks)
- Apply dither or other inserts to all tracks sent to a common output or bus

Creating Master Faders

You may want to use a Master Fader to control submix levels, a send mix level, or a main output. Master Faders control levels feeding either audio interface outputs or internal mix bus destinations without consuming any of your system's audio processing power.

To use a Master Fader as a stereo master volume control:

1. Create a stereo Master Fader track.
2. Set the outputs of all Audio, Instrument, and Aux Input tracks in the session to the main output bus (e.g., outputs 1–2 of your audio interface).
3. Set the AUDIO OUTPUT PATH SELECTOR on the Master Fader to the same main output bus.

You can apply inserts to any Master Faders you create. Unlike inserts on other tracks, though, Master Fader inserts are post-fader.

 Meters on Master Faders always show post-fader levels, regardless of the Pre-Fader Metering setting in the Options menu.

Inserts added to a Master Fader will globally affect all tracks routed to the corresponding destination. This conserves processing power in your system and also allows an effect to be added to your overall mix. Since Master Faders are final destinations for audio, they have no sends.

Master Faders can be assigned to main paths or subpaths as defined in the I/O Setup dialog box. However, each Master Fader must have a unique output bus or mix bus assignment. If you attempt to assign a Master Fader to a bus that has already been assigned to another Master Fader, Pro Tools will make the Master Fader inactive until you select another unused output bus or mix bus.

Lesson 8 ■ Basic Mixing and Signal Flow **223**

Review/Discussion

1. Where can you assign the color-coding that Pro Tools will automatically apply for tracks and clips? How can you display track color bars in the Mix and Edit windows? (See "Track Color Coding" beginning on page 204.)

2. Describe the track icons used for each type of track (Audio, Aux Input, MIDI, Instrument, and Master Fader) in the Mix window. (See "Track Type Icons" beginning on page 205.)

3. How many inserts are available on a track in Pro Tools? Why is it important to consider the order in which inserts are arranged on a track? (See "Using Inserts for Effects Processing" beginning on page 207.)

4. Are inserts pre-fader or post-fader on Audio tracks, Instrument tracks, and Aux Input tracks? Are inserts any different on Master Fader tracks? Explain. (See "Inserts on Audio Tracks and Aux Inputs" and "Inserts on Master Faders" beginning on page 207.)

5. Are sends pre-fader or post-fader on Audio tracks, Instrument tracks, and Aux Input tracks? Are sends any different on Master Fader tracks? Explain. (See "Using Sends and Returns for Effects Processing" beginning on page 209.)

6. How many sends are available on a track in Pro Tools? (See "Using Sends and Returns for Effects Processing" beginning on page 209.)

7. What is the difference between an Output send and a Bus send? When would you use each? (See "Choosing a Send Type" beginning on page 209.)

8. What level does a send default to when it is first created? How can you change this default? (See "Setting the Send Level" and "Changing the Default Send Level Preference" beginning on page 210.)

9. What is the difference between standard view and expanded view for sends? What keyboard modifier can you use to toggle between view modes by clicking a Send selector? (See "Send Display Options" beginning on page 211.)

10. How can you prevent a "return" track from muting when one of the source tracks is soloed? What modifier key is used to enable this function? (See "Using Solo Safe Mode" beginning on page 214.)

11. What is the effect of enabling the PRE button in a Send window? What is the effect of enabling the FMP button? (See "Send Controls" beginning on page 216.)

12. How can you visually determine whether the Inverse Pan option is enabled for a send? What button(s) will be highlighted? (See "Send Panner Options" beginning on page 217.)

13. How can you copy a send from one track to another track and duplicate its settings? What considerations might apply? (See "Moving and Copying Sends" beginning on page 218.)

14. Which type of plug-in effects are generally used on inserts? Which are generally used with sends? Why? (See "Using Native Plug-Ins" beginning on page 219.)

15. What is the Librarian menu used for in a plug-in window? What is displayed in the Librarian menu when you first assign a plug-in? Why? (See "Using the Plug-In Window" beginning on page 220.)

16. What are some of the uses of a Master Fader? How can you assign a Master Fader to the desired output or bus? (See "Master Fader Tracks" beginning on page 221.)

To review additional material from this chapter, see the PT110 Study Guide module available through the Elements|ED online learning platform at ElementsED.com.

EXERCISE 8

Adding Music and Effects Processing

The mixing and signal-routing features in Pro Tools provide powerful capabilities for both music production and video post-production projects. In this exercise, you will work with a video podcast session to add a music bed and signal processing to polish the audio.

Duration: 25 Minutes

Getting Started

To get started with this exercise, you will create a session from a template file provided with the course exercise media and save it to the class files location specified by your instructor.

Open the template and save the session:

1. Launch Pro Tools and choose **FILE > OPEN SESSION** (or choose **OPEN FROM DISK** from the Dashboard).

2. Navigate to the Exercise Media folder and open the *Ex08-Starter.ptxt* template file [PT110 Exercise Media (v12.8) > 06 Inferno > Ex08-Starter.ptxt].

   A dialog box will open displaying default parameters based on the template.

3. Name the session 110 Exercise 8 [Your Initials] and select the **PROMPT FOR LOCATION** option near the bottom of the dialog box.

4. Click **CREATE** to proceed. A second dialog box will open, prompting you to choose a save location.

5. Navigate to an appropriate location and click **SAVE**. The session will open with the Edit window displayed.

Adding a Music Bed

In this part of the exercise, you will be adding music to the video podcast using provided audio clips and loops. You will use a standard intro music clip for the opening and closing sequences. You will also build a music bed for the episode narration using loops.

Add music to the opening sequence:

1. Press **COMMAND+=** (Mac) or **CTRL+=** (Windows) to display the Edit window, if not already shown, and press **RETURN** (Mac) or **ENTER** (Windows) to return to the start of the session.

2. Double-click on the **ZOOMER** tool to zoom the Edit window out and show the entire session.

3. Place the session in **GRID** mode and enable the **SMART TOOL**.

4. Deselect **AUTOMATION FOLLOWS EDIT** under the **OPTIONS** menu.

226 PT110: Pro Tools Fundamentals II

 The Edit window toolbar includes a button for toggling Automation Follows Edit on/off. This button displays in blue when active and orange when inactive. For this part of the exercise, the button should be orange.

5. Locate the **TitleMusic** clip in the Clip List and drag it to the start of the **MX01** track.

6. With the Smart Tool positioned near the end of the **TitleMusic** clip, trim the clip to end around 01:00:29:20. If needed, zoom in to work with greater precision.

7. Use the **SMART TOOL** to add a short fade-out (approx. 3 seconds) at the end of the **TitleMusic** clip. (Click in the upper-right corner and drag left.)

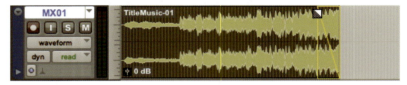

Figure 8.27 Adding a fade-out with the Smart Tool

Duplicate the music clip for the closing sequence:

1. Using the Smart Tool as a Grabber, click on the **TitleMusic** clip to select it.

2. Press **COMMAND+D** (Mac) or **CTRL+D** (Windows) to duplicate the clip.

3. Using the **SMART TOOL** as a Grabber, drag the duplicate clip toward the end of the **MX01** track. Position the clip to begin at the Title Music Cue marker location (1:04:02:13).

   If needed, use the Nudge function to fine-tune the clip placement.

4. Press **RETURN** (Mac) or **ENTER** (Windows) when finished to return to the start of the session.

Add a music bed for the narration:

1. Audition the three music loops in the Clip List by **OPTION-CLICKING** (Mac) or **ALT-CLICKING** (Windows) on each one to select your preferred option. (See Figure 8.27.)

   The clips are labeled **MXLoop01**, **MXLoop02**, and **MXLoop03**, respectively.

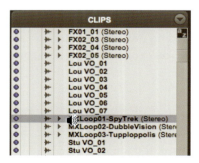

Figure 8.28 Auditioning the first music loop in the Clip List

2. Drag your preferred music loop to the MX01 track, a short distance after the first **TitleMusic** clip.

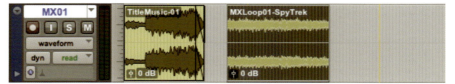

Figure 8.29 Music loop clip placed on the MX01 track

3. Right-click on the music loop and choose **SNAP TO PREVIOUS** from the pop-up menu.

4. With the music loop still selected, choose **CLIP > LOOP** to open the Clip Looping dialog box.

5. In the Clip Looping dialog box, select the option to **LOOP UNTIL END OF THE SESSION OR NEXT CLIP** and click **OK**. (See Figure 8.30.)

   A clip loop will be created, extending to the second **TitleMusic** clip.

Figure 8.30 Looping options selected in the Clip Looping dialog box

6. Use the **SMART TOOL** to add a fade-in and fade-out on either end of the clip loop. Extend your fades to approximately 3 seconds each. (See Figure 8.31.)

   You may have to scroll the Edit window to access either end of the clip loop.

Figure 8.31 Adding a fade-out on the clip loop using the Smart Tool

Discussion Point #1

Can you think of a way to quickly navigate between the start and end of the clip loop to add or adjust the fades at either end? What steps would be required?

Adding Room Reverb

For this part of the exercise, you will add reverb to your mix to create a sense of realism for the audio. By placing the reverb on an Aux Input track, you will be able send track signals to the processor, as desired.

Create the return track:

1. Press **COMMAND+=** (Mac) or **CTRL+=** (Windows) to display the Mix window.

2. Add a stereo Aux Input track to the session by holding **CONTROL** (Mac) or **START** (Windows) while double-clicking on a blank area of the Mix window (to the right of the existing tracks).

3. Click on Insert selector A at the top of the Aux Input track and select **MULTICHANNEL PLUG-IN > REVERB > D-VERB (STEREO)**. The D-Verb plug-in window will open.

4. Click on the **LIBRARIAN** menu in the D-Verb plug-in window and select **LARGE ROOM**.

Figure 8.32 Selecting the Large Room preset for the D-Verb plug-in

5. Close the plug-in window to reduce on-screen clutter.

6. Enable Solo Safe mode on the Aux Input track by **COMMAND-CLICKING** (Mac) or **CTRL-CLICKING** (Windows) on the track's **SOLO** button. The Solo button will become dimmed.

Discussion Point #2

Why is it important to enable Solo Safe mode on the Aux Input track? In what way might this be helpful when setting send levels?

Create sends to the Aux track:

1. Select each of the voice-over tracks (VO01 and VO02).

2. While holding **OPTION+SHIFT** (Mac) or **ALT+SHIFT** (Windows), click on Send selector A for one of the selected tracks and choose **BUS > BUS 3-4 (STEREO)**. A send will be created at position A on each of the selected tracks, and a Send window will open.

3. Close the Send window to reduce on-screen clutter.

4. Right-click on the Send Assignment A button on either of the VO tracks and choose **RENAME** from the pop-up menu.

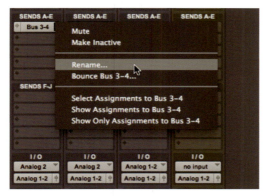

Figure 8.33 Choosing Rename from the Send Assignment pop-up menu

5. In the ensuing dialog box, rename the bus path to Verb Bus and click **OK**.

6. Click on the **AUDIO INPUT PATH SELECTOR** for the Aux Input track and choose **BUS > VERB BUS** to route the send signal into the track.

> ### Discussion Point #3
>
> What is the purpose of holding Option/Alt and Shift in Step 2 above? What would be the result if you did not use these modifiers while assigning the send?

Adjust the send levels:

1. Display the Send A controls in the Mix window by choosing **VIEW > EXPANDED SENDS > SEND A**. The send controls will display in the Sends A–E view area.

2. Press **RETURN** (Mac) or **ENTER** (Windows) to return to the beginning of the session.

3. Begin playback and adjust the send levels as you feel appropriate. You may need to solo each track and toggle the send Mute on/off to hear the contribution that each send is making.

    Try setting the send levels around the following values for each track:

    - VO01 track: -2.9 dB
    - VO02 track: -7.9 dB

4. When satisfied with the result, stop playback.

Wrap Up

To finish this project, you will create a bounce to QuickTime. First, you should save your work to prevent data loss and protect your session for future use or to submit for a grade.

Finalize the session:

1. Press **COMMAND+=** (Mac) or **CTRL+=** (Windows) to display the Edit window.
2. Re-enable **AUTOMATION FOLLOWS EDIT** using the **OPTIONS** menu or the button on the Edit window toolbar.
3. Using the **SMART TOOL** as a Grabber, click on the clip on the Video track to select it.
4. Play through the selection, listening carefully to the audio transitions and reverb processing levels. Make adjustments to fades and/or send levels as necessary.
5. When satisfied, save the session.

Create a bounce to QuickTime:

1. With your selection still active, choose **FILE > BOUNCE TO > QUICKTIME**. The QuickTime Bounce dialog box will open. (See Figure 8.34.)
2. Set the audio parameters to **Interleaved**, **16 Bit**, and **44.1 kHz**. Also, ensure that **ADD TO ITUNES LIBRARY** is unchecked.
3. In the video section of the dialog box, make sure that **INCLUDE VIDEO** and **SAME AS SOURCE** are checked. Then verify the **FILE NAME** and **DIRECTORY** location for the bounce file.
4. At the bottom of the dialog box, check the **OFFLINE** option; then click **BOUNCE**.

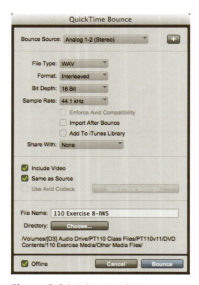

Figure 8.34 The QuickTime Bounce dialog box configured for bouncing the session

5. When the bounce completes, save and close the session. That concludes this exercise.

 Remember that you cannot close a Pro Tools session by closing its windows. You must choose **CLOSE SESSION** from the **FILE** menu.

LESSON 9

Writing and Editing Automation

After you have finished editing and adding plug-in effects to your tracks, you are ready to create the final mix of your session. The automation features of Pro Tools allow you to record your mixing moves in real time, then go back and edit those moves with great precision. Automation data can be recorded and edited using many of the same tools and techniques you have already learned and used for recording and editing audio.

GOALS

- Understand Pro Tools' automation features
- Write automation for different track parameters
- Work with automation displays
- Edit automation data graphically
- Suspend writing and playback of automation

Key topics from this lesson are included in the *Pro Tools 12 Essential Training: 110* course on Lynda.com, available here: alpp.us/PT110_Online.

When preparing for final mixdown, many of your tracks may require changes in level, panning, and effects throughout various parts of the session. Using automation, you can record these changes and fine-tune them prior to mixdown. This lesson discusses different ways of writing, editing, and playing back automation data.

Understanding Automation

Pro Tools lets you automate the following controls in real time during playback of a session:

- **Track Controls**
    - Volume, Pan, and Mute on Audio tracks, MIDI and Instrument tracks, and Aux Inputs
    - Volume controls on Master Faders
- **Send Controls**
    - Send Volume, Send Pan, and Send Mute
- **All Plug-In Controls**

Automation is written and played back exactly as you perform it. Since Pro Tools creates a separate automation playlist for each type of automation you write, you can edit and modify each automatable control individually. This allows you to build up a complex mix in stages and ensures that your automation will play back accurately every time.

Groups and Automation

If you are working with tracks that are part of an active Mix group, recording automation to one member of the group will generally record the same automation for all other members of the group. Mix groups affect the recording of automation for any linked attributes of the group.

Depending upon your automation goals, you may wish to enable or disable groups for specified tracks.

     Mix and Edit groups are covered in Lesson 10 of this book.

Automation Playlists

Automation playlists are the graphs that affect parameters during playback of your tracks. Both Audio tracks and MIDI/Instrument tracks support playlists for automating their controls. However, automation graphs are different for audio automation than their corresponding controller graphs for MIDI data.

Audio Tracks

Each Pro Tools Audio track includes a single automation playlist for each automatable control. You cannot store multiple takes of automation for a single control in an Audio track. Although an Audio track can have several different edit playlists (arrangements of clips), the track's automation playlist applies to all of the edit playlists for that track.

     Details on using multiple edit playlists are covered in the *Pro Tools 210M* and *Pro Tools 210P* course books.

MIDI and Instrument Tracks

On MIDI tracks and Instrument tracks, all MIDI-based continuous controller automation data (except for MIDI Mute) is stored within the associated MIDI clip. Each edit playlist on the track is separate and represents a distinct performance, complete with continuous controller automation.

All MIDI information, including notes, velocities, controller values, program changes, and SysEx events, are stored within MIDI clips and therefore reside in the edit playlist. Most MIDI continuous controller data has a resolution of 127 steps across the range of the control.

Audio Automation versus Continuous Controller Automation

Pro Tools audio automation offers much higher resolution than MIDI continuous controller automation. When you are using a MIDI track in conjunction with an Aux Input track, you can automate the Aux Input track's volume, pan, and mute controls for more precise control of these parameters. Likewise on Instrument tracks, you can use the track's audio volume, pan, and mute controls rather than the corresponding MIDI controls for greater precision.

Working with Automation

Pro Tools provides various modes and functions for working with automation. Having the ability to write automation selectively, suspend automation writing and playback, audition automation changes, and view automation graphs can be very powerful in helping perfect your automation moves.

Automation Modes

Pro Tools offers five main automation modes (Pro Tools HD software includes additional modes). You can set the automation mode from the Automation Mode selector on each track. The Automation Mode selector is available in both the Mix and Edit windows.

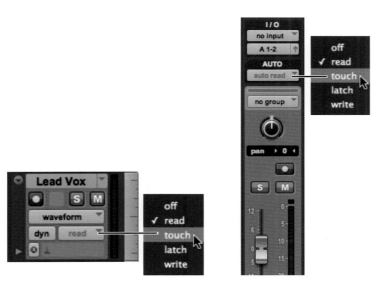

Figure 9.1 Selecting Touch mode from the Automation Mode selector (Edit window, left; Mix window, right)

The five automation modes available in Pro Tools are **OFF**, **READ**, **TOUCH**, **LATCH**, and **WRITE**. You've learned about Off, Read, and Write mode in the Pro Tools 101 course. Touch and Latch modes allow you to control when automation is written to each parameter during an automation pass. These modes begin writing automation only when you touch (or move) an automatable control, such as a volume fader in the Mix window or a touch-sensitive fader on a control surface.

Table 9.1 describes each of the automation modes and provides examples of when to use each.

Table 9.1 Pro Tools Standard Automation Modes

Automation Mode	Description	Automation Writing Stops	Usage Examples
Off	Automation playback and writing disabled.	n/a	Temporarily disabling automation to hear a complex session or provide local control without changing automation.
Read	Automation play-only mode. Automation writing disabled.	n/a	Playing a final automated mix with all automated parameters write-protected to prevent accidental alteration.
Touch	Automation writing starts when an enabled parameter is modified. Modified parameters only writing automation while being held.	Writing stops when modified parameter is released; the parameter returns to previously automated value.	Updating and writing automation parameters in select areas, returning parameters to their previous values when released.
Latch	Automation writing starts when an enabled parameter is modified. Modified parameters continue writing automation after being released.	Writing stops for all modified parameters when playback stops.	Automating parameters over long areas, with controls remaining put when you release them.
Write	Automation writing starts for all enabled parameters immediately when playback starts, overwriting any previous automation data.	Writing stops for all parameters when playback stops.	Overwriting existing automation on a track, or deleting all previously automated parameters while writing new automation.

Enabling and Suspending Automation

Pro Tools allows you to enable or suspend the writing and playback of automation in several ways. Globally suspending automation allows you to temporarily ignore all automation in the session so that you can freely adjust volume, pan, and other parameters without affecting the underlying automation. Disabling individual parameters allows you to write-protect those parameters against changes during an automation pass.

Suspending and disabling automation is done using the controls in the Automation window.

To access the Automation window:

- Choose WINDOW > AUTOMATION. The Automation window will open.

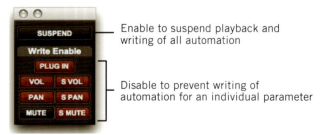

Figure 9.2 Automation window (standard Pro Tools software shown)

Example 9.1: Controlling Parameters in a Session with Existing Automation

Once a parameter has been automated, it becomes locked to its automation graph. As a result, you no longer have free, real-time control over that parameter. This will be true even if the automation graph has no dynamic automation and only a single automation breakpoint.

When you receive a session that has existing automation, it can be hard to set levels, adjust panning, or modify sends or plug-in parameters, because controls that have automation will immediately snap back to their automated levels upon playback. And oftentimes it will be difficult to determine whether the existing automation is meaningful or not until you become familiar with the session.

To gain hands-on control over all the tracks, you can click the SUSPEND button at the top of the Automation window. This has the same effect as putting all tracks into OFF mode. The Suspend function lets you experiment with the mix without discarding or overwriting any existing automation.

The Automation window has the following options:

- **Suspend Button:** Globally enables or suspends writing and playback of all automation parameters for all tracks in your session. When the button is highlighted, all automation is suspended.

- **Write Enable Buttons:** Enable or disable writing for the corresponding automation parameter across all tracks in your session. When a button is highlighted, the parameter is enabled for automation. Note that the buttons enable or suspend *writing* of automation only; they have no effect on automation *playback*.

Writing Automation Selectively

As you learned in the Pro Tools 101 course, you can use Write mode to write automation during playback. The downside to using Write mode, however, is that as soon as the transport is rolling, you are writing automation for all enabled parameters, whether you make any changes or not.

By contrast, Touch and Latch modes write automation only to parameters that are changed, allowing you to be much more selective when automating a mix.

Latch mode is effective when you want to set a parameter and let it ride through long sections of a mix. This can be useful for an initial automation pass, to set levels for the different parts of a song (intro, verse, chorus, solo, etc.).

Touch mode is effective when you need to touch up small sections of existing automation, such as to boost a vocal for a specific line or word. In this mode, when you release the fader or other control, it returns to the existing automation level.

To write automation selectively:

1. Choose WINDOW > AUTOMATION.

2. Enable any parameters you plan to automate using the Write Enable buttons.

3. Put the target tracks into TOUCH or LATCH mode using the tracks' Automation Mode selectors.

4. Begin playback.

5. To begin writing automation, click on the control you wish to automate (or touch the control on a touch-sensitive control surface).

Playing Automation

After creating automation, you will naturally want to listen to the automation you created, to decide if changes or updates are needed.

1. Play back the session to listen to the automation you just created.

2. If you are satisfied with your automation pass, make sure you save your session (**File > Save**). Alternatively, if you do not like the automation you just wrote, you can undo the automation pass (**Edit > Undo**).

3. To write additional automation or to change your existing automation, use either Touch or Latch mode, start playback, and move the controls as desired.

Viewing Automation

At times it's helpful to view and manually edit automation. In the Edit window, each track has a separate playlist for each type of automation (e.g., pan, volume, mute, send level, and send mute). As you create sends and enable plug-in parameters for automation, additional automation graphs are automatically created and added to the Track View selector menu for the corresponding track.

You can change a track's view to display the desired automation parameter at any time using the **Track View selector** pop-up menu. You can also display automation playlist lanes under a track, independent of the selected track view.

To display an automation playlist in the main track view:

1. In the Edit window, click on the **Track View selector** for the track on which you want to view or edit automation.

2. From the pop-up menu, choose the automation type you want to view, such as **Volume**.

Figure 9.3 Using the Track View selector to display the Volume automation graph

The track's graphical display will change to show the automation graph for the selected parameter.

To display automation and controller lanes for a track:

1. In the Edit window, click the **Show/Hide Lanes** button at the head of the track. (See Figure 9.4.) The track's Volume automation playlist (Audio tracks) or Velocity view (MIDI and Instrument tracks) will display in a lane below the track.

Lesson 9 ■ Writing and Editing Automation   237

Figure 9.4 Controls for displaying automation/controller lanes

2. To change the type of automation displayed, click the **AUTOMATION TYPE** selector and select the automation type that you want to view from the pop-up menu.

3. If desired, click the **ADD LANE** button to view additional automation lanes.

 Hold OPTION (Mac) or ALT (Windows) before choosing a track view or showing automation lanes to make the display change across all tracks in the session.

Before automation has been written for a control, the automation playlist will show a single breakpoint at the beginning of the track and a straight line indicating the initial position of the control.

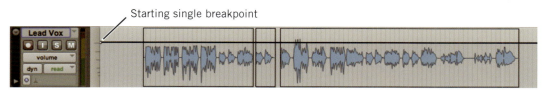

Figure 9.5 Volume graph with no breakpoint in the automation data

After automation has been created, the automation graph will show automation breakpoints wherever automation has been written.

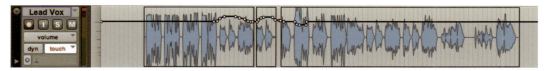

Figure 9.6 Volume graph with multiple breakpoints in the automation data

Graphical Editing of Automation Data

Automation data is represented in the form of a line graph with editable breakpoints. Breakpoints can be added, deleted, moved, copied, pasted, and nudged using many of the same editing techniques you already use to edit audio waveforms.

To edit automation data graphically, set the track view or automation lane to show the automation graph you want to edit.

When you drag a breakpoint, Pro Tools will either numerically or textually indicate the change in the automation value. This provides a convenient visual reference while you are performing the edit.

Automation Displays

Some automation graphs have a continuum of possible vertical breakpoint positions (such as a volume graph); others may have only five or six discrete options (such as an EQ Type graph), while some have only two choices (such as a Mute graph). The following sections describe some basic automation playlists you are likely to use.

Volume Graph

The Volume graph enables you to edit volume automation using the Grabber and other Edit tools. The Grabber tool allows you to create new breakpoints by clicking on the graph line or to move existing breakpoints by dragging them. Dragging a breakpoint up or down changes the dB value, while dragging left or right adjusts the timing of the dB change earlier (left) or later (right).

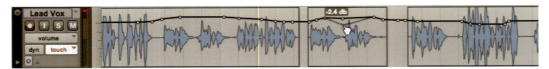

Figure 9.7 Volume graph display

Pan Graph

Pan automation appears as shown in Figure 9.8. Dragging a breakpoint up pans to the left, dragging down pans to the right, and dragging near the middle pans center. Dragging horizontally left or right adjusts the timing of the Pan change earlier (left) or later (right).

Figure 9.8 Pan graph display

Mute Graph

The Mute graph has stepped controls that toggle between two different states (muted or unmuted). To mute the audio, drag down; to unmute the audio, drag up. Dragging left or right adjusts the mute timing.

Figure 9.9 Mute graph display

Creating and Adjusting Breakpoint Automation Data

All automation graphs display time on the horizontal axis and the current parameter setting on the vertical axis. For easier editing of the automation graphs, you can zoom in and out, as well as increase the track height.

After displaying the type of automation data you want to edit, you can make changes with the Grabber tool.

To add or move a breakpoint:

- To create a new breakpoint, click the **Grabber** tool on the line graph. (See Figure 9.10.)

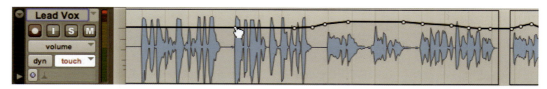

Figure 9.10 Adding a breakpoint with the Grabber tool

- To move a breakpoint, click on an existing point on the line graph with the **Grabber** tool and drag it to a new position.

You can also move a range of breakpoints together as a group.

To move or nudge one or more breakpoints earlier or later in a track:

1. Select the range that contains the breakpoints you want to nudge.

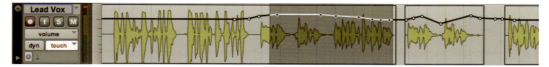

Figure 9.11 Breakpoints selected on the Volume automation graph

2. Choose a nudge value from the **Nudge value pop-up** menu in the Edit window toolbar.

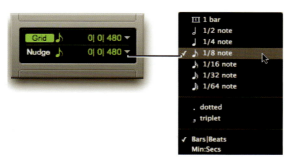

Figure 9.12 Setting the Nudge value

3. From the numeric keypad, press the Plus key **[+]** to nudge the breakpoints later (to the right) or the Minus key **[–]** to nudge them earlier (to the left) in the track.

 Creating and editing automation data on an Audio track that is a member of an active group will affect all other members of the group. To affect automation data on only one member of an active group, hold down the **Control** key (Mac) or **Start** key (Windows) while performing the edit.

Drawing Automation

In addition to creating and adjusting automation using the Grabber and Trim tools, you can also draw automation using the Pencil tool. You can use the Pencil tool to draw or redraw breakpoint automation data on any automation graph. The Pencil tool's different drawing modes can be used to create a wide variety of automation shapes.

To draw a freehand automation shape:

1. Click and hold the **Pencil** tool icon; in the Pencil tool pop-up menu, verify that the **Free Hand Pencil** mode is active.

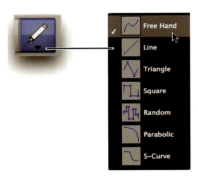

Figure 9.13 Selecting the Free Hand Pencil tool

2. Click and drag on an automation graph to draw a new shape or automation curve.

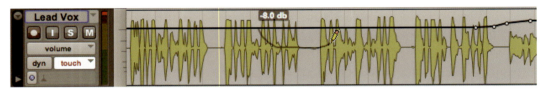

Figure 9.14 Drawing automation with the Pencil tool

A series of new automation breakpoints are created, matching the shape you draw.

To draw a smooth ramp (for example, in a volume automation playlist):

1. Click and hold the **Pencil** tool icon and choose the **Line Pencil** from the pop-up menu.

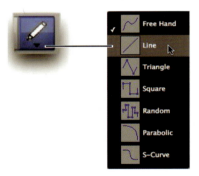

Figure 9.15 Selecting the Line Pencil tool

2. Click and drag on an automation graph to create a breakpoint and draw a new line segment. (See Figure 9.16.)

Figure 9.16 Drawing automation in line segments with the Pencil tool

3. Release the mouse at the point where you want to add the next breakpoint. Line segments will be added on either side, connecting to the previous and next breakpoints.

Any Pencil tool mode can be used for drawing automation except for the Parabolic or S-Curve modes.

> ### Example 9.2: Automating Pan and Tremolo Effects
>
> The Triangle and Square modes of the Pencil tool are useful for drawing automation that alternates between two extreme settings. When used on a Pan graph, for example, the Triangle Pencil tool lets you draw panning changes that sweep back and forth from left to right. When used on a Volume graph, the Triangle or Square Pencil tools let you draw graphs that modulate amplitude for a tremolo effect.
>
> Both of these Pencil tool modes use the current Grid setting as the basis for their modulation rate. To change the modulation rate, choose a Grid value prior to drawing automation with the Pencil tool.

Cutting, Copying, and Pasting Automation Data

Just as you can cut, copy, and paste audio waveform data, you can also apply the same techniques when editing automation data. When you make a selection in an automation playlist and then cut- or copy-and-paste the data into a new location, breakpoints will be added at the beginning and ending points of the pasted data.

When you use the cut command, breakpoints will also be added to the beginning and ending points of the original selection of automation data. This is done to preserve the slope of the automation data both inside and outside of the selection.

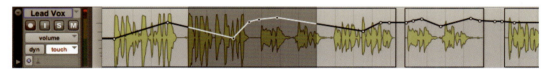

Figure 9.17 Selecting a range of automation data

Cutting Automation Versus Deleting Automation

Cutting a selection of automation data (using the **Cut** command in the Edit menu) has a different effect than deleting a selection of automation data (using the **Delete** key on the keyboard). Both operations will remove the selected breakpoints. However, the Cut command will add breakpoints at the start and end of the selection, while the Delete key will not. (See Figures 9.18 through 9.20 below.)

These two options can have very different results, so it is important to consider your intended outcome when removing a range of breakpoints.

Figure 9.18 Automation playlist prior to editing

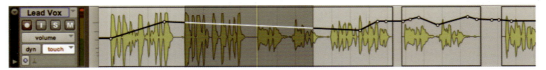

Figure 9.19 (Option 1) Automation playlist after removing selected automation data using the Delete key

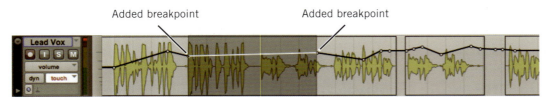

Figure 9.20 (Option 2) Automation playlist after removing selected automation data using the Cut command instead

Using Cut, Copy, and Paste Commands

You can use standard Cut, Copy, and Paste commands for automation. These operations let you copy automation levels or moves to another location on the same track or to a matching automation playlist on another track.

To cut (or copy) and paste automation data:

1. Select the automation data you want to cut or copy.

2. Do one of the following:

    - Choose **EDIT > CUT**, or press **COMMAND+X** (Mac) or **CTRL+X** (Windows).
    - Choose **EDIT > COPY**, or press **COMMAND+C** (Mac) or **CTRL+C** (Windows).

3. Place the cursor where you want the pasted automation to begin.

4. Choose **EDIT > PASTE**, or press **COMMAND+V** (Mac) or **CTRL+V** (Windows).

When cutting (or copying) and pasting automation data, the following rules apply:

- Automation data is always pasted to the same automation graph that it originated from, even if the corresponding automation graph is not currently displayed on the target track.

- When a track view is set to Waveform and audio is cut, copied, or pasted, all corresponding automation data is also cut, copied, and pasted with the audio.

> The Pro Tools setting **AUTOMATION FOLLOWS EDIT** is enabled by default. This setting can be toggled on/off under the **OPTIONS** menu (or using the **AUTOMATION FOLLOWS EDIT** button). When off, editing audio will **not** affect the corresponding automation data.

- Cutting or copying data from an automation playlist that contains no data (a playlist with a single breakpoint at the beginning of the track) will not add breakpoints to the playlist.

- Automation data for plug-ins or sends that do not exist on the target track will be ignored when pasted.

Lesson 9 ■ Writing and Editing Automation   243

Using Paste Special Mode

Pro Tools provides three Paste Special modes, two of which provide options for working with automation data.

Repeating Automation Across a Selection

The Repeat to Fill Selection option allows you to paste multiple iterations of copied automation data to a selection range. If your destination selection is not an exact multiple of the copied selection size, the remaining selection area will be filled with a partial iteration of the copied selection.

 Repeat to Fill Selection can also be used to paste a section of audio or MIDI data to fill a selected area.

Pasting to a Different Automation Type

Normally, when you paste automation data into Pro Tools, the automation data is pasted into matching automation playlists (for example, *pan* data is pasted into the *pan* playlist, *volume* data is pasted to the *volume* playlist, and so on). However, at times you may want to paste from one type of automation playlist to another (for example, to copy volume automation to a send).

To paste between playlists, you need to use the **PASTE SPECIAL > TO CURRENT AUTOMATION TYPE** command. This allows you to copy and paste between automation playlists on the same track or to copy automation data from one track and paste it to a different type of playlist on another track.

To paste automation data into a different automation playlist:

1. Use the **TRACK VIEW SELECTOR** to display the automation playlist that you want to copy from.

2. Select the automation and choose **EDIT > COPY** or press **COMMAND+C** (Mac) or **CTRL+C** (Windows).

3. Display the automation playlist that you want to paste into on the destination track.

4. Choose **EDIT > PASTE SPECIAL > TO CURRENT AUTOMATION TYPE**, or press **CONTROL+COMMAND+V** (Mac) or **START+CTRL+V** (Windows).

For this paste special mode to function, the following must be true:

- Every track selected for pasting must be displaying the automation playlist you wish to affect.

- There must be only one automation playlist on the Clipboard for each target track. (The Paste Special function cannot copy multiple automation playlists for a single track.)

> ### Using Merge Mode for MIDI Data
>
> The third Paste Special option, Merge mode, lets you add copied MIDI data from the Clipboard to existing MIDI data in a track. This can be useful for consolidating MIDI data from different tracks into a single track. For example, you could copy the performance from a MIDI snare track and merge it with the performance on a MIDI kick drum track. The MIDI notes from the snare track are added to the existing MIDI notes on the kick drum track. This option is similar to recording in MIDI Merge mode.

 You cannot interchange automation data between Audio and MIDI tracks or between continuous controls (such as faders or pans) and switched or stepped controls (such as mute or MIDI controllers).

Removing Automation from a Track

As you have learned, Pro Tools provides multiple ways to delete breakpoints in an automation playlist. You can delete individual breakpoints with the Grabber tool or delete a range of breakpoints with the Delete command.

At times, you may want to remove automation across an entire track. This may involve clearing all automation for a single, displayed automation graph on a track or clearing the automation across all automation graphs.

Deleting Breakpoints on the Displayed Automation Graph (Recap)

In the Pro Tools 101 course, you learned how to delete individual breakpoints with the Grabber tool. If you need to delete multiple consecutive breakpoints, it can be faster to select across the range of target breakpoints.

To delete one or more breakpoints on the displayed automation graph:

- **OPTION-CLICK** (Mac) or **ALT-CLICK** (Windows) on individual breakpoints with the **GRABBER** tool.
- Select a range of breakpoints with the **SELECTOR** tool and do one of the following:
  - Press the **DELETE** key on the keyboard.
  - Choose **EDIT > CLEAR**.

Clearing Automation for the Displayed Automation Graph

Once a parameter has been automated, that parameter will be locked to its automation graph. Clearing the automation graph for the entire track allows you to regain free control over the parameter.

To clear the displayed automation graph:

1. With the automation graph you wish to clear displayed, do one of the following to select the entire graph:
   - Triple-click on the automation graph with the Selector tool.
   - Place the Edit cursor on the automation graph and press **COMMAND+A** (Mac) or **CTRL+A** (Windows).
2. Press the **DELETE** key on the keyboard or choose **EDIT > CLEAR**.

Clearing Automation for All Automation Graphs

To regain full control over a track, you may need to remove automation for multiple parameters. Pro Tools provides a quick way to reset a track and start mixing fresh, without any parameters locked to an automation graph. Often this is the easiest way to start a remix project, especially if the original automation was done elsewhere.

To remove automation for all automation graphs on a track:

1. With any automation playlist displayed, select the range of automation data to be removed. To select across the entire track, triple-click with the **SELECTOR** tool.

   To clear automation from multiple tracks, extend the selection across all of the target tracks.

2. Press **CONTROL+DELETE** (Mac) or **CTRL+BACKSPACE** (Windows). The automation data on all automation playlists will be deleted in the selected range.

   When deleting automation across multiple tracks, be sure that each track is displaying an automation graph.

Lesson 9 ■ Writing and Editing Automation   **245**

Review/Discussion

1. What are some of the parameters that you can automate in Pro Tools? (See "Understanding Automation" beginning on page 232.)

2. What are some of the differences between MIDI continuous controller data and Pro Tools audio automation? What kinds of tracks can Pro Tools audio automation be used on (Audio, MIDI, Instrument, Aux Input)? (See "Automation Playlists" beginning on page 232.)

3. What selector can you use to set the automation mode for a track? Where is this selector located? (See "Automation Modes" beginning on page 233.)

4. What is the difference between the Write, Touch, and Latch automation modes? (See Table 9.1 beginning on page 234.)

5. When might you suspend automation? What is the difference between the Suspend button and the Write Enable buttons? (See "Enabling and Suspending Automation" beginning on page 234.)

6. What are the advantages of using Touch or Latch mode over using Write mode? In what scenarios would you use Latch mode? When would it make more sense to use Touch mode instead? (See "Writing Automation Selectively" beginning on page 235.)

7. What are two ways to display an automation playlist in the Edit window? (See "Viewing Automation" beginning on page 236.)

8. What are some common automation graphs that you may work with? How might automation graphs be different for different types of parameters, with respect to the available vertical positions? (See "Automation Displays" beginning on page 238.)

9. What are some ways that the Grabber tool can be used to edit an automation playlist? How would you go about Nudging automation breakpoints? (See "Creating and Adjusting Breakpoint Automation Data" beginning on page 238.)

10. What are some ways that the Pencil tool can be used to edit an automation playlist? (See "Drawing Automation" beginning on page 239.)

11. How is cutting automation data different from deleting automation data? (See "Cutting Automation Versus Deleting Automation" beginning on page 241.)

12. What will be the result if you copy automation (Edit > Copy) from a track displaying the Volume automation graph and paste the automation (Edit > Paste) on a track displaying Pan automation? (See "Using Cut, Copy, and Paste Commands" beginning on page 242.)

13. How would you go about duplicating the volume automation for a track onto Send B for the track? (See "Pasting to a Different Automation Type" beginning on page 243.)

14. How can you delete individual breakpoints in an automation graph? How can you delete a range of automation breakpoints? (See "Deleting Breakpoints on the Displayed Automation Graph" beginning on page 244.)

15. How can you clear all automation on a displayed automation graph? What modifier can you use to clear the automation across all automation graphs for a track? (See "Clearing Automation for the Displayed Automation Graph" and "Clearing Automation for All Automation Graphs" beginning on page 244.)

To review additional material from this chapter, see the PT110 Study Guide module available through the Elements|ED online learning platform at ElementsED.com.

EXERCISE 9

Using Automation

Pro Tools offers extremely powerful automation features for both music and video post-production. Fortunately, these automation features are also relatively easy to learn. Mastering the basic automation concepts is the first step to using more sophisticated automation in your own sessions.

In this exercise, you will enable and record real-time automation, view and edit automation data, and draw automation data with the Pencil tool.

Duration: 25 Minutes

Getting Started

For this exercise, you will add some basic automation to the commercial that you used for Exercise 5. To get started, you will open the session you created for Exercise 5. If that session is not available, you can use the *Ugly Duckling.ptxt* session template to create a new session.

Open the session and save a copy:

1. Locate and open the 110 Exercise 5 [Your Initials].ptx session file that you created previously.

> If your Exercise 5 session is not available, open the *Ugly Duckling.ptxt* session template [PT110 Exercise Media (v12.8) > 04 Ugly Duckling > Ugly Duckling.ptxt) to create a new session.
>
> Name the new session 110 Exercise 9 [Your Initials] and save it to the class files location for your course. Then skip to the next section.

2. Choose FILE > SAVE AS.

3. Navigate to the class files location for your course and create a new folder named 110 Exercise 9 [Your Initials].

4. Save the session in the newly created folder as 110 Exercise 9 [Your Initials].

Enabling Automation

Before recording real-time automation on a track, you'll need to verify that the parameters and tracks you want to affect are automation-enabled. For this part of the exercise, you will enable volume automation for the Music track.

Verify that volume automation is globally enabled:

1. Open the Automation window by selecting WINDOW > AUTOMATION or pressing COMMAND+[4] (Mac) or CTRL+[4] (Windows). (See Figure 9.21.)

Figure 9.21 Automation window (standard Pro Tools shown)

2. Verify that the **VOL** button is lit red, indicating that volume automation is enabled for the session.

3. When finished, close the Automation window.

Set the Automation mode for the Music track:

1. Locate the **Music** track.

2. Click the **Automation Mode selector**. The Automation Mode selector menu will appear.

3. Select **Touch** automation mode. The track is now ready to begin recording automation.

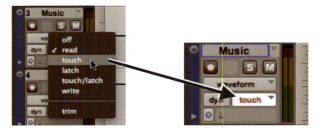

Figure 9.22 Using the Automation Mode selector to enable Touch mode

> **Discussion Point #1**
>
> Why is it important that the Vol button is enabled (lit red) in the Automation window? Will it matter whether the other buttons in this window are enabled? Why or why not?

Recording Touch Automation

In this section, you will ride the Volume fader on the **Music** track to create a better balance between the music and the dialog.

Record volume automation on the Music track:

1. Choose **Window > Memory Locations** to open the Memory Locations window.

2. In the Memory Locations window, click on location **99 MX Fader** to display the fader window for the **Music** track and locate the cursor to the beginning of the session.

3. Press **Zoom Preset 2** to set an appropriate zoom level.

4. Press Return (Mac) or Enter (Windows) and play back the session to review the music and identify areas to automate. The overall goals for your automation pass should include the following:

- Keep the music relatively loud (near current levels) at the very beginning to introduce the guitar theme.
- Lower the music during the middle section so it doesn't obscure the actor's dialog (around –7dB).
- Raise the music again under the narrator's voice-over at the end.
- Fade the music out before reaching the END marker on the Markers ruler.

5. Play back the session a second time to perform the automation. Click and drag the Music track's fader to modify the level of the music.

   Note: Because you are working in Touch mode, you will need to hold the mouse down while writing automation.

6. Stop playback when you've played through the entire session.

7. Play the session again to verify that your automation was successfully recorded.

> **Discussion Point #2**
>
> What would happen if you were to release the mouse during your automation pass in Step 5 above? Would the result be any different if you were working in Latch mode? Why or why not?

Viewing and Editing Automation

After recording volume automation, you can graphically view and edit the data using the volume automation playlist. You can also draw automation on any available automation playlist and use standard editing techniques to clean up existing automation.

Viewing Volume Automation

To get started, you will display the volume automation on the MUSIC track.

View the volume playlist on the Music track:

1. Click the **TRACK VIEW SELECTOR** on the MUSIC track. The Track View menu will appear.

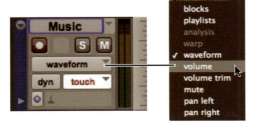

Figure 9.23 Using the Track View selector to select Volume view

2. Select **VOLUME**. The volume automation playlist will display on the track.

3. Click on **ZOOM PRESET 1** to zoom out so you can see the entire automation playlist.

Figure 9.24 Music track with the volume automation playlist visible

Nudging Automation

Next, you will use nudging to make subtle changes to the existing automation.

Nudge the volume automation on the Music track:

1. Set the Nudge value to **1 FRAME** (**00:00:00:01.00**).

   Figure 9.25 Setting the Nudge value

2. Using the **SELECTOR** tool, select the final curve of volume automation on the Music track.

   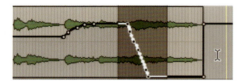

   Figure 9.26 Selecting automation

3. Use the **[+]** and **[-]** keys on the numeric keypad to nudge the automation and fine-tune your fade-out. Try to make the fade-out conclude precisely at the **END** marker.

Drawing Automation

In this part of the exercise, you will automate a reverb plug-in on the **FX** track using drawing techniques. To get started, you will display the automation playlist for the Wet/Dry parameter of the D-Verb plug-in.

Draw automation for the Wet/Dry parameter:

1. Click the **TRACK VIEW SELECTOR** on the FX track and choose **(FX A) D-VERB > WET/DRY**.

   The Wet/Dry automation playlist will display on the track.

   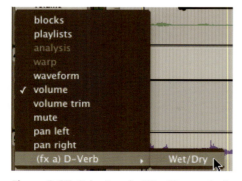

   Figure 9.27 Selecting the Wet/Dry track view

2. Locate the Explosion clip near the **ADD REVERB** marker.

3. Click and hold on the **PENCIL** tool and choose Line from the pop-up menu. The Line Pencil tool will become active.

4. Using the Pencil tool, draw an upwards line on the Wet/Dry automation graph to increase the mix from 0% to around 50 or 60% across the beginning of the Explosion clip.

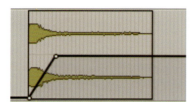

Figure 9.28 Wet/Dry mix automation

5. Play the explosion to hear the result. Feel free to redraw and experiment with the automation.

Deleting Automation

The **ATMOS** track includes some unwanted automation data. In this section, you will delete the automation using either the Grabber or the Selector tool.

Delete an automation breakpoint:

1. Locate the **ATMOS** track and set its track view to **VOLUME**. An errant breakpoint is causing the Wind clip to become gradually quieter over course of the session.

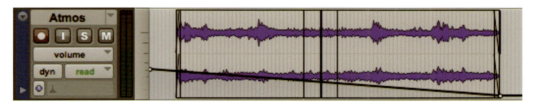

Figure 9.29 Volume view on the Atmos track

2. Delete the breakpoint at the end using one of the following methods:

   - Using the **SELECTOR** tool, make a selection that includes the breakpoint and press the **DELETE** key.
   - Using the **GRABBER** tool, hold **OPTION** (Mac) or **ALT** (Windows) and click on the breakpoint.

With the breakpoint deleted, the **ATMOS** track can now be heard throughout the session.

> **Discussion Point #3**
>
> What is the difference between using the Selector tool and the Grabber tool in Step 2 above? Does it matter which method you use in this scenario? Would your choice of tools be different in a different scenario? If so, why?

Finishing Up

Before exiting Pro Tools, you should play through the session to make sure you are satisfied with the results. You will also need to save your work for future use or to submit for a grade.

Listen to the results and save the session:

1. Press **RETURN** (Mac) or **ENTER** (Windows) to return to the start of the session.

2. Play back the session to hear the final results.

3. When finished, save and close the session. That concludes this exercise.

Remember that you cannot close a Pro Tools session by closing its windows. You must choose CLOSE SESSION from the FILE menu.

LESSON 10

Using Advanced Mixing Techniques and Creating Final Media

The advanced mixing features in Pro Tools enable users to work efficiently, maximizing the power of their system while achieving optimum audio results. Having the ability to work with groups of tracks, create submixes, and modify a mix at any level—from high-level balancing to granular-level tweaking—opens worlds of possibilities for shaping a Pro Tools mix.

GOALS

- **Work with sets of tracks**
- **Create submixes**
- **Create Mix and Edit groups**
- **Modify Mix and Edit groups**
- **Create final media for deliverables and archives**

Key topics from this lesson are included in the *Pro Tools 12 Essential Training: 110* course on Lynda.com, available here: alpp.us/PT110_Online.

254 PT110: Pro Tools Fundamentals II

This lesson introduces some of Pro Tools' advanced mixing options, such as working with submixes, creating Mix and Edit groups, and creating final mixes and archives. The processes discussed in this lesson will help you to speed up your mixing workflow, simplify your mixing environment, easily modify subsets of tracks, and create final deliverables for your projects.

Working with Track Subsets

When you work on sessions with large numbers of tracks, you will commonly find yourself needing to apply the same action to multiple tracks simultaneously. In the Pro Tools 101 book, you learned that the **OPTION** modifier (Mac) or **ALT** modifier (Windows) can be used for a Do-To-All function, allowing you to easily apply a change across all of your tracks at once. In cases where you need to apply a change to a select subset of tracks, you can use the Do-To-Selected modifier set instead.

Alternatively, you can create a submix of selected tracks and control their output using an Aux Input track.

Using the Do-To-Selected Function

To simultaneously perform an action across a subset of tracks in a session, you need to first select the target tracks so their nameplates are highlighted. You can select an individual track by clicking on its track nameplate or by clicking on its track name in the Track List.

To select multiple tracks, do the following:

- Select the first track; then **SHIFT-CLICK** to extend the selection across a contiguous range of tracks.

- Select one or more tracks; then **COMMAND-CLICK** (Mac) or **CTRL-CLICK** (Windows) to add or remove tracks non-contiguously.

With the target tracks selected, holding the Do-To-Selected modifiers will let you apply a change to the selected tracks only:

- **OPTION+SHIFT** (Mac)

- **ALT+SHIFT** (Windows)

Example 10.1: Soloing and Resizing Drum Tracks (without Groups)

In a session with multi-track drums, you will commonly need to hear the drums in isolation for mixing or editing purposes. One way to accomplish this is to select all the drum tracks (click on the first drum track in the Track List; then Shift-click on the last drum track), and then hold **OPTION+SHIFT** (Mac) or **ALT+SHIFT** (Windows) while clicking on the **SOLO** button for any individual drum track. All selected tracks will be soloed.

When working in the Edit window, you can use the same technique to resize the drum tracks: select the tracks; then hold **OPTION+SHIFT** or **ALT+SHIFT** while selecting a track height for any drum track. All selected tracks will resize to the selected height.

Submixing Tracks

To help control levels and processing in a large mix, you can assign a group of related tracks to a single fader. This process, known as creating a submix, allows a single Aux Input track to control the overall output of multiple combined tracks that are routed through it. Summing to an Aux Input enables you to easily apply effects to a group of tracks and centralizes volume, panning, and send control for the submix.

The following example illustrates how to create a submix to control the volume of all elements in a set of tracks (for example, a group of vocals, a set of sound effects, or a drum kit).

To use an Aux Input to control a mono or stereo submix:

1. Choose **TRACK > NEW**, select a Mono or Stereo Aux Input track, and click **CREATE**.

   It can be helpful to rename the track as well. For example, you might name the track for a vocal submix Vox Sub.

2. Set the output for all tracks that you want included in the submix to an available mix bus using the tracks' **AUDIO OUTPUT PATH SELECTORS**. Route the output for each included track to the same bus.

> To assign an output for multiple tracks at the same time, you can select each of the tracks and then hold OPTION+SHIFT (Mac) or ALT+SHIFT (Windows) while assigning the output on one of the tracks.

Figure 10.1 Vocal tracks routed to a common internal mix bus (Bus 3–4)

3. Set the input for the Aux Input track to correspond to the internal mix bus you chose in Step 2, using the **AUDIO INPUT PATH SELECTOR**. (See Figure 10.2.)

Figure 10.2 The bus used for the submix (Bus 3–4) is routed to the input of the Aux Input track (Vox Sub).

4. Set the output of the Aux Input track to your main stereo outputs using the **Audio Output Path selector** (typically, this will be analog outputs 1–2 of your audio interface).

Figure 10.3 The Aux Input track's output is routed to the main stereo outputs.

5. Solo-safe the Aux Input track by **Command-clicking** (Mac) or **Ctrl-clicking** (Windows) on the track's **Solo** button. (This will allow the track to stay live when you solo one of the tracks in the submix.)

The Volume Fader on the Aux Input track will now control the output levels of all tracks in the submix. You can also apply inserts and sends to the track, globally affecting all tracks in the submix. This conserves processing power and also allows an effect to be quickly added to multiple tracks simultaneously.

Routing Signals Using Paths and Selectors

In the process of routing a subset of tracks to a common destination, such as a submix track or an effects return, you often have to use Input, Output, and Send selectors on multiple different tracks. For routing within a session, you can use any available internal mix bus. You learned in Lesson 1 that the mix busses you configure in I/O Setup appear as available choices in track selector menus.

To simplify common signal routing tasks, you can also use the **TRACK** or **NEW TRACK** options that appear in an Output or Send selector menu.

Routing with Busses (Recap)

To route signals internally, you typically choose an existing bus path using the Input, Output, or Send selectors on the associated tracks. When configuring a submix or an effect return, this signal path will need to be connected from each of the source tracks and also connected to the input of the destination track.

Bus paths that are already in use and fully routed will display with orange text in selector menus.

To route a signal to or from a track using an existing bus path:

1. Click on the track's Input, Output, or Send selector. The associated selector menu will appear.

2. Select the desired internal mix bus from the Bus submenu.

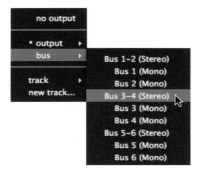

Figure 10.4 Selecting Bus 3-4 from a track's Output Path selector menu

Routing to Tracks

To speed up the process of creating submixes and effects returns, Pro Tools lets you use Output and Send selectors to route signals directly to an existing track or to a new track. When routing to an existing track, you can select the desired destination from the **TRACK** submenu. To create a new track to use as a send or submix destination, you can select the **NEW TRACK** option instead.

Figure 10.5 Existing track destinations available from a Send selector menu

Routing to an Existing Track

Selecting an existing track will automatically connect the output or send to the selected track as follows:

1. If no input is assigned on the destination track:

   - A new bus will be added to the I/O settings and named to match the destination track.

   - The bus will be routed to the input of the selected destination track.

2. The source track's output or send will be assigned to the bus connected to the destination track's input.

To route an output or send to an existing track:

1. Click on the Output or Send selector on the source track.

Figure 10.6 Clicking to assign a send at position F (top of the image)

2. Select **TRACK** from the pop-up menu and choose the desired destination track from the submenu.

Figure 10.7 Selecting the Fat Delay track as the send destination

A bus will be assigned, routing the signal from the output or send of the source track to the input of the destination track.

Routing to a New Track

Selecting **NEW TRACK** from an Output or Send selector will open the New Track dialog box, where you can configure the details for the destination track. As above, Pro Tools will create a new bus routed to the destination track's input, name the bus to match the track, and assign the bus to the output or send of the source track.

To route an output or send to a new track:

1. Click on the Output or Send selector on the source track.

Figure 10.8 Assigning a second send on the track, at position G

2. Select **New Track** from the pop-up menu. The New Track dialog box will appear.

Figure 10.9 The New Track dialog box

3. Configure the track parameters and enter a name for the track.

4. Click **Create**. A new track will be created and a bus will be assigned, routing the signal from the output or send of the source track to input of the new track.

 To quickly route a set of tracks to a common destination, select the tracks and then hold the Do-To-Selected modifiers (Option/Alt+Shift) while selecting Track or New Track from a Send or Output selector for one of the tracks.

Grouping Tracks

While submixing gives you one method of controlling the output of a set of tracks, another method is to link the parameters on a set of tracks using Mix and Edit groups. Edit groups are useful to ensure that a certain set of tracks is always edited in an identical manner. Mix groups are useful when you want to affect several faders at once across multiple tracks, allowing you to keep the relative volume of the tracks consistent to preserve their balance.

The track grouping functions in Pro Tools link tracks and their controls, allowing you to manipulate any set of tracks as a group. You can create a group as either a Mix group or an Edit group, or both.

Understanding Mix and Edit Groups

Pro Tools provides the following grouping features:

- The ability to create up to 104 groups, in four banks of 26 Group IDs (a through z)
- The ability to create Mix groups, Edit groups, or combined Mix/Edit groups
- The ability to create nested groups (groups can contain subgroups)

Mix groups allow you to preserve relative fader or controller levels among a set of tracks as you adjust or automate your mix. Edit groups allow you to apply edit operations, AudioSuite processing, and Elastic Audio operations consistently across a set of tracks.

Edit Group Parameters

Edit groups affect the following track parameters:

- Track views
- Track heights
- Track timebase settings
- Elastic Audio plug-in assignments

- Audio and MIDI editing functions
- Playlist views
- Selection-based processing (such as AudioSuite processing and the Consolidate command)
- Automation editing functions

 Edit operations are not applied to members of a group that are hidden in the Track List. Be sure that all group members are displayed when performing edits that could affect the timing between tracks.

Mix Group Parameters

Mix groups can be configured to affect the following track parameters, based on the selected group attributes:

- Main volume level
- Track panning
- Automation mode settings
- Track mute settings
- Track solo settings
- Record enables
- Send levels
- Send panning
- Send mute settings
- Insert controls (plug-ins)

 Unlike editing operations, mix operations are applied to hidden tracks.

Example 10.2: Soloing and Resizing Drum Tracks using Groups

Creating a group for multi-track drums will simplify the processes of isolating the drums in the mix and resizing the drum tracks. To link the solo controls across the drum tracks, create a Mix group for the tracks. In the Create Group dialog box, be sure to enable the **SOLOS** checkbox.

To link the track heights across the drum tracks, create an Edit group for the tracks. To add track height control to the above-described solo control for a group, create the group as an Edit and Mix group with the **SOLOS** checkbox enabled.

After you've created the Edit and Mix group, soloing any member track will solo the entire group, and changing the track height of any member track will change the height of all tracks in the group. To regain independent control over a member track, you can either hold **CONTROL** (Mac) or **START** (Windows) while making a change on the track or disable the group prior to making the change.

Creating a Mix or Edit Group

You can create a track group anytime to make adjustments that affect multiple tracks simultaneously.

To create a track Mix or Edit group:

1. In the Mix or Edit window, select all of the tracks you wish to include in the group. You can use **SHIFT-CLICK** to select a range of adjacent tracks or **COMMAND-CLICK** (Mac) or **CTRL-CLICK** (Windows) to add or remove individual tracks.

   Figure 10.10 Selecting tracks to include in a group

2. Do one of the following:

   - Choose **TRACK > GROUP**.
   - Choose **NEW GROUP** from the **GROUP LIST POP-UP** menu (Edit or Mix window).
   - Press **COMMAND+G** (Mac) or **CTRL+G** (Windows).

   Figure 10.11 Creating a new group from the Group List pop-up menu

   The **CREATE GROUP** dialog box will open. (See Figure 10.12.)

3. In the dialog box, enter a name for the group, choose a Group ID from the dropdown list, and select a group type. You can create an Edit group, a Mix group, or a dual-type Mix/Edit group.

   Figure 10.12 Create Group dialog box

If you do not select a Group ID in the Create Group dialog box, Pro Tools will automatically assign the next available ID to the new group.

4. If needed, add or remove tracks for the group by selecting tracks in the Available list or the Currently in Group list and clicking the appropriate button (**Add** or **Remove**).

 With tracks selected in the Create Group dialog box, press A or R on your keyboard to add or remove the tracks, respectively.

5. Select the group attributes (linked mixing parameters) under the **Attributes** or **Globals** tab.

 The settings under the Globals tab will be in effect if the Follow Globals checkbox is selected. Otherwise, the settings under the Attributes tab will be in effect.

6. When finished, click **OK**. The new group will be added to the appropriate Group List; dual-type groups will appear in both the Edit Group List (Edit window) and the Mix Group List (Mix window).

Activating and Deactivating Groups

When a group is active, its members' controls are linked. Moving a fader of any member of an active Mix group will cause the faders for all other members to move relative to it. Likewise, changing other linked Mix parameters, such as solos or mutes, will affect all members of the group, and performing Edit operations will simultaneously affect all members of any active Edit groups.

Toggling the State of Individual Groups

Groups become active (enabled) when they are created. You can disable and re-enable groups at any time as needed.

To enable/disable an individual group:

- In the **Group List**, click the name of a group to enable/disable the group. The group name becomes highlighted when the group is enabled (active) and becomes unhighlighted when disabled (inactive).

Figure 10.13 Active groups in the Group List

 You do not need to Shift-click to enable or disable multiple groups.

Globally Suspending Groups

You can also globally suspend all groups, making any enabled groups temporarily inactive.

To temporarily suspend all groups, do one of the following:

- Click on the **Group List pop-up** selector at the top of the Group List and choose **Suspend All Groups**.

– Or –

- Press **Command+Shift+G** (Mac) or **Ctrl+Shift+G** (Windows).

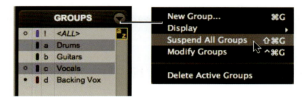

Figure 10.14 Suspending groups from the Group List pop-up menu

When groups are suspended, the Group List will be dimmed. Enabled groups will temporarily be ignored (inactive) without being toggled to a disabled state.

Figure 10.15 Group names dimmed to indicate that they are currently suspended

To re-activate all enabled groups again, repeat the previous step.

Unlinking Mix and Edit Group Enables

By default, group enabling is linked between the Mix and Edit windows for dual-type Mix/Edit groups. These groups appear in both the Edit window and the Mix window and are enabled/disabled in both windows in tandem—when you enable the group in one window, it also becomes enabled in the other.

In some cases, however, you might prefer not to have enabling of the Mix/Edit groups linked. For example, a large group you use in the Mix window might contain smaller, nested groups. In the Edit window, you might want to perform editing tasks within one of the smaller groups while leaving the larger group enabled in the Mix window.

By disabling the Link Mix/Edit Group Enables preference, you can work with different groups enabled in each of the two windows. To change this preference, choose **Setup > Preferences** and click the **Mixing** tab. The Link Mix/Edit Group Enables checkbox is available under the Setup section in the upper left.

Working with Groups

Once you've created your Mix and Edit groups, you can use them to show and hide tracks and select tracks based on group membership. You can also modify or delete any of your groups at any time.

Identifying Group Membership

When a track is a member of an active group, its Group ID displays the active group name with a lowercase letter. If a track is a member of more than one active group, an uppercase letter is displayed with the name of the topmost group, or parent group, to which the channel belongs.

The Group ID displays in the Group ID Indicator just above the pan controls in the Mix window.

Figure 10.16 Group IDs Indicators for tracks that belong to various groups

To display a list of the active groups that a channel belongs to, click the channel's Group ID Indicator in the Mix window. A pop-up menu will appear listing the group names. Each group name, in turn, will have a submenu that provides a list of available actions for the group, including options for showing and hiding tracks in the group.

To display a list of member tracks for a group, mouse over **TRACKS** in the submenu.

Figure 10.17 Displaying a list of active groups that a track belongs to and the actions available for each group

---

Determining Group Priority

Group priority on each track is determined based on two factors: the size of each active group and the creation order of the active groups.

Group Size. Larger groups will always have priority over smaller groups. For example, if group **c** includes 7 members and group **d** includes 10 members, group **d** will take priority on any tracks that the two groups share.

Creation Order. Older groups will have priority over newer groups of the same size. If group membership is subsequently modified, older membership will have priority over newer membership on a track-by-track basis. For example, if groups **d** and **e** both have 10 members, the group that was created first will take priority on any tracks that they share. Assuming the groups have been created in order, group **d** will take priority.

If the membership of an older group **c** is increased from 7 tracks to 10 tracks, group **c** will take priority over groups **d** and **e** for any shared tracks that it originally included (tracks with older membership in group **c**); group **d** or **e** will take priority for any shared tracks that have been newly added (tracks with older membership in one of those groups).

Selecting Members of a Group

You can quickly select all the tracks in a group from the Groups List.

To select the members of a group:

- Click in the column to the left of a group name to select the tracks in the group. A filled-in circle will appear next to the group name, and the included tracks will become selected in the Mix and Edit windows.

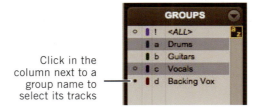

Click in the column next to a group name to select its tracks

Figure 10.18 Selecting members of a group

A filled-in circle next to a group name indicates that all of the members of the group are currently selected, and no members from outside the group are selected. A hollow circle indicates that only some members of the group are currently selected.

It is also possible to have a circle with a dot displayed next to a group name. This symbol indicates that all members of the group are currently selected as well as some tracks that are not group members.

> ### Example 10.3: Routing Group Members to a Send
>
> Setting up groups early on in a session can simplify signal routing tasks. This is especially true when you need to route multiple tracks to the same send destination for effects processing or other purposes. If the target tracks are already members of a Mix or Edit group, you can easily route the tracks as a group, even though send routing is not linked via group membership.
>
> To route all tracks that are members of a **Dialog** group to a reverb send, for example, you can click to the left of the Dialog group in the Group List to select all of the member tracks. You can then hold **OPTION+SHIFT** (Mac) or **ALT-SHIFT** (Windows) while clicking on a send selector for one of the tracks and selecting the reverb bus. All selected tracks will route to the same send destination, effectively sending the entire group to the reverb.

Modifying a Group

You can rename groups, add or remove group members, and make any other modifications necessary at any time. Pro Tools provides multiple methods for modifying a group.

 The one group characteristic you cannot modify is the Group ID; to change a Group ID, you need to delete the group and recreate it with the desired new ID.

To modify a group:

1. Do one of the following:
   - Choose **MODIFY GROUPS** from the Group List pop-up menu. (See Figure 10.19.)

- In the Mix window, click the **GROUP ID** indicator on a track and choose **MODIFY** from the Group ID indicator pop-up menu.

- Right-click on a group name in the Group List and choose **MODIFY** from the pop-up menu.

Figure 10.19 Modifying groups using the Group List pop-up menu

The Modify Groups dialog box will open.

2. In the dialog box, choose the Group ID for the group that you want to update. (See Figure 10.20.)

3. Modify the group name, type, options, and track membership for the selected group as desired.

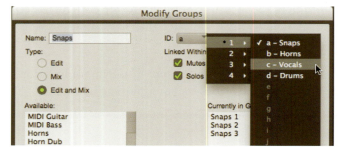

Figure 10.20 Selecting a group to modify

4. Choose additional Group IDs, if desired, and modify each as needed.

5. Click **OK** to close the dialog box. The groups will be updated to reflect the changes you made to each.

Deleting a Group

You can delete a single group or delete multiple groups at once.

To delete a single group, do one of the following:

- In the Mix window, click the **GROUP ID** indicator on a track and choose **DELETE** from the Group ID indicator pop-up menu.

  – Or –

- Right-click on the group name in the Group List and choose **DELETE** from the pop-up menu.

To delete multiple groups:

1. In the Group List, activate the groups you wish to delete so that they are highlighted. All groups you wish to keep should be inactive (not highlighted).

2. From the Group List pop-up menu, choose **DELETE ACTIVE GROUPS**.

Lesson 10 ■ Using Advanced Mixing Techniques and Creating Final Media   267

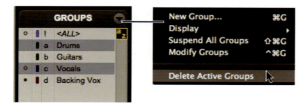

Figure 10.21 Deleting active groups from the Group List pop-up menu

The Delete Groups Warning dialog box will appear.

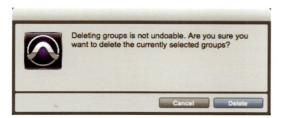

Figure 10.22 The Delete Groups Warning dialog box

3. To proceed, click **DELETE**. The active groups will be deleted from the Group List. To make your remaining groups active again, highlight the desired groups to activate them.

 This command deletes ALL ACTIVE groups. Use this command with caution; be sure to deactivate any groups you wish to keep prior to proceeding.

Using the All Group

In every session, Pro Tools automatically creates a special group known as the **ALL** group. When this group is active, it overrides all other groups in the session, combining all tracks in the session into a single large group. The All group is useful for applying global changes to all tracks in the session.

All group enable/disable

Figure 10.23 The All group displays at the top of the Group List in both the Mix and Edit windows.

Membership in the All group cannot be modified and the group cannot be deleted.

Example 10.4: Attenuating a Mix with the All Group

As you add tracks to a session, the levels hitting your main outputs will gradually increase. If you find that you need to lower the overall output to prevent clipping midway through your work on a session, you can turn to the All group for help.

Rather than trying to lower each individual fader in the session by a set amount and struggling to maintain the current balance, you can enable the All group and then pull a single fader down. All faders in the session will attenuate equally, maintaining their levels relative to one another.

When finished, disable the All group to regain individual control over each track.

Groups and Automation

Recording automation to one member of an active group will record the same automation for all other members of the group. Track grouping can affect the recording of Volume fader automation, mute automation, and send level and send mute automation. Depending upon your automation goals, you might want to enable or disable grouping for specified tracks and/or parameters.

Groups and Elastic Audio

Elastic Audio–enabled tracks can be included in Edit groups. Applying Elastic Audio processing to a track that is part of an active Edit group likewise applies it to all other tracks that are members of the Edit group.

Editing Event markers on a track that is part of an Edit group will affect all other member tracks for the group. Similarly, adding or moving Warp markers on a member track will add new Warp markers on all other Elastic Audio–enabled tracks within the Edit group.

Creating Final Media

When you are working in the final stages of a project, you will often need to create a mixdown of a CD-ready disk file. You may also need to create a compact, self-contained copy of the entire session for archive and backup purposes and/or for delivery to the client. Each of these processes requires certain steps to optimize your results.

Creating a CD-Compatible Bounce

To create a CD-ready mixdown from a 24-bit or 32-bit floating point session will require a bit-depth reduction during the bounce, to create a 16-bit file. To maintain the highest possible audio quality when reducing bit depth, it is necessary to apply *dither* to your audio. Dither is a form of randomized noise used to minimize quantization artifacts in digital audio systems. Quantization artifacts are most audible when an audio signal is near the low end of its dynamic range, such as during a quiet passage or fade-out.

By introducing dithering, you can reduce quantization artifacts with very low-level noise, minimizing artifacts as audio reaches low levels. With dithering, you make a trade-off between signal-to-noise performance and less-apparent artifacts. Proper use of dithering allows you to squeeze better subjective performance out of 16 bits (or whatever your destination bit depth is).

Adding Dither to the Master Fader

The most common application of dithering is on a master output as the last processor in the signal path when preparing a high bit-depth session for a mixdown that will subsequently be burned directly to an audio CD. In this case, you would insert the dither plug-in on a Master Fader to optimize the final output for a 16-bit word length.

 If you will be sending your mixed file to a mastering house, you'll want to keep it at 24-bit or 32-bit floating point resolution to retain the highest quality for the mastering process. (Check with the mastering house for their format requirements.) In this case, you should NOT apply dither.

The POW-r Dither Plug-In

The POW-r Dither plug-in utilizes an advanced type of dither that provides optimized word length reduction, allowing you to maintain the highest audio quality possible when reducing bit depth.

POW-r stands for Psychoacoustically Optimized Wordlength Reduction.

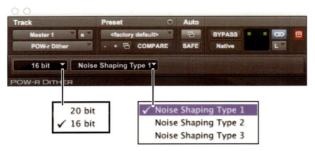

Figure 10.24 POW-r Dither plug-in

The POW-r Dither plug-in includes adjustable settings for bit resolution and noise shaping.

Bit Resolution

The Bit Resolution pop-up menu allows you to choose either 16- or 20-bit resolutions for POW-r Dither processing. Set this parameter to the maximum bit resolution of your destination.

- **16-bit:** Recommended for output to devices with a maximum resolution of 16 bits, such as DAT and audio CD recorders.

- **20-bit:** Recommended for output to devices that support a full 20-bit recording data path, such as certain ADATs and DAT recorders.

Noise Shaping

Noise shaping is a method of improving the signal-to-noise ratio of dither. Noise shaping exploits the Fletcher-Munson loudness contours, which graph the sensitivity of the human ear (in dB) across the frequency spectrum.

POW-r Dither noise shaping improves audio performance and lessens the perceptible noise inherent in dither by shifting noise components into a less audible range.

 The POW-r Dither plug-in is not appropriate for truncation stages that are likely to be further processed. POW-r Dither should be used only as the LAST insert in the signal chain (especially when using Type 1 Noise Shaping).

The POW-r Dither plug-in provides three types of noise shaping, each with its own characteristics. To optimize the results, you should try each noise shaping type and choose the one that adds the least amount of coloration to the audio being processed.

- **Type 1:** Has the flattest frequency spectrum in the audible range of frequencies. Type 1 dither uses a gentle second-order noise curve that is designed for less stereophonically complex material and material that has a fairly narrow dynamic range.

    Type 1 is generally recommended for solo instrument recordings and spoken-word recordings.

- **Type 2:** Has a psychoacoustically optimized noise-shaping curve. This is a slightly more aggressive fifth-order curve that uses additional noise shaping over a wide frequency range.

    Type 2 is recommended for material with moderate stereophonic complexity and is often suitable for rock and pop music.

- **Type 3:** Has a psychoacoustically optimized high-order noise-shaping curve. This is a more severe ninth-order curve, designed for full-spectrum, wide-stereo field material.

  Type 3 is especially suited to material with a broad dynamic range, such as classical and orchestral music; however, it can also be effective for rock and pop music.

Creating an Archive

After completing work on a session, it is useful to create a compact, self-contained archive of the session and all related media files. To facilitate file transfer and backup, you will want to reduce file sizes as much as possible by removing any unneeded content. However, it is important to follow certain precautions to protect against accidental data loss.

The recommended workflow for creating a final archive involves a three-step process:

1. Clear all unused files from the session without permanently deleting any audio.

2. Create a copy of the session, including all necessary parent files.

3. Compact the parent files to eliminate unused portions of the files.

You have already learned how to complete the first two steps in this process.

Step 1: Clear Unused Clips (Recap)

To clear the unused clips from your session, follow the steps outlined in Lesson 7 for selecting unused clips and removing them from your session. The steps are summarized below.

To remove unused clips:

1. From the Clip List pop-up menu, choose SELECT > UNUSED.

2. With the unused clips selected, choose CLEAR from the Clip List pop-up menu.

3. In the resulting dialog box, click REMOVE to remove the unused clips from the session without deleting them from disk.

Step 2: Create a Session Copy (Recap)

After clearing the unused clips, you can make a copy of the session with all of the remaining (used) clips. You will use this session copy for your final archive.

By using the Save Copy In command for this process, you can ensure that all of the files needed for the archive session are copied into the corresponding Audio Files and Video Files folders. This will also protect the original files against accidental data loss.

To create a self-contained session copy:

1. Choose FILE > SAVE COPY IN.

2. In the resulting dialog box, set the Session Parameters as desired.

3. In the Items to Copy section at the bottom of the dialog box, enable the AUDIO FILES checkbox. If the session contains video, also enable the MOVIE/VIDEO FILES checkbox.

4. Click OK to create the copy and navigate to the desired save location.

Step 3: Compacting Sound Files

The final step of the process is to reduce the size of the parent audio files in the copy by eliminating any unused portions of the files. This is a process known as compacting sound files. When you compact files, Pro Tools irretrievably deletes any portions of the parent files that are not currently used by a clip in the session.

When you compact files, you can include padding to retain extra audio on either side of the subset clip boundaries. This will allow you to add crossfades later or to trim the clip boundaries, should you need to make any edit adjustments in your session archive.

To compact sound files for the archive session:

1. Open the session copy that you created for your archive in Step 2 above.

    Be sure to use the session copy that you created and not the original session. Compacting files in the original session could lead to permanent data loss in any shared files referenced by the session.

2. From the Clip List pop-up menu, choose **SELECT > ALL** to select all of the clips currently in your session.

3. Choose **COMPACT** from the Clip List pop-up menu. The Compact Selected dialog box will open.

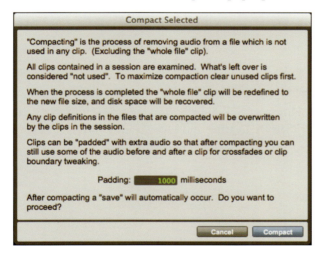

Figure 10.25 The Compact Selected dialog box

4. Choose a padding amount in milliseconds (1000 milliseconds=1 second).

5. Click **COMPACT**.

When the Compact operation completes, the session will automatically save. The compacted files will include only the portions of audio that you are currently using, plus any padding you selected.

 Never compact audio files that are referenced in other Pro Tools sessions.

 Because the Compact Selected command permanently deletes audio data, use this command only if you are sure that you have no further use for the unused audio data in any of your Pro Tools sessions.

Review/Discussion

1. How is the Do-To-Selected function useful? What keyboard modifier set is used to access Do-To-Selected functionality? (See "Using the Do-To-Selected Function" beginning on page 254.)

2. Describe the process of creating a drum submix. What kind of track is commonly used as a submix destination? (See "Submixing Tracks" beginning on page 255.)

3. What processes can you use to route the outputs of a set of tracks to a destination track? (See "Routing Signals Using Paths and Selectors" beginning on page 256.)

4. What is the purpose of grouping tracks? How many track groups can you create in a session? (See "Grouping Tracks" beginning on page 259.)

5. What are some of the parameters that are affected by Edit groups? What are some of the parameters that can be included in a Mix group? (See "Understanding Mix and Edit Groups" beginning on page 259.)

6. What is the keyboard shortcut to create a Mix or Edit group from selected tracks? (See "Creating a Mix or Edit Group" beginning on page 261.)

7. How can you enable or disable a single group? How can you globally suspend all groups? How can you visually tell when groups have been suspended? (See "Activating and Deactivating Groups" beginning on page 262.)

8. How can you identify group membership of tracks in the Mix window? (See "Identifying Group Membership" beginning on page 263.)

9. How can you quickly select all members of a group? How might this be useful? (See "Selecting Members of a Group" beginning on page 265.)

10. What are some options for modifying or deleting a group? (See "Modifying a Group" and "Deleting a Group" beginning on page 265.)

11. What is the purpose of the All group? Can you modify track membership or delete this group? (See "Using the All Group" beginning on page 267.)

12. When is it necessary to apply dither? Where should you insert a dither plug-in? (See "Creating a CD-Compatible Bounce" beginning on page 268.)

13. What is noise shaping used for in a dither plug-in? How is noise shaping used by the POW-r dither plug-in? (See "Noise Shaping" beginning on page 269.)

14. What are the steps involved in creating a session archive? Why is it important to use the Save Copy In command before compacting sound files? (See "Creating an Archive" beginning on page 270.)

 **To review additional material from this chapter, see the PT110 Study Guide module available through the Elements|ED online learning platform at ElementsED.com.**

EXERCISE 10

Mixing Techniques

Pro Tools a complete set of mixing tools for projects of all types and sizes. Even a modest Pro Tools system offers a sophisticated mixing feature set that will bring your project to completion with style.

In this exercise, you will use Mix and Edit groups, send and return effects, and processing on a Master Fader.

Duration: 25 Minutes

Getting Started

For this exercise, you will work with the same session you used for Exercise 6 and perform various mixing tasks. To get started, you will open the session you created for Exercise 6 and save a copy to a new location. If that session is not available, you can use the *Exercise 10.ptxt* session template to create a new session.

Open the session and save a copy:

1. Locate and open the 110 Exercise 6 [Your Initials].ptx session file that you created previously.

> If your Exercise 6 session is not available, open the *Exercise 10.ptxt* session template
> [PT110v12 Exercise Media (v12.8) > 05 Trouble Trouble > Ex10.ptxt] to create a new session.
>
> Name the new session 110 Exercise 10 [Your Initials] and save it to the class files location for your
> course. Then skip to the next section.

2. Choose FILE > SAVE AS.

3. Navigate to the class files location for your course and create a new folder named 110 Exercise 10 [Your Initials].

4. Save the session in the newly created folder as 110 Exercise 10 [Your Initials].

Using Mix Groups

In this section, you will set up a Mix group to create a proportional joining of the faders on the drum tracks.

Create a group for the drum tracks:

1. Press COMMAND+= (Mac) or CTRL+= (Windows) to toggle to the Mix window.

2. Select all of the drum tracks by clicking on the track nameplate for the first drum track (Kick), then holding SHIFT while clicking the track nameplate for the last drum track (Room Mics). The eight drum tracks will become selected.

Figure 10.26 Drum tracks selected in the Mix window

3. Choose **Track > Group** or press **Command+G** (Mac) or **Ctrl+G** (Windows) to create a new Mix and Edit group. The Create Group dialog box will appear.

4. Name the group "Drums" and deselect (uncheck) the **Follow Globals** option.

Figure 10.27 Unchecking Follow Globals in the Create Group dialog box

5. Click on the **Attributes** tab to configure the linked mixing attributes.

6. Enable the **Volume** checkbox to link the volume faders for the member tracks. (See Figure 10.28.)

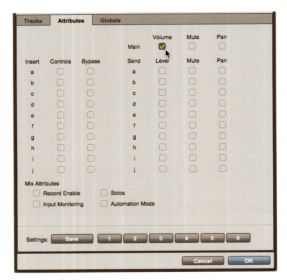

Figure 10.28 Checking the Volume attribute to enable it for the group

7. Click **OK** to close the dialog box.

    The **Drums** group will be created and made active in the Group List.

Balance the mix using active groups:

1. Locate the **Snaps** and **Horns** groups in the Group List (bottom left of the Mix window); click on each so that all three groups are active (highlighted).

Figure 10.29 Active groups in the Group List

2. Play back the session to monitor the mix as you make adjustments.

3. Balance the **Horns** group, **Drums** group, and **Snaps** group against the **MIDI Guitar** and **MIDI Bass** tracks. Try raising the level of each group by 3 to 5 dB and adjusting the overall balance between groups to taste.

4. When satisfied with the results, stop playback.

> **Discussion Point #1**
>
> What is the purpose of enabling each of the groups in Step 1 above before rebalancing the mix? How would you go about deactivating a group? Why might you want to deactivate a group?

Creating Send and Return Effects

In this section, you will create a send and return setup to add a delay to the session using the Route to Tracks feature in Pro Tools.

Route a Send to a New Track

To get started, you will create a new send on one of the Snaps tracks and route it to a new Aux Input. Then you will copy the send to the other two Snaps tracks.

Create a send to an Aux Track:

1. Click on the track nameplate for the **Reverb** track to select it. This will allow the new track you create to be placed adjacent to the **Reverb** track.

2. Locate the **Snaps 1** track and click on Send Selector B.

Figure 10.30 Clicking on Send Selector B for the Snaps 1 track

3. Select **NEW TRACK** from the Send Selector pop-up menu.

Figure 10.31 Selecting New Track from the Send Selector pop-up menu

The New Track dialog box will open.

4. Configure the dialog box for a stereo Aux Input track. Name the track **DDelay** and uncheck the **CREATE NEXT TO CURRENT TRACK** option.

Figure 10.32 The New Track dialog box configured for the Delay track

5. Click the **CREATE** button to create the new track and establish the send.

   A send window will open for the **Snaps 1** track.

6. In the Send window, raise the Send level to around -7.5. Close the send window when finished.

Duplicate the send to adjacent tracks:

1. **OPTION-DRAG** (Mac) or **ALT-DRAG** (Windows) on the **SEND ASSIGNMENT** button to copy it from the Snaps 1 track to the Snaps 2 track.

2. Repeat for the Snaps 3 track.

Figure 10.33 Copying a send by Option/Alt-dragging

Configure the Delay effects return:

1. Click on **INSERT SELECTOR A** on the DDelay track and select **MULTI-MONO PLUG-IN > DELAY > MOD DELAY III (MONO)**. The Mod Delay III plug-in window will open.

Figure 10.34 The Mod Delay III plug-in

2. In the Sync section towards the bottom of the plug-in window, click on the ¼ **NOTE** icon so that it becomes highlighted.

Figure 10.35 Enabling the ¼-note sync control

3. Raise the **FEEDBACK** (**FBK**) control to around **15** to **25%**; then close the plug-in window.

> ### Discussion Point #2
> What is the advantage of setting up the delay plug-in on an Aux Input track over placing the plug-ins on the Snaps tracks? When would you not want to use an Aux Input for a plug-in processor?

Enable Solo Safe Mode

Next you will need to enable Solo Safe mode for the DDelay effects return track.

Make the return Solo Safe:

1. COMMAND-CLICK (Mac) or CONTROL-CLICK (Windows) on the DDelay track's SOLO button to place the track in Solo Safe mode. The button will gray out on screen.

2. Play through the session to audition the delay effect, toggling SOLO on/off for each of the Snaps tracks.

3. Adjust the Volume fader for the Delay Aux Input track while playing back to set an appropriate level for your mix. (You may want to reduce the overall level of the delay by 5 dB or so.)

Adding Processing on the Master Fader

Now it's time to manage the overall output of your session. For this task, you'll be using the existing Master Fader track.

Add a Maximizer

In this section, you will add a maximizing plug-in to the Master Fader.

Add a maximizing plug-in:

1. Click INSERT SELECTOR A for the Master 1 track and select MULTICHANNEL PLUG-IN > DYNAMICS > MAXIM (STEREO). The Maxim plug-in window will open.

2. While playing back the session, configure the settings to get a consistently loud signal. Try setting the THRESHOLD between -5.0 and -8.0 dB and the CEILING around -0.3 dB.

Figure 10.36 The Maxim plug-in window

3. Stop playback and close the plug-in window when satisfied with the results.

Add Dither to the Session

In this section, you add the POW-r Dither plug-in to the Master Fader.

Add dither to the Master Fader:

1. Click on **INSERT SELECTOR B** for the Master 1 track and select **MULTICHANNEL PLUG-IN > DITHER > POW-R DITHER (STEREO)**. The POW-r Dither plug-in window will open.

2. In the plug-in window, select the options for **16-BIT** resolution and **NOISE SHAPING TYPE 2**.

Figure 10.37 The POW-r Dither plug-in configured on the Master Fader

3. Close the POW-r Dither plug-in window when finished.

> **Discussion Point #3**
>
> What is the purpose of using dither? Why might it be important to add dither to this session? When would you not want to add dither? Why not?

Finishing Up

To complete this exercise, you will need to save your work and, optionally, create a bounce to disk.

Bounce the session and save:

1. If directed by your instructor, bounce the session as follows:
   - Create an interleaved stereo 16-bit bounce of your session (**FILE > BOUNCE TO > DISK**).
   - Save or copy the bounce to the location specified by your instructor.

2. When finished, save and close your session. That completes this exercise.

 Remember that you cannot close a Pro Tools session by closing its windows. You must choose CLOSE SESSION from the FILE menu.

INDEX

A

AAC files, 41
absolute Time Scale, 90
ACID files, 41
ADAT, 7
Add Meter Change button, 65
Add Tempo Change button, 65
Advanced Search, 42
AES/EBU, 7
Aggregate I/O, 4
AIFF files, 40
alternate takes, 79
    Alternate Takes List, 79–80, 84–85
Alternates Match Criteria, 79, 84–85
Analysis view, 119, 121
archiving
    creating an archive, 270
audio channels, 53
audio clips, 100
audio files
    batch import, 49
    importing, 44
Audio Files Conform to Session Tempo, 60, 118
Audio Files folder, 41
audio interface, 4, 7
AudioSuite
    plug-ins, 12
    X-Form plug-in, 117
AudioSuite processing, 178–195
    applying processing, 184
    AudioSuite features, 178
    AudioSuite file naming, 185
    configuring AudioSuite controls, 181
    configuring plug-in parameters, 183
    Handle Length and Whole File options, 185
    using AudioSuite plug-ins, 179, 180
auditioning
    and waveform displays, 35
    audio files, 34
    Audition Path, 12, 36
    clip groups, 53
    during playback, 36
    from a Workspace browser, 35
    in a waveform display, 37
    in the Clip List, 49

    loop record takes, 85
    MIDI, 98, 99, 100
Automatically Copy Files on Import, 41
Automatically Create New Playlists When Loop
    Recording, 78
automation, 32
    adding and moving breakpoints, 238
    audio automation versus Continuous Controller
        automation, 233
    automatable controls, 232
    automation modes, 234
    automation playlists on Audio tracks, 232
    automation playlists on MIDI and Instrument
        tracks, 233
    clearing all graphs, 244
    clearing the displayed graph, 244
    cutting versus deleting, 241, 245
    cutting, copying, and pasting, 242
    deleting breakpoints, 244, 246
    drawing automation, 239
    enabling, 234
    Latch mode, 235
    Mute graph, 238
    nudging breakpoints, 239
    Pan graph, 238
    Paste Special mode (for pasting to a different
        automation type), 243, 246
    playing automation, 236
    Suspend button, 235
    suspending, 234
    Touch mode, 235
    viewing automation, 236
    Volume graph, 238
    Write Enable buttons, 235
auto-name memory locations, 73
Avid Audio Engine, 5
Avid Media Composer, 33

B

batch import, 49
Beat Detective, 50, 68
bit depth, 32
BPM, 66, 90, 91, 119

C

Cache Size, 5
Calculate Waveform, 36
Capture clip command, 192
Catalogs, 35
channel width, 14
clearing MIDI, 101
Click II plug-in, 69
click track
    alternative click sounds, 69
Click/Countoff Options dialog box, 69–70
clip groups, 45, 49, 51–53, 121
    channels, 53
    clip icons, 52
    file extension, 50
    file icon, 50
    file type, 50
    rules, 50
Clip List
    auditioning clips, 12, 186
    auditioning files, 49
    auditioning MIDI clips in, 100
    clip groups in, 51–53
    Compact command, 271
    deleting audio files, 191
    exporting clips as files, 193
    Find command, 186
    importing to, 40–41, 43, 46
    loop record takes in, 78–79
    MIDI clips in, 96
    removing clips, 191
    selecting multiple clips in the Clip List, 188
    selecting unused clips, 189
    working with, 185–194
clip loops
    creating, 171
    editing, 172
    editing with the Loop Trim tool, 173
    editing with the Trim tool, 173
    enable crossfades, 171
    flattening, 175
    modifying settings, 172
    removing, 175
    unlooping clips, 175
    working with, 170, 174
Clip Rating, 80
Clip Start and End, 80, 84
Clips view, 95, 100

clock source, 6–7
    external, 7
    internal, 7
Close Session command, 61, 88, 113
collaboration tools, 19
color-coding
    options, 204
    Preferences settings, 204
    track color bars, 205
Comments view, 18–19
Compact command, 271
compacting sound files, 271
Conform to Session Tempo, 37–38
Conform to Tempo command, 120
Consolidate Clip command, 192
Consolidate command, 49
Continuous Controller automation, 233
continuous controller events, 95
controller lane, 97
Counters, 83
countoff, 69–70
    enabling and disabling countoff, 69
Current Cursor display, 105
Current Meter display, 65
cutting MIDI, 101

D

DB-33, 93
Default Note Duration, 102, 103
Default Output Bus, 13
Default Thru Instrument, 99, 100
digital video, 32
disk cache, 5
dither
    adding dither, 268
    noise shaping, 269
    the POW-r Dither plug-in, 268
Do-To-Selected function, 254
Down arrow key, 71
drag-and-drop rendering (MIDI), 93–94
duplicate selected notes, 105

E

Edit cursor, 42, 96
Edit Window View selector, 16_17
Edit Window Views, 16

editing operations
  Layered Editing, 177
  MIDI versus Audio, 100
effects sends, 9
Elastic Audio, 91–92, 116–121
  Accordion Warp, 125
  analysis, 119
  Elastic Audio Plug-in selector, 116
  Elastic Audio processor, 37
  Elastic Properties window, 132–133
  Enable Elastic Audio on New Tracks, 118
  for pitch transposition, 133
  improving results, 129
  markers, 121
  plug-ins, 117
  quantizing, 127–128, 136
  Range Warp, 126
  Telescoping Warp, 124
  undoing pitch transposition, 135
  using Elastic Audio for tempo changes, 128
  using X-Form, 133
error suppression, 5
Event markers, 119–122, 157
  adding, 130
  deleting, 131
  editing, 130
  repositioning, 131
Event Sensitivity
  adjusting, 131
  and event confidence, 131
Expanded Transport, 83
Export Clips as Files command, 193
external clock, 7

F

fade settings
  Preferences, 145
  selecting, 148
Fades
  deleting fades, 153
  disabling fade linking, 150
  editing fades, 151–152
  Equal Gain, 149–150
  Equal Power, 149–150
  Equal Power versus Equal Gain, 150
  keyboard shortcut, 146
  slope/link settings, 149
  using presets, 150–151
  with the Smart Tool, 145

Fades dialog boxes, 146
  audition and preview controls, 147
  audition controls, 147
  fade shape settings, 148
  preview controls, 148
  slope/link settings, 149
file
  audition, 34–37
  search, 34
Follows First Selected MIDI Track setting, 99
force-copy, 41
Formant preservation, 117

G

General Properties, 74
Global Track Collaboration tools, 19
Graphic Tempo Editor, 64
Grid mode, 68
  Absolute Grid mode, 176
  Relative Grid mode, 176
Grid value, 102–103
Groups
  activating/deactivating Mix and Edit groups, 262
  creating Mix and Edit groups, 259
  deleting Mix and Edit groups, 266
  modifying Mix and Edit groups, 265
  selecting group attributes, 262
  the All Group, 267

H

H/W Buffer Size, 4–5, 99
Hardware Setup, 6–7
hiding tracks, 20
host-based performance, 4

I

I/O
  capacity, 32
  customizing I/O settings, 8
  I/O settings, 12, 24, 27
  I/O Setup, 10–13, 25–28, 36
  Last Used I/O settings, 9
  Stereo Mix I/O settings, 8
  the I/O view, 18, 29, 112–113
import
  audio, 46, 49
  import audio from a video file, 47

MIDI, 44
video, 33, 43, 56
Import commands, 45
Import Options, 44–47, 49
Import Session Data, 47–48, 58
Match Tracks, 48
inactive tracks, 48
index
update index, 35
inserts
hardware inserts, 208
on Audio tracks, 207
on Aux Input tracks, 207
on Master Fader tracks, 207, 221
plug-in inserts, 207
Inserts view, 110–111, 113
Instruments view, 98
internal clock, 7

J-L

key signature map, 44
Last Used I/O settings, 27
Latch automation mode, 235
Launch Control Panel, 7
Launch Setup App, 7
Layered Editing, 177–178
level meter, 98
Librarian menu, 111–112
link timeline and edit selection, 71, 76, 78
Loop Playback, 81, 85–86
Loop Preview, 38
Loop Record, 77–81, 86
loop record takes, 78, 84
low-latency domain, 4, 99

M

Main Timebase ruler, 71
markers, 74
Markers ruler, 65, 72, 74
Marquee Grabber, 102
Master Faders
creating, 222
uses of, 222
Match Tracks, 48
Mbox Pro, 7
memory locations, 72
auto-naming, 73
general properties, 72

recalling, 74
Memory Locations window, 72, 74–75
meter
default meter, 64
Meter Change window, 66
meter events, 64, 66
Meter Ruler, 64
Metronome button, 69
MIDI
connecting via a MIDI port, 86
connecting via a USB port, 86
drag-and-drop rendering, 93–94
MIDI channels, 53
MIDI clips, 95, 100
MIDI Controls, 65, 69, 83
MIDI Input selector, 97
MIDI keyboard, 85, 86, 87
MIDI Merge button, 81, 86
MIDI Merge mode, 81, 85, 86
MIDI Merge recording, 87
MIDI nodes for virtual instruments, 93
MIDI notes, 96, 100
MIDI Output selector, 97, 112, 113
MIDI Thru option, 98, 100
MIDI velocity meter, 98
MIDI volume, 98
rendering with Track Freeze, 94
triggering MIDI instruments, 92
MIDI Editor window, 20, 95
MIDI files
batch import, 49
importing, 44
import options, 43–44
mini-keyboard, 96, 104
Mix and Edit groups
activating/deactivating groups, 262
and Automation, 268
and Elastic Audio, 268
creating groups, 261
deleting, 266
Edit group parameters, 259
features, 259
Group ID indicator, 264
identifying group membership, 263
Mix group parameters, 260
modifying, 265
selecting group attributes, 262
selecting member tracks, 265
suspending groups, 262
the All Group, 267

Mix Window View selector, 16
Mix Window Views, 16
mixed multitrack clip group, 52
monitoring
    MIDI input, 99
monitoring latency, 4
Monophonic processor, 117
moving MIDI, 101
MP3 files, 41
multitrack clip groups, 50, 53
MXF files, 41

N

Narrow Mix view, 18
Native plug-ins, 5
    processing, 4
new tracks
    adding, 14–15, 28
New Workspace, 42
non-contiguous clip group, 52
note duration, 101
Notes view, 95–96, 102, 107

O

open session, 35
organ plug-in, 93

P

Pan Controls, 98
Paste Special Mode, 243
Pencil tool, 101
piano-roll, 96
placing MIDI, 101
playback, 98
Playback Engine, 4–5, 9
playlist, 78
    track playlist, 44
Playlists view, 78
plug-ins
    the plug-in window, 220
    using gain-based processors, 219
    using time-based processors, 219
Polyphonic processor, 117
post-fader sends, 209
pre- and post-roll
    disabling, 76
    enabling pre-roll, 76

flags, 75, 77
post-roll button, 75
pre-roll and loop recording, 78
pre-roll field, 75
setting and enabling, 76
settings, 70
toggling on/off, 77
values, 75
preamp, 93
pre-fader sends, 209
Preferences, 41, 99, 118–119
Pre-Separate Amount dialog box, 177
preserve note start times, 105
Preserve Tempo After Selection, 67
preview at the session tempo, 37
preview in context, 37
Pro Tools|First, 119
Pro Tools|HD Native, 32
Pro Tools|HDX, 32
Pro Tools Aggregate I/O, 7
Pro Tools HD software, 33
project documents, 2, 8, 14, 19
pulses per quarter note, 92
punch-in, 70, 75
punch-out, 70, 75

Q

quantizing, 121
    after recording (Quantize function), 155
    audio and MIDI, 154
    audio clips, 156
    Elastic Audio events, 157
    Input Quantize, 154
    MIDI data, 155
    MIDI note attributes, 158
QuickTime files, 41
    importing audio from, 47

R

RAM cache, 6
Real-time Elastic Audio processing, 116
Real-Time Properties
    enabling, 160
    floating window, 159, 160
    quantize, 161
    quantize options, 162
    track-based properties versus clip-based
        properties, 160

types of, 159
view in the Edit window, 159
Record Enable button, 86–87, 97
recorded takes, 79
Regroup command, 53
Change All, 53
relative Time Scale, 90, 93
Remove Warp command, 120
Rendered Elastic Audio processing, 116–117
Rendering
drag-and-drop rendering (MIDI), 93–94
using Track Freeze, 94
using Track Freeze, 94–95
Restore Previously Shown Tracks, 21
ReWire, 93
REX files, 41
Rhythmic Elastic Audio plug-in, 116
Rhythmic processor, 117
rotary-speaker cabinets, 93
routing signals
routing to paths, 257
routing to tracks, 257
rubato, 119
Ruler View selector, 16, 17, 64
Rulers, 16
Meter Ruler, 64
Tempo Ruler, 64

S

S/PDIF, 7
sample rate, 6, 32
default, 6
sample-based
changing to tick-based, 91
files, 119
timebases, 90
timing, 92
tracks, 50
saving selections, 74
Score Editor window, 20, 95
SD I files, 41
SD II files, 41
search, 34
selection-based memory locations, 74–75
sends
changing and removing sends, 219
choosing a send type, 209
copying a send, 218
creating a return, 212

default send level (Preferences setting), 210
expanded sends view, 211
FMP button, 217
Inverse Pan button, 217
Link button, 217
moving a send, 218
panner options, 217
send controls, 216
sends view areas, 211
setting the send level, 210
using send selectors, 209
using the Send window, 215
Separate command, 105
Separate Notes, 106
session data, 45
session documents, 2, 8, 14
session files, 34
Session Setup, 33
Show/Hide Lanes button, 97, 106
Shuffle mode, 52
signal paths
default signal paths, 11
renaming, 12, 15, 25
Smart Tool
creating fades with, 145
enabling, 144
using, 144
Snap To Bar, 65–66
Solo and Mute buttons, 97
Solo Safe mode, 214
sound effects, 44
Sound Libraries, 38, 39
Soundbase, 38–40
Spot dialog box, 44–45, 59–60
Spot mode, 44
stand-alone virtual instruments, 93
start point, 92
status indicators
Global Freeze Tracks indicator, 206
in the Edit window, 206
Mute indicator, 207
Solo indicator, 206
Task Manager Status indicator, 206
Submaster Tracks, 255
submixing, 9
subset clips, 49
surround mixing, 32
suspend the grid, 102
synthesizers, 92

T

Tags for Soundbase, 38–40
tempo
    applying tempo changes with Elastic Audio, 129
    default tempo, 64
    tempo change, 92
    Tempo Ruler, 64
tempo analysis, 116
Tempo Change window, 66
tempo changes
    conforming to, 119
    inserting, 65
Tempo Detection, 119
Tempo Event–generated Warp markers, 121, 122
tempo events, 64, 66
tempo map, 44, 119, 120, 121
Tempo Operations window, 64, 67, 68
Tempo ruler, 116, 119
tick values
    ticks per 1/8 note, 92
    ticks per quarter note, 92
tick-based
    changing to sample-based, 91
    files, 119
    tick-based timing and Elastic Audio, 128, 136
    timebases, 90
    timing, 92
    tracks, 50
Time Compression and Expansion, 92, 116
Time Operations window, 64
Time Properties, 74
Time Stamps, 80
timebase ruler
    main, 33
timecode, 44, 45
    Timecode ruler, 33
Timeline Out Point, 71
timeline selection, 71
Timeline Selection In Point, 71
Timeline Selection Out Point, 71–72
time-stamp, 84
Touch automation mode, 235
Track Collaboration controls, 19–20
Track Collaboration view, 20
Track controls, 98
Track Freeze, 94, 95
track height, 96

Track List, 20–21, 44, 48, 99–100, 112, 118
    importing to, 40
    pop-up menu, 21
track playlist, 76, 95
Track Show/Hide, 20–21
track timebase, 92
Track View selector, 96, 102
Track views
    for MIDI and Instrument tracks, 95
tracks
    track type icons, 205
transient detection, 116, 119
transient events, 119, 121
Transport controls, 79
transpose MIDI notes, 105
Transpose window, 133–134
Trim command, 105
Trim Notes, 106
Trim tool, 105
trimming MIDI, 101

U

Unfreezing a track, 95
Ungroup All command, 53
Ungroup command, 52
Up arrow key, 71

V

Vacuum plug-in, 112
Varispeed processor, 117
velocity
    Velocity controller lane, 107
    velocity stalks, 97, 106
    Velocity Trimmer, 102, 106
    Velocity view, 95, 97, 106–107
video
    clips, 32
    edit video clips, 32
    editing, 32
    importing video files, 45
    Video Engine, 57
    video file batch import, 49
    video file import options, 43, 44
    video playback, 33
    Video track, 32
    Video window, 33, 57

virtual instruments, 4–5, 92
   DB-33, 93
   Vacuum, 112
   Xpand!2, 93
Volume Fader, 98

W

Warp indicator, 120
Warp markers, 120–122, 157
   adding, 123
   deleting, 124
   repositioning, 124

Warp view, 120–121, 123
WAV files, 40
WaveCache, 35–36
waveform display, 35
Waveform view, 95, 120
Word Clock, 7
Workspace browsers, 34–35, 38–44, 48, 59

X-Z

X-Form processor, 117
Xpand!2, 70, 85, 93, 111–112